IMAGES
of America

PLATTEVILLE

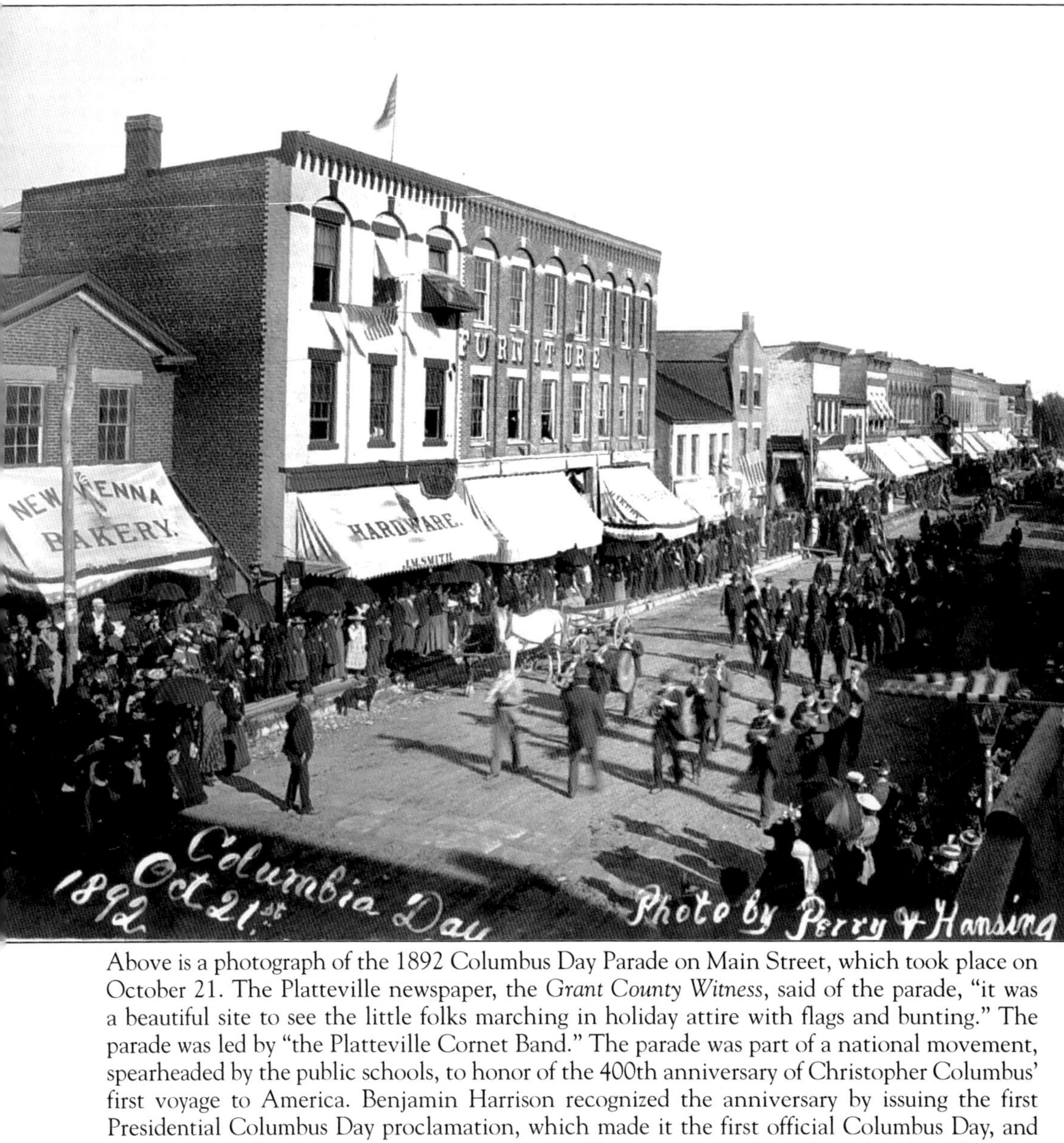

Above is a photograph of the 1892 Columbus Day Parade on Main Street, which took place on October 21. The Platteville newspaper, the *Grant County Witness*, said of the parade, "it was a beautiful site to see the little folks marching in holiday attire with flags and bunting." The parade was led by "the Platteville Cornet Band." The parade was part of a national movement, spearheaded by the public schools, to honor of the 400th anniversary of Christopher Columbus' first voyage to America. Benjamin Harrison recognized the anniversary by issuing the first Presidential Columbus Day proclamation, which made it the first official Columbus Day, and the World's Columbian Exposition buildings in Chicago were dedicated on that day. The date of October 21 was selected because the schools wanted historical accuracy: Columbus had first sighted land on October 12, 1492, under the Julian, "old style," calendar; that date became October 21 under the Gregorian, "new style," calendar.

(*Cover image*) The Platteville Legion Band leads the parade down Main Street during the dedication of the Masonic Temple, Saturday, June 27, 1925. The members of the Tripoli Shrine of Milwaukee immediately followed. For more details on this subject see pages 79 and 80.

IMAGES
of America

PLATTEVILLE

James B. Hibbard

ARCADIA
PUBLISHING

ISBN 978-0-7385-3317-9

Published by Arcadia Publishing
Charleston, South Carolina

Printed in the United States of America

Library of Congress Catalog Card Number: 2004107606

For all general information contact Arcadia Publishing at:
Telephone 843-853-2070
Fax 843-853-0044
E-mail sales@arcadiapublishing.com
For customer service and orders:
Toll-Free 1-888-313-2665

Visit us on the Internet at www.arcadiapublishing.com

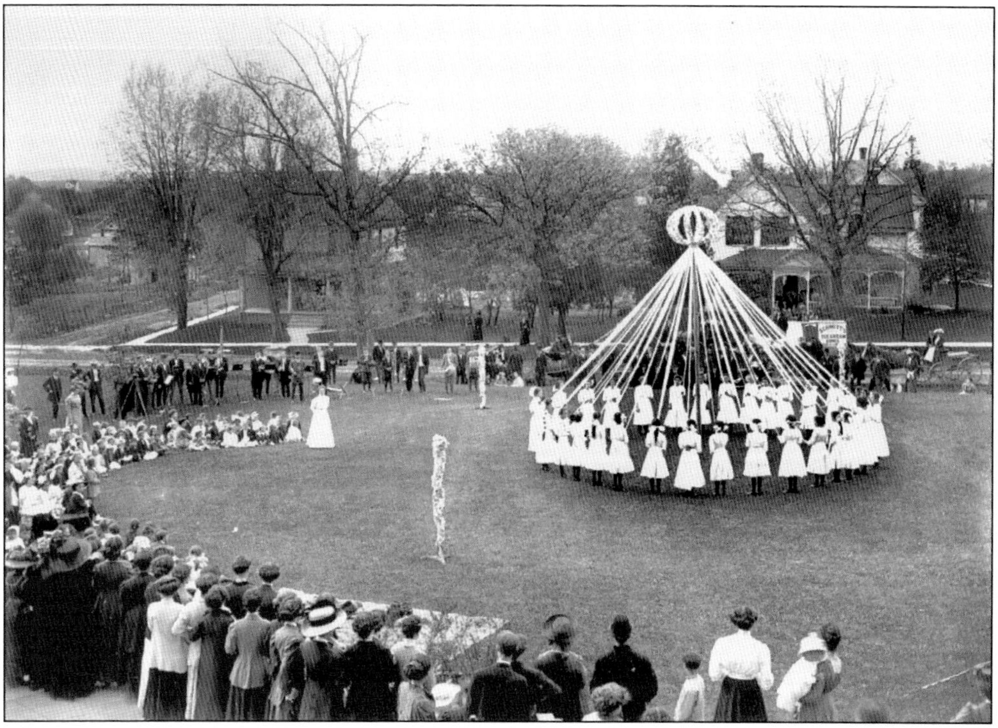

Above is an image of May Day exercises, *c.* 1908, held on the north lawn of the Normal School's Main Building. The participating children would have been Training School students of the Normal School. At that time, the Normal School operated a Training (or grade) School for the Normal School students to practice teaching. It was probably no coincidence that "Schmitt's Ice Cream Cones" carriage was parked on Main Street. It is the white carriage in the distance.

Contents

ACKNOWLEDGMENTS

This book is dedicated to my dear wife Dori. Your love, patience, and understanding (especially for all the evenings and weekends spent on this book) have been an inspiration. And to Sadie Mae for her love and warmth.

To research and write history is to locate the relevant primary sources, accurately interpret them, and present them in such a way that captures the essence of the past. I hope that my attempt is successful. Unless noted otherwise, all of the images are from the photograph collection of the University of Wisconsin-Platteville's Southwest Wisconsin Room, in the basement of the Karrmann Library.

This book could not have been written without the assistance of many organizations and individuals. I owe a great debt of gratitude to the following: Paula Nelson and Tom Lundeen for reading the manuscript, your suggestions improved it; Phyllis Shipley and Angie Reinecke of the Southwest Wisconsin Room; John Krogman; Stephanie Saager-Bourret, Mary Huck, and Steve Kleefisch of the Rollo Jamison Museum; Grant County Historical Society; Daryl Watson and the Galena History Museum; Gary Tuescher, Dick Brockman, Karen Reese, Jon Angeli, Jerry Daniels, John Dutcher, and Larry Bowden; John, "Jack," Tiedemann and Kay T. Young for your wonderful family photographs, ledgers, and visit; Loren Farrey, Mort Stephens and, last but not least, the wonderful people of Platteville—you opened your homes and hearts to Dori and me when we came here four years ago—thank you.

I would especially like to thank Mary Freymiller, my predecessor, for her advice and years of dedication to preserving and expanding the collections in the Southwest Wisconsin Room and the Wisconsin Historical Society's Area Research Center. Those collections, with their precious Southwest Wisconsin materials, made this book possible. I hope that I am as successful in preserving and expanding those collections for the next generation to enjoy.

–James B. Hibbard
Lancaster, Wisconsin, May 2004

INTRODUCTION

"On the morning of the 4th of July 1827, we concluded to visit the Mounds (called the Platte Mounds) and as it was a Beautiful, clear, Bright day, we could have a fine view of the surrounding country, and spent our Nation's 51st Birth day on the most commanding position that we had ever seen."

–Major John H. Rountree, 1870

More than the commanding position, what brought Rountree and his fellow miners to the Platte Mound was the prospect of lead ore. What he saw on that day must have pleased him. The future site of Platteville had the three necessary ingredients for mining: lead ore, the Platte River to clean the lead, and trees as fuel to smelt the ore. Opportunity presented itself and Rountree took it.

Throughout the last 175 years, two themes have been constant throughout the history of Platteville: opportunity and education. Opportunity first came in the form of lead ore mining. From 1827 until 1849, when the California gold rush hit, Platteville was a major mining town in the "Lead Region," a region that encompassed Southwest Wisconsin, Northeast Iowa, and Northwest Illinois. By the turn of the century and lasting through World War I, Platteville again rose to prominence by becoming a major zinc ore mining center. Supporting all of this was the heart of Platteville—its people and their entrepreneurial talent.

Opportunity came in other forms as well. Emma Dorothy Eliza Nevitte Southworth, for example, lived here for only a brief time. Abandoned by her husband in the early 1840s, she moved to the Washington, D.C. area and became a very successful novelist. One of her first books was entitled *The Deserted Wife*. There were numerous residents, however, who came and stayed. An almost forgotten person, Judge Stephen O. Paine, came to Platteville as a miner during its lead mining era. He eventually served as president (mayor) of Platteville and county judge. And another resident, Henry Kleinhammer, became a noted architect with his designs—Frank Burg's house, the Armory, and Clarence Gribble's house to name a few.

Educationally, Platteville has been a leader in both public schools and higher education. Lorenzo Bevans, a Platteville attorney and lead miner, had the foresight to call for, "suitable and ample provisions for the education of the children of the state," at the state's constitutional convention. Hanmer Robbins, a former superintendent of the public schools, and Josiah Pickard, the most influential principal of the Platteville Academy, secured the state's first Normal School for Platteville in 1866 and the Mining School was established in 1907. The successor of these schools, the University of Wisconsin-Platteville, remains a major educational leader.

Platteville, like the rest of the hills of Southwestern Wisconsin, has been a paradox since its settlement in the 1820s. It is in a northern state, but the first pioneers who ventured into the area were predominantly southerners who came up the Mississippi from Kentucky and Tennessee. It is on the western side of Wisconsin, but was one of the earliest parts of the state settled, defying the general east to west settlement pattern in the United States. It is also in the middle of the glaciated section of North America, but the glaciers went around this area, creating the Driftless Area—without glacial deposits or drift. Because of these paradoxes, it is fitting that Southwest Wisconsin also gave Wisconsin its nickname. Many of the first lead miners lived in dugouts that reminded people of badger holes, hence we became the Badger State.

Writer's Note

Since coming here in 2000, I have been looking for a vehicle to tell the story of Platteville. This book is that vehicle. In writing it, I wanted to present the story in an appealing way that would place each image in the context of Platteville's history. This is why I wrote the captions in a narrative style, whenever possible connecting each image with the next. This approach allows the images to move the narrative along, each chapter to have a storyline, and the narrative itself to have a cadence.

It should also be noted that to keep the quotations in the text as readable and unencumbered as possible, I have made only minor punctuation changes to them. Thus, on page 13, for example, I have retained the writer's original spelling of Plattville, without the middle "e," and did not use [sic] to indicate a spelling error. This retains the freshness of the original quotation.

I used four criteria in choosing each image. First, the image had to be rare or unique. Because of this, I placed a higher value on photographs over postcards; second, the image had to be clear and well preserved; third, the image must contribute to the story; and fourth, I used only those images that I could positively identify through research.

There are two timelines used in this book. For Platteville, except for the last photograph in the book, I chose 1827 to 1945, with an emphasis on 1827 to 1925. This was a natural ending, for the Platteville of 1945 is still recognizable today. For the university, except for the image of the Pioneer Student Center, I chose 1839 to 1971, again with an emphasis on an earlier period of 1839 to 1945. The date of 1971 was selected because that was when it became the University of Wisconsin-Platteville.

Finally, for me one of the most satisfying things to do is to locate a scene in a historic photograph. Hence, an alternative use for this book would be that of a tour guide of Platteville. If you notice, I give the date of each image, who is in it, and, if relevant, the location of the building in the image. Take the image on page 102, for example. I state that, "August [Kettler] had this house, located at the southwest corner of Furnace and Water Streets, built in 1868. The photograph, *c.* 1905, shows, from left to right, August. . . ." From this the reader knows who is in the photograph, and where and when it was taken. To save on space, the reader can presume that the buildings in the photographs still exist unless it is implied in the text or directly mentioned that they have been razed. Enjoy your tour.

One

The Pioneer Era

"In the winter of 1828&9, on the Petition of myself and Neighbors. . . a Post office was Established at Platteville, named at my Suggestion, because of its Location in the vicinity of the Platte River."
–Major John H. Rountree, 1870

The beginning of Platteville can be traced back to the spring and summer of 1827, when miners from Gratiot's Grove, New Diggings, and other mining towns and camps in the Lead Region came to the area to prospect for lead ore. The following spring, John H. Rountree, one of the few individuals who had remained in the area during the first winter, opened the town's first store and lead smelting furnace.

In due course, more miners arrived and gradually a town began to develop. A miner traveling through the Platteville area in 1834 recorded what the area looked like, "It is true there were . . . settlements and cultivated fields in view, but the prairie was cut up by numerous mineral holes, piles of dirt, and windlasses, which marred the beauty of the landscape, but showed great activity and industry."

By 1835, the original pioneers of Platteville, who were mostly Kentuckians and Tennesseans, were joined by miners from Cornwall, England, called "cousin Jacks," and by New Yorkers, Pennsylvanians, and others from eastern states.

The heyday of the lead mining era came to an end in 1849. The majority of lead above the watertable had been mined and many of the miners, upon learning about gold in California, participated in the gold rush. The miners, however, left an indelible mark on Platteville—mining holes, not a surveyor's compass and chain, determined the course of many of its streets. By mid-century, Platteville had become an established town. It had nearly 1,500 inhabitants, public schools, an academy, a newspaper (the *Independent American*), eight churches, a small commercial base, and telegraph service as of November 1849.

Over the next 40 years, Platteville sent its sons off to war to save the Union, heard the first steam engine chug into town in 1870, became an educational center, and witnessed the rise of a growing commercial and industrial base. On June 30, 1890, John H. Rountree, one of the founders of Platteville, died. His passing marked the end of Platteville's pioneer era.

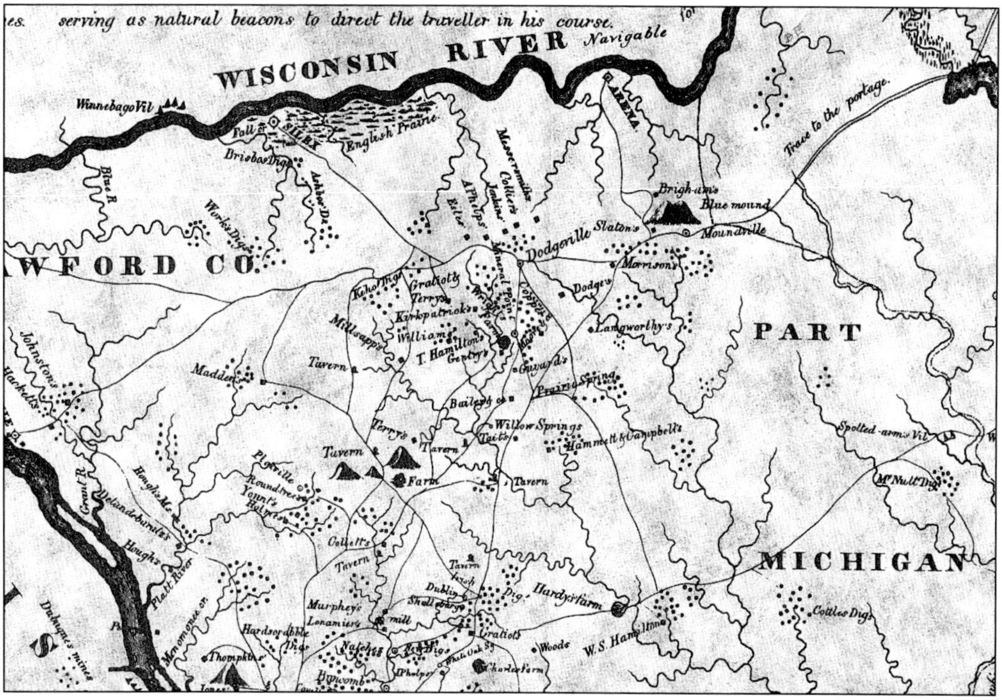

One of the things that facilitated the miners' movement into the Lead Region was R.W. Chandler's "Map of the United States' Lead Mines on the Upper Mississippi River." Issued in 1829, it showed the principal roads, natural features (such as the Platte Mound), and, most importantly, dots indicating "Discoveries of Mineral or Lead ore" (known as diggings). Notice that "Platville" is shown, as well as "Roundtree's" diggings.

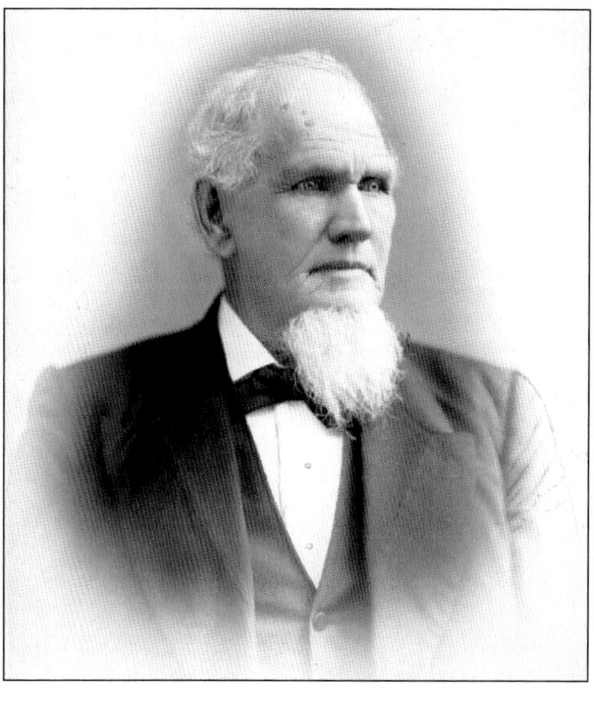

One of the most influential persons in Platteville's pioneer era was John Hawkins Rountree, shown here around 1880. Popularly known as Major Rountree, he was born in Kentucky in 1805, and arrived in Platteville in November 1827. Miner, soldier, legislator, businessman, Rountree's entrepreneurial activities made him a very wealthy man. Married twice, Roundtree outlived both of his wives, Mary Mitchell and Lydia Southworth. He remained deeply involved in the affairs of Platteville until his death in 1890.

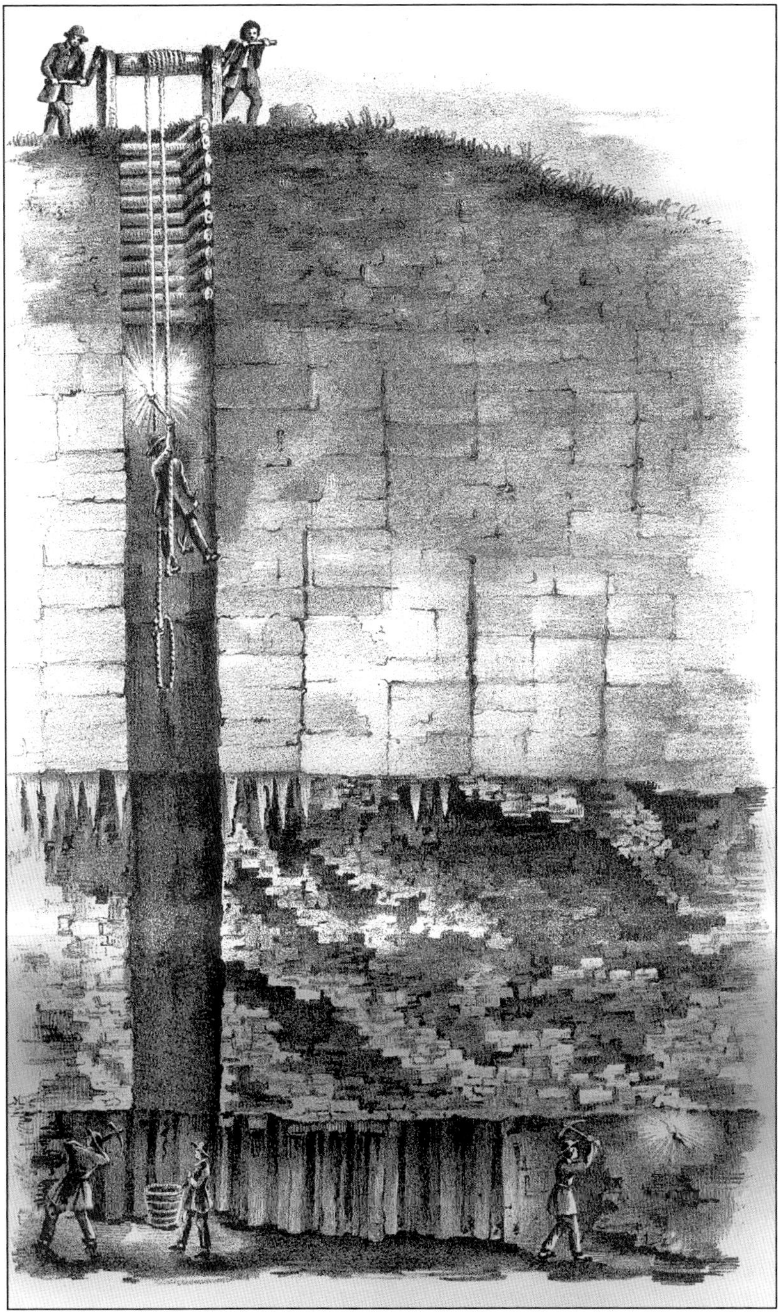

Commonly referred to as mineral, lead, or sometimes Galena, by the miners, lead ore was a very marketable and profitable commodity. Lead mining, moreover, in the 1820s, 1830s, and 1840s was a simple process. Once a miner found evidence of some mineral or a previous digging on the surface, he would dig a hole, comparable to a hole for a water well. When he struck a vein of lead ore, he would dig a shaft that followed the vein. The mined lead was placed in a wood bucket and brought to the surface with a windlass. The lead ore was then cleaned and smelted into 70 pound pigs or plats of lead, which were shipped to market. This image, from David Dale Owen's 1839 report on the Upper Mississippi lead mines, shows a lead mining operation in the 1830s.

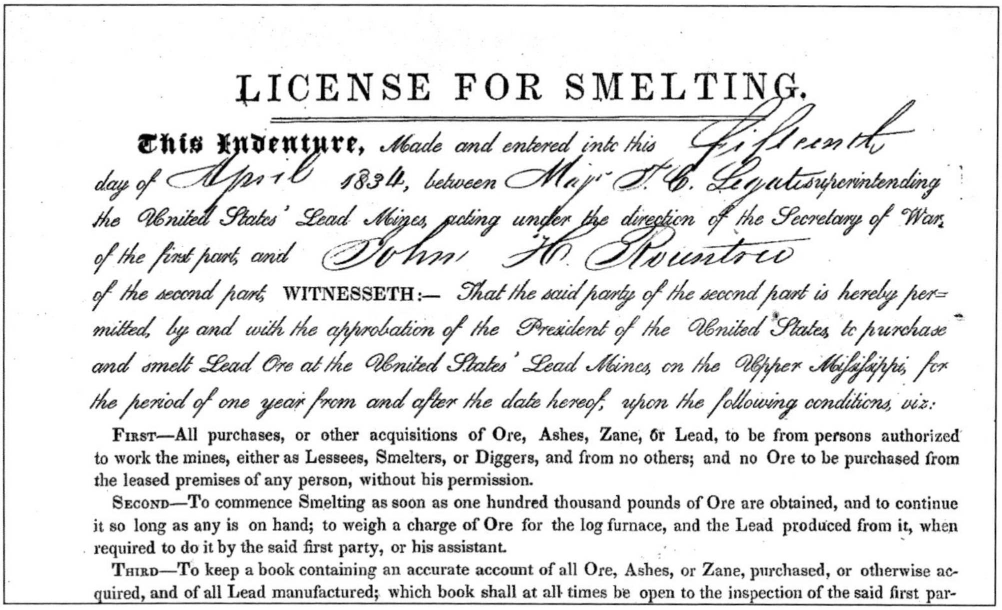

LICENSE FOR SMELTING.

This Indenture, Made and entered into this Fifteenth day of April 1834, between Majr. T. C. Legate superintending the United States' Lead Mines, acting under the direction of the Secretary of War, of the first part, and John H. Rountree of the second part, WITNESSETH:— That the said party of the second part is hereby permitted, by and with the approbation of the President of the United States, to purchase and smelt Lead Ore at the United States' Lead Mines, on the Upper Mississippi, for the period of one year from and after the date hereof, upon the following conditions, viz:

FIRST—All purchases, or other acquisitions of Ore, Ashes, Zane, or Lead, to be from persons authorized to work the mines, either as Lessees, Smelters, or Diggers, and from no others; and no Ore to be purchased from the leased premises of any person, without his permission.

SECOND—To commence Smelting as soon as one hundred thousand pounds of Ore are obtained, and to continue it so long as any is on hand; to weigh a charge of Ore for the log furnace, and the Lead produced from it, when required to do it by the said first party, or his assistant.

THIRD—To keep a book containing an accurate account of all Ore, Ashes, or Zane, purchased, or otherwise acquired, and of all Lead manufactured; which book shall at all times be open to the inspection of the said first par-

The United States government regulated the Lead Region by requiring each miner to sign a lease and by licensing each smelter. This is Major Rountree's lead smelting permit, dated April 15, 1834. (Courtesy of Wisconsin Historical Society, hereafter WHS.)

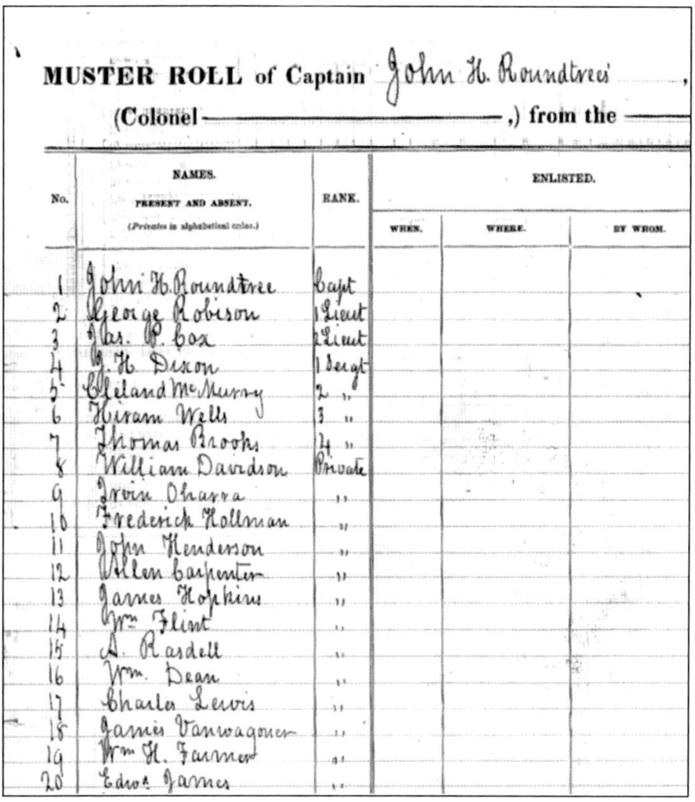

MUSTER ROLL of Captain John H. Roundtree, (Colonel ,) from the

No.	NAMES. PRESENT AND ABSENT. (Privates in alphabetical order.)	RANK.	ENLISTED. WHEN.	WHERE.	BY WHOM.
1	John H. Roundtree	Capt			
2	George Robison	1 Lieut			
3	Jas. P. Cox	2 Lieut			
4	J. H. Dixon	1 Sergt			
5	Cleland McMurry	2 "			
6	Hiram Wells	3 "			
7	Thomas Brooks	4 "			
8	William Davidson	Private			
9	Irvin Oharra	"			
10	Frederick Hollman	"			
11	John Henderson	"			
12	Allen Carpenter	"			
13	James Hopkins	"			
14	Wm. Flint	"			
15	A. Rasdell	"			
16	Wm. Dean	"			
17	Charles Lewis	"			
18	James Vanwagoner	"			
19	Wm. H. Farmer	"			
20	Edwd. James	"			

In the spring and summer of 1832, the pioneering settlements in the Lead Region were thrown into a panic when a band of Sauk and Fox Indians, led by Black Hawk, crossed the Mississippi River into Illinois and returned to their ancestral lands, precipitating the Black Hawk War. Major Rountree commanded a company of 35 mounted volunteers from Platteville that fought against Black Hawk in the Battles of Wisconsin Heights and Bad Ax. For posterity, Major Rountree had a muster roll of his men recorded in 1870. This image shows part of that muster roll. (Courtesy of WHS.)

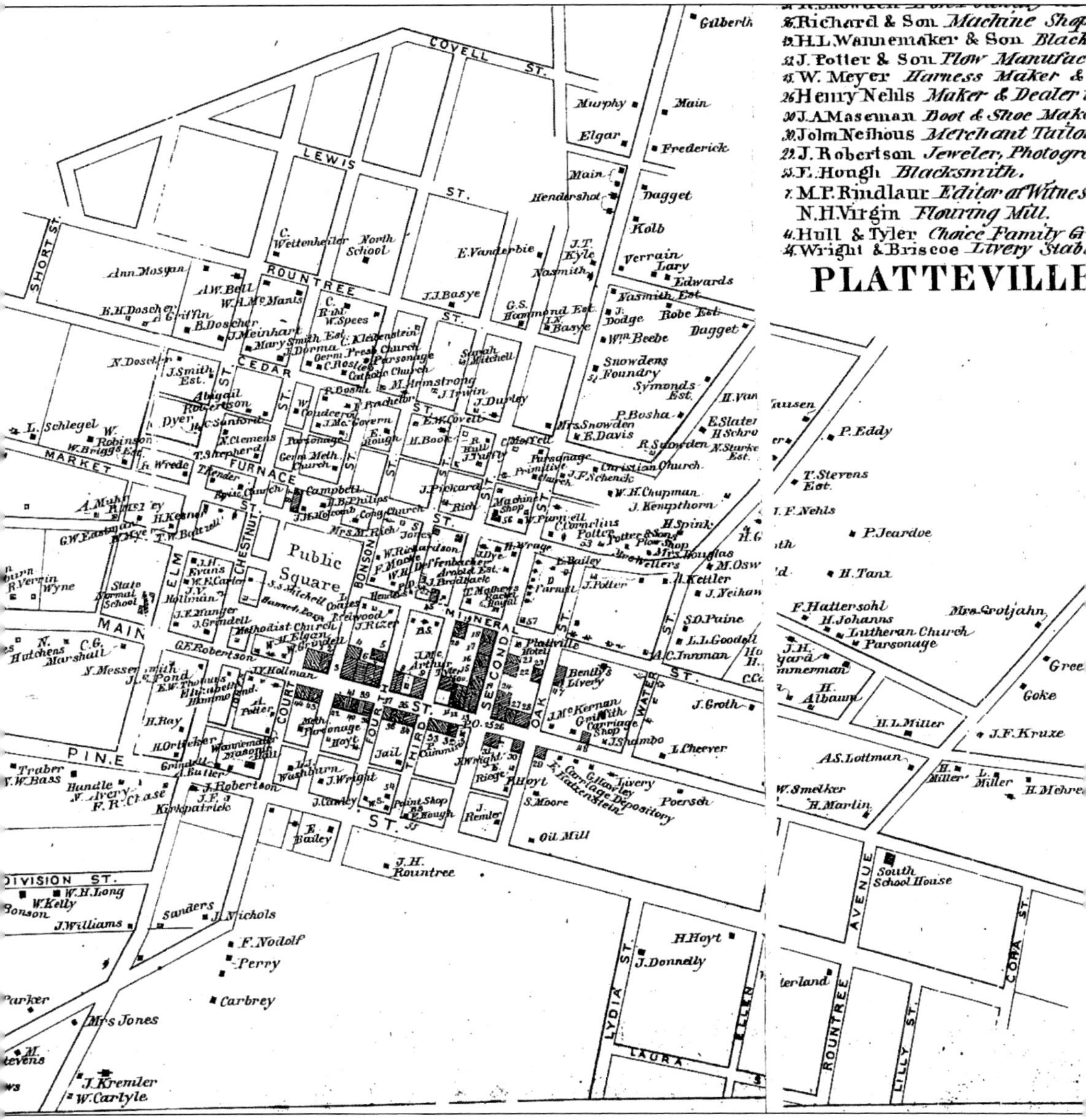

Once the Black Hawk War was over, Platteville started to grow. In 1834, a United States Land Office was established in Mineral Point, opening the land for permanent settlement. Never one to pass up an opportunity, in 1835 Major Rountree had Platteville, which was little more than a frontier camp, surveyed and platted. On September 19, 1835, he advertised in the *North Western Gazette & Galena Advertiser* that, "Plattville is handsomely situated on the border of the Prairie, in a grove that connects with the extensive Forest on the Platte Rivers . . . The surrounding country is inferior to none, in fertility of soil, and adaptedness to agriculture." Above is a section of an 1868 map of the village of Platteville. Notice that most of the streets do not run true north and south, east and west. The surveyor platted it that way to avoid mining holes.

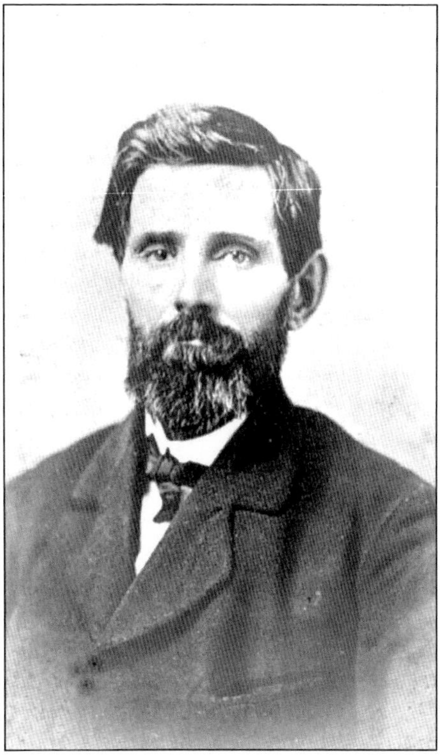

Several of Platteville's prominent pioneers arrived during the 1830s. Hanmer Robbins, shown here *c.* 1865, was one of them. Among his many accomplishments, Hanmer operated a schoolhouse from 1837 to 1839, served as Town Superintendent of Schools from 1854 to 1860, served in the state legislature in the 1850s and 1860s, and was on the Board of Regents for Normal Schools.

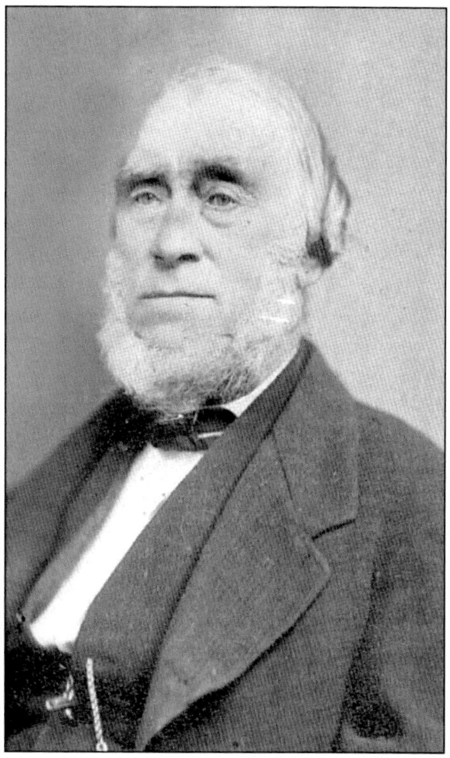

In 1836, another prominent pioneer came to Platteville, Leonard Coates. Coates, shown here around 1875, made a living as a lead miner and then as a smelter. Born in Yorkshire, England, in 1814, Coates came directly to Platteville in June 1836. In 1852, he not only became president (mayor) of Platteville, but also married a local lady, Caroline Gear. They had one child, Lucy. Leonard Coates died on April 25, 1894.

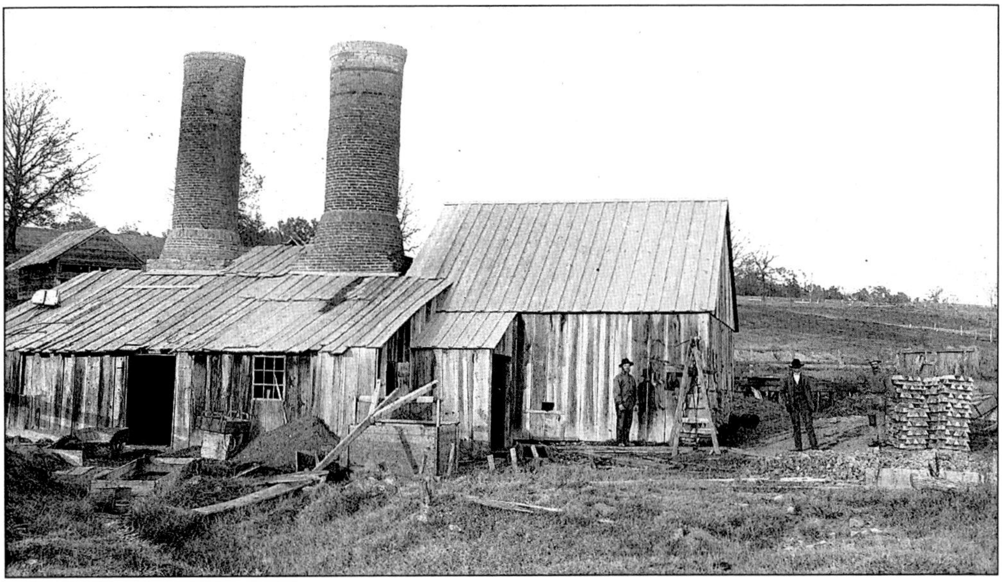

Coates' smelting furnace, located at the Rountree Branch on the southwest side of town, is shown here c. 1880. Popularly known as the "Straw Furnace," it exchanged ownership several times before Richard Straw & Company purchased it in 1851 and operated it for decades. It could smelt 350 pigs of lead ore per week.

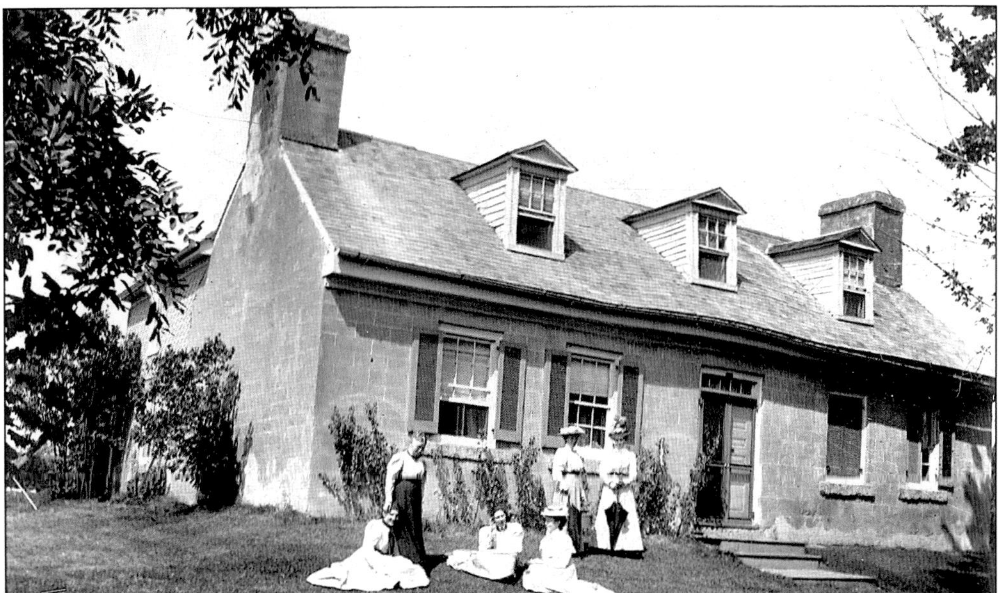

In 1837, Major Rountree's parents-in-law, Reverend Samuel and Eleanor Mitchell, also arrived in Platteville. Upon arrival, they constructed this limestone house, called the Mitchell-Rountree Stone Cottage (shown here c. 1900). The house's Colonial tidewater architectural style was derived from the Mitchell's places of origin—Samuel from Virginia and Eleanor from Maryland. Located at the northeast corner of Madison and Lancaster Streets, it is Platteville's oldest surviving building. The Grant County Historical Society conducts tours of it. (Courtesy of Grant County Historical Society, hereafter GCHS.)

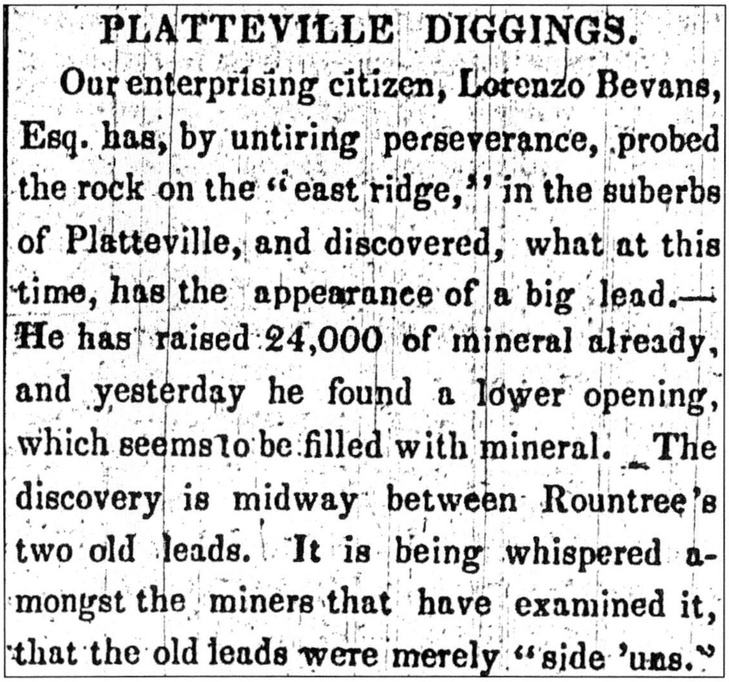

PLATTEVILLE DIGGINGS.

Our enterprising citizen, Lorenzo Bevans, Esq. has, by untiring perseverance, probed the rock on the "east ridge," in the suberbs of Platteville, and discovered, what at this time, has the appearance of a big lead.—He has raised 24,000 of mineral already, and yesterday he found a lower opening, which seems to be filled with mineral. The discovery is midway between Rountree's two old leads. It is being whispered amongst the miners that have examined it, that the old leads were merely "side 'uns."

One of the biggest lead discoveries in Southwest Wisconsin took place in Platteville in 1845. Prospecting on the east side of town, Lorenzo Bevans, a lawyer and poverty stricken lead miner, struck a rich vein of lead ore—nearly two million pounds were removed from his mine in 1845 alone. This article is from the July 4, 1845, issue of the *Independent American* newspaper. Today, the Mining Museum conducts tours of the Bevans Mine.

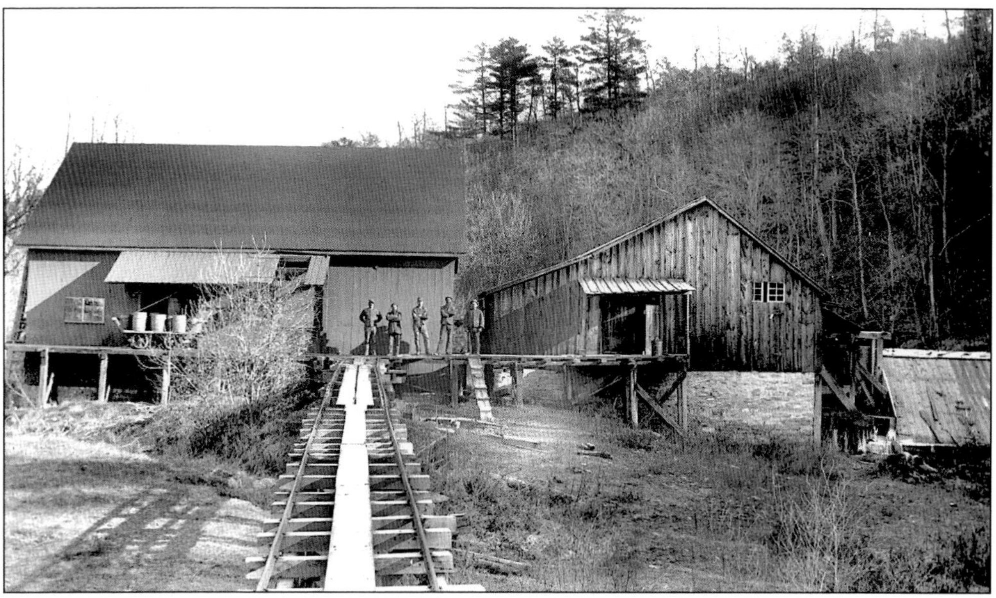

The mining industry created the need for blasting powder. The first powder mill was established by Edward and Francis Stowell about a mile-and-a-half northwest of town on the Little Platte River in 1849. This was the Coining Mill, c. 1891, when the Laflin & Rand Powder Company operated the mill. In the Coining Mill, the powder was ground into small particles. (Courtesy GCHS.)

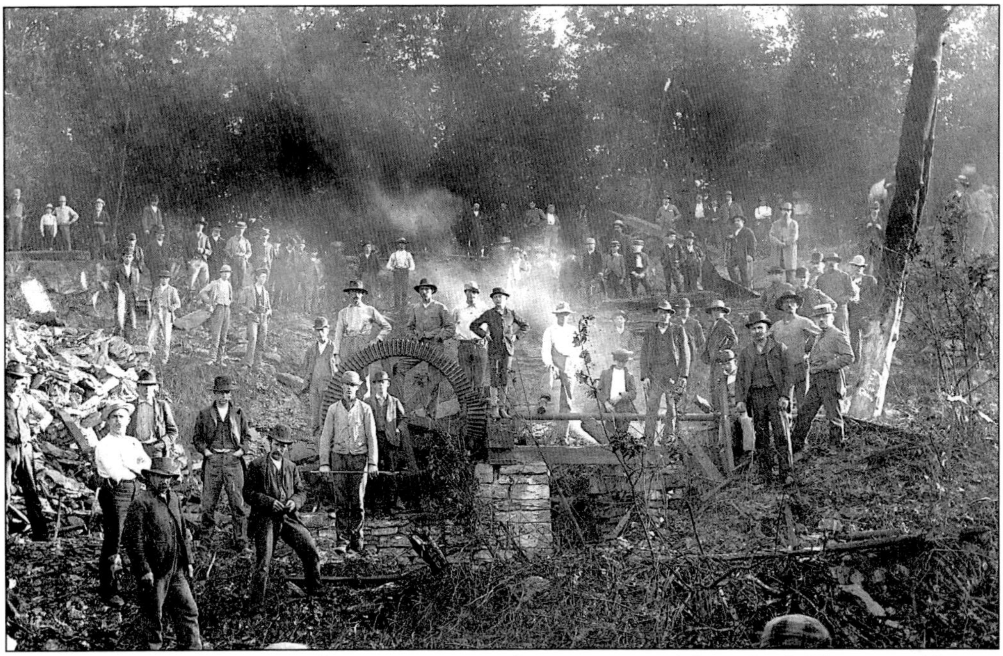

Unfortunately, the powder mill was prone to explosions, some of them fatal. This image depicts the explosion of the cylinder mill on July 27, 1891. In February 1900, the powder mill exploded one last time. It was never reopened.

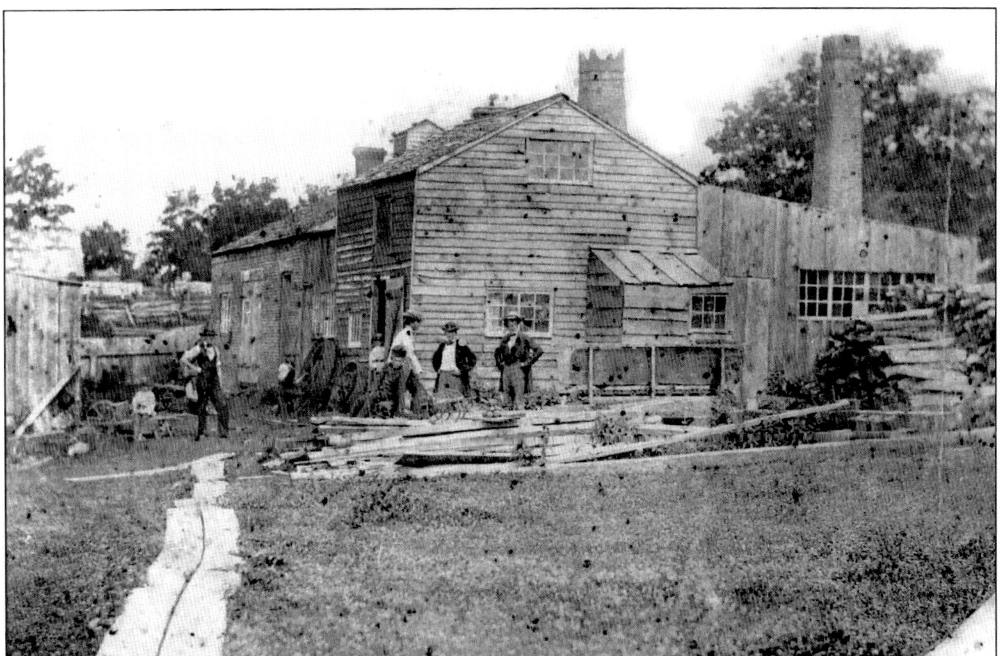

Another small business that got its start during the antebellum years was Randolph Snowden's Iron Foundry & Machine Shop, established in 1849. It was located near the intersection of Adams and Second Streets. This photograph was taken in 1861. Randolph operated it until his death in 1883.

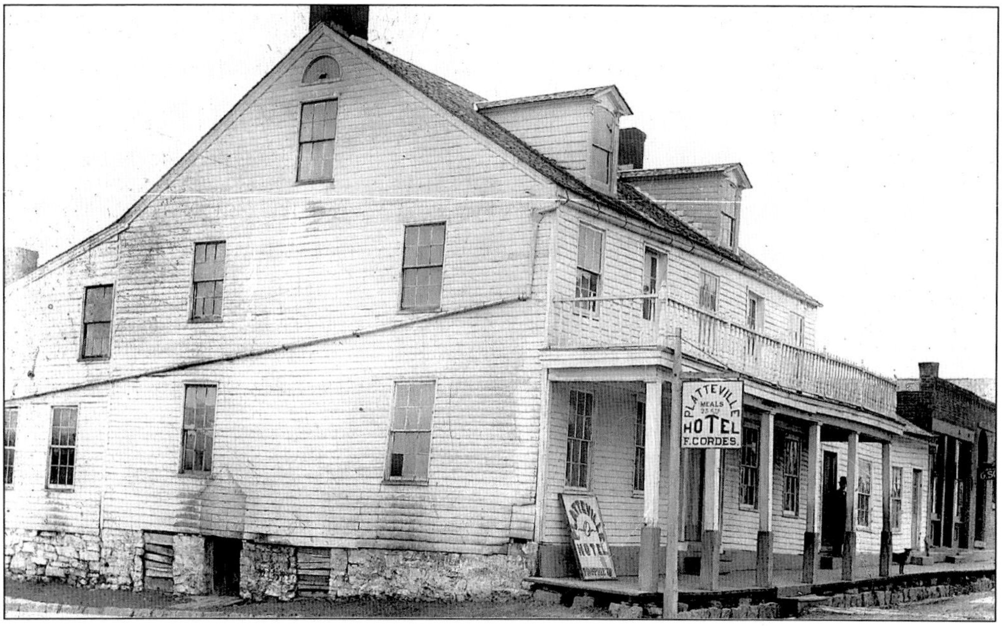

Bevans' lead discovery gave a huge boost to Platteville's economy. Platteville's population swelled from around 800 in 1844 to about 1,500 by 1850, thus creating a need for hotels and other businesses. Above is the Platteville Hotel, located at the southeast corner of Mineral and Second Streets from 1840 to about the turn of the century. This photograph (*c.* 1888) shows it when Friedrich Cordes operated it as a "$1.00 a day house."

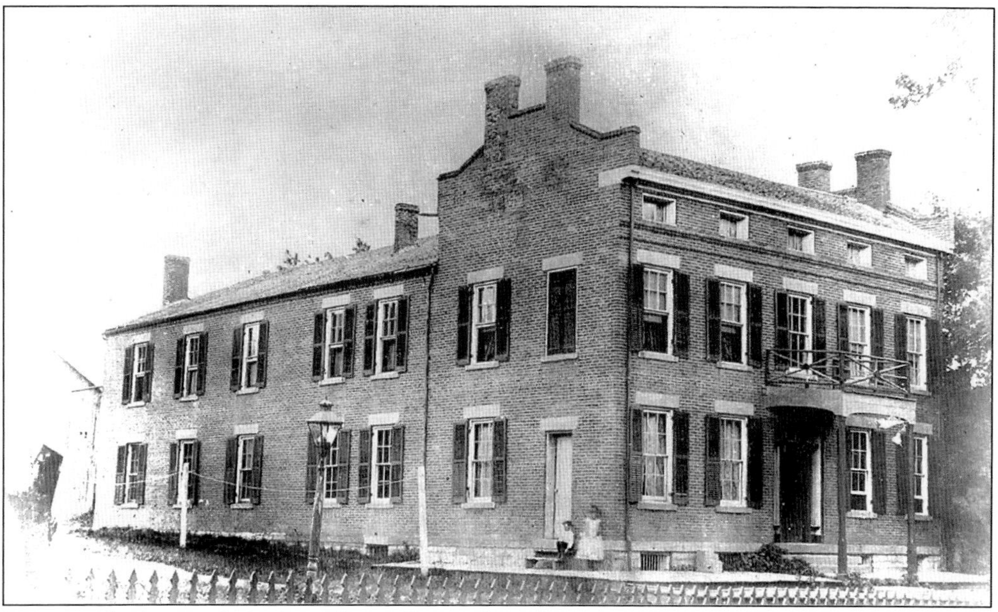

It was in the latter 1840s that Platteville residents began to construct brick buildings. A good example of this is the Campbell House, shown here around 1890, located on the north side of City Park. Built by Dr. James Campbell around 1846–47, it served as a hospital and hotel. Dr. Campbell moved his medical practice to St. Louis in the early 1850s, but did return to Platteville occasionally, passing away here in 1881. Today, this is a two-story building.

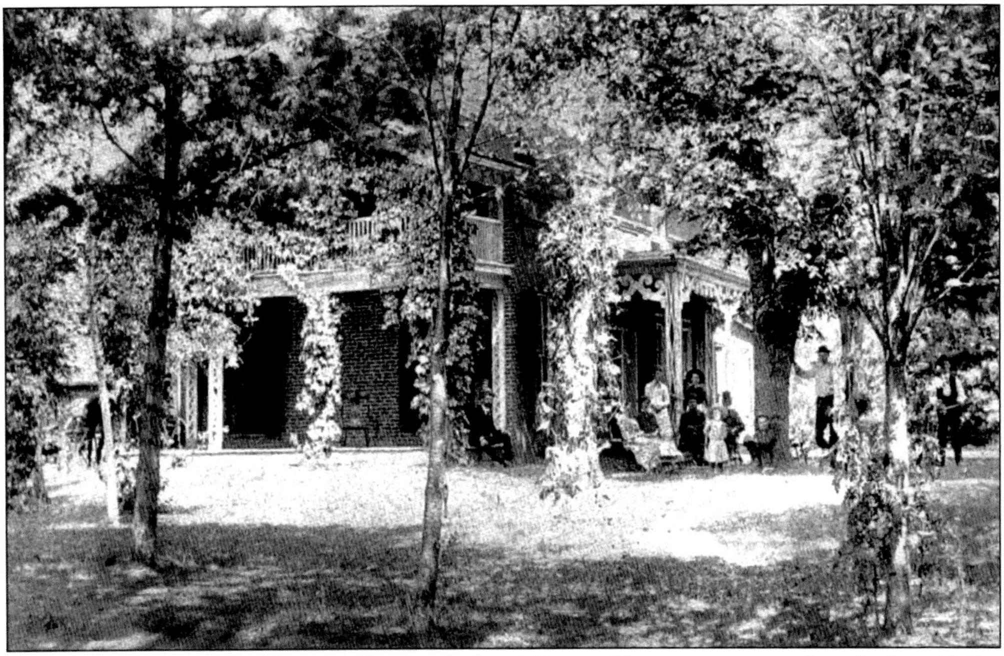

For his part, Hanmer Robbins had his brick Greek Revival house constructed in the late 1840s. By the time of this photograph, taken in August 1887 at a family gathering, Robbins had probably added a few improvements. The house, which is now gone, was located on the south side of East Mineral Street, near its intersection with old Highway 151.

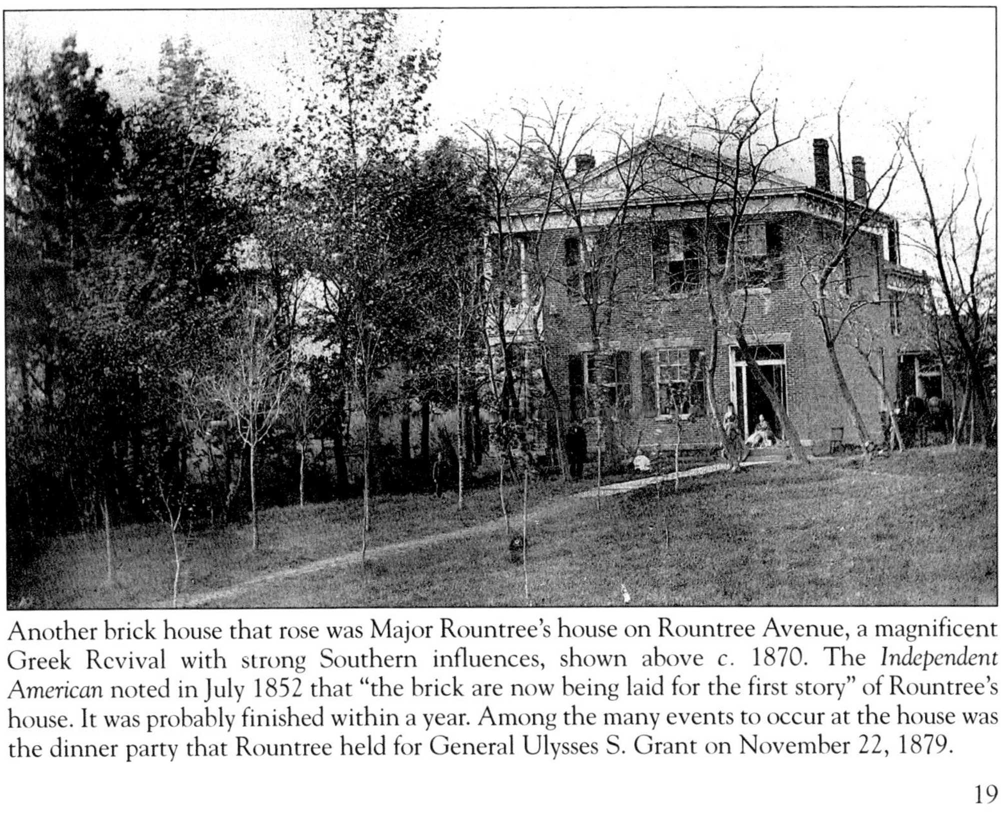

Another brick house that rose was Major Rountree's house on Rountree Avenue, a magnificent Greek Revival with strong Southern influences, shown above *c.* 1870. The *Independent American* noted in July 1852 that "the brick are now being laid for the first story" of Rountree's house. It was probably finished within a year. Among the many events to occur at the house was the dinner party that Rountree held for General Ulysses S. Grant on November 22, 1879.

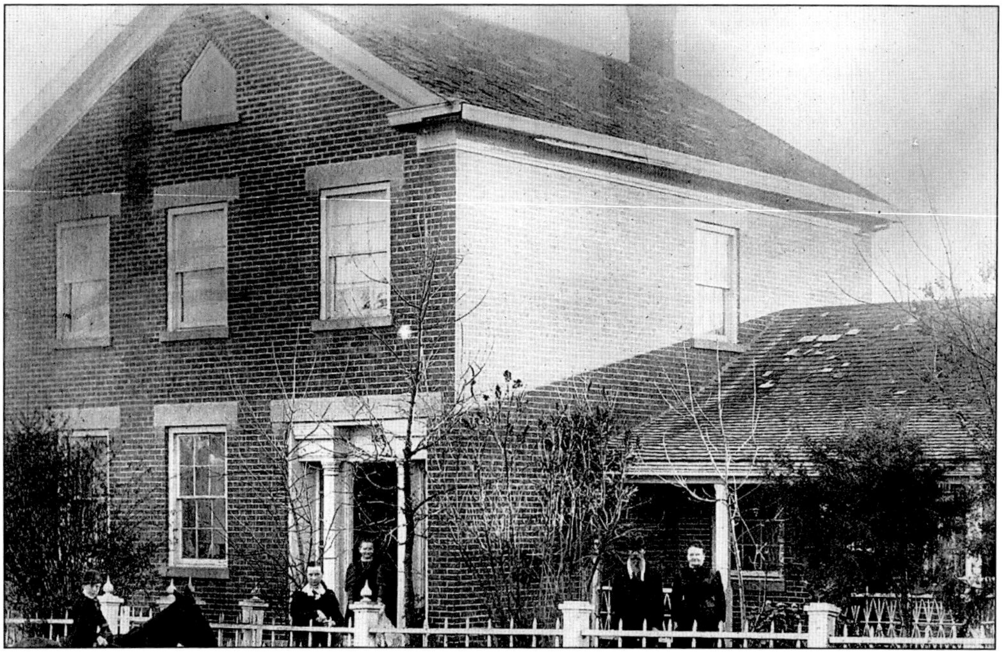

And on the eve of the Civil War in 1858, Philip Hendershot, a harness maker, and his wife Sarah had this more modest Greek Revival house constructed at the southwest corner of Furnace and Third Streets. Philip and Sarah, standing at right, are the only identifiable people in this photograph, taken around 1880. The house no longer stands.

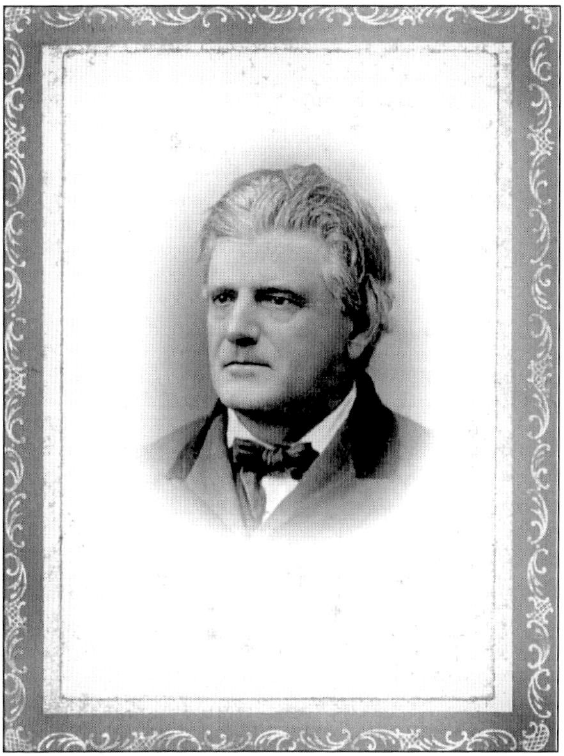

From 1858 to 1863, Platteville was also the home of Wisconsin's first governor, Nelson Dewey, shown here *c.* 1865. Dewey, an attorney, practiced law and lived with his wife Catherine and their two children in a house on Mineral Street, on the east side of City Park.

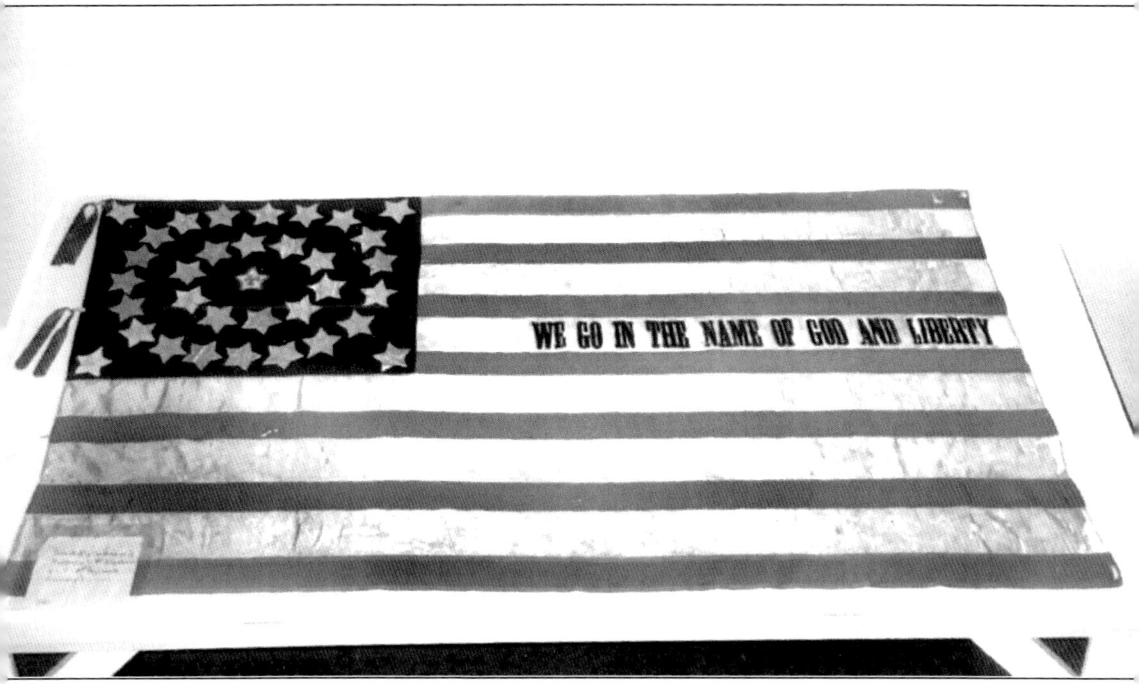

When the Civil War began in April 1861, Plattevillians immediately responded. On the evening of April 18, Major Rountree, Hanmer Robbins, and a few others held a meeting at Rountree's Hall on Main Street. At that meeting, the nucleus of what would become Company F, 3rd Wisconsin Infantry was formed. In all, 41 of Platteville's sons joined the company. On Sunday, April 21, the company was given a great send-off from Platteville, full of speeches and music. In early May, while the company was encamped at Boscobel, the ladies of Platteville presented it with "a very pretty silk flag [shown here], nine feet long by four wide. The motto is, 'We go in the name of God and liberty.' " It is currently housed in the Wisconsin Veterans Museum in Madison. More than 100 men served in the Civil War from Platteville Township. (Courtesy of Mort Stephens.)

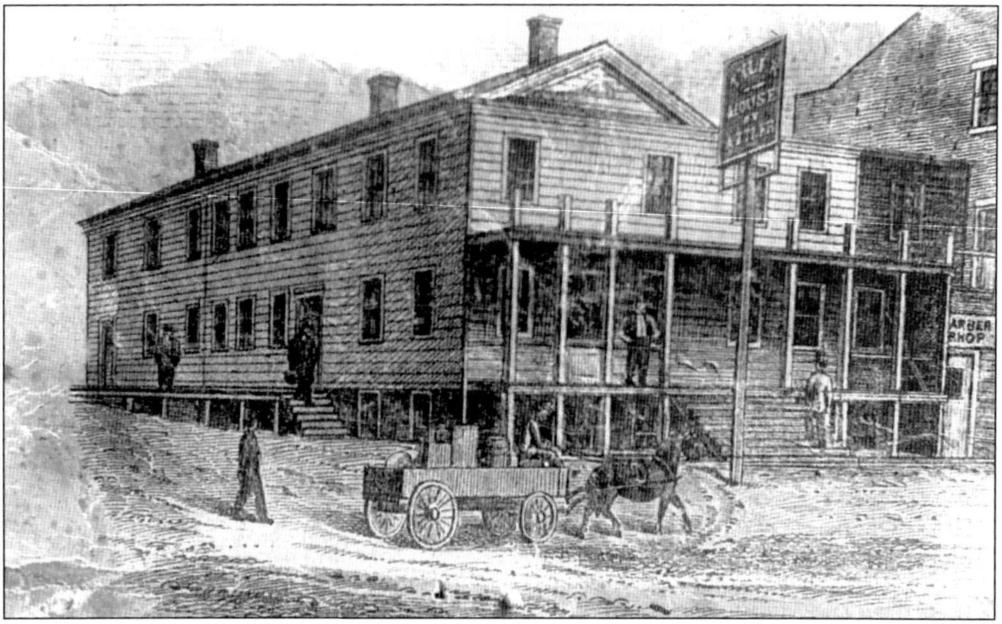

The Rewey House (shown above in 1868 when it was the Tyler House) served as the recruitment headquarters for the area. Located at the northeast corner of Main and Third Streets, over 1,000 men from the area enlisted in the Union Army in this hotel. This naturally brought many people into Platteville to say good-bye. On August 20, 1861, the young lady pictured below, Susan Williams of Paris Township, came to town and watched her brother march off to war with Company C, 7th Wisconsin Infantry.

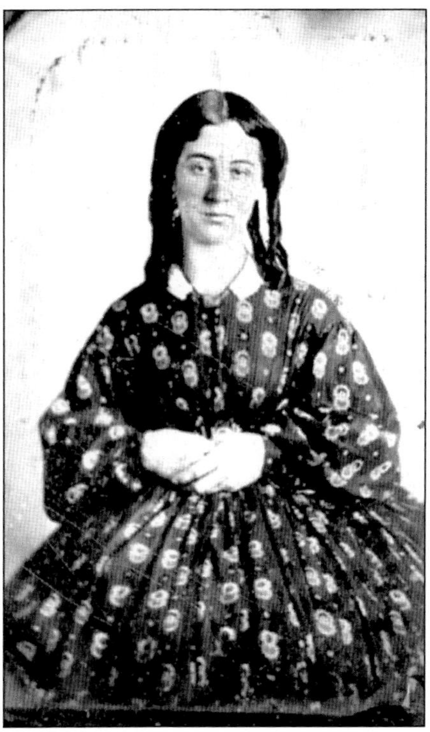

In her diary for that day, Susan wrote, "All the soldiers were cutting up all kind of shines to keep up their spirits. I think at half past 7 the drum was heard and they fell in rank and we shook their hands for the last time and kissed them. Oh what a time it was . . . Oh my dear Brother Lewis if he is only spared to come home what a joyful time we shall have. The town was full of folks and soldiers." Lewis survived the war; Susan died in February 1862 of Typhoid Fever.

The 25th Wisconsin Infantry regiment was another unit well represented by area men. Nelson Beckwith of Ellenboro joined the Platteville Guards, Company E, on August 11, 1862. In 1863, he fell ill and was transferred back to Platteville. Tragically, he died of Bilious Fever on July 16 in the care of his family at the Rewey House—he was 19. His family buried him at Buckwheat Ridge Cemetery, near his home in Ellenboro Township. His mother died just a month later and was buried beside him.

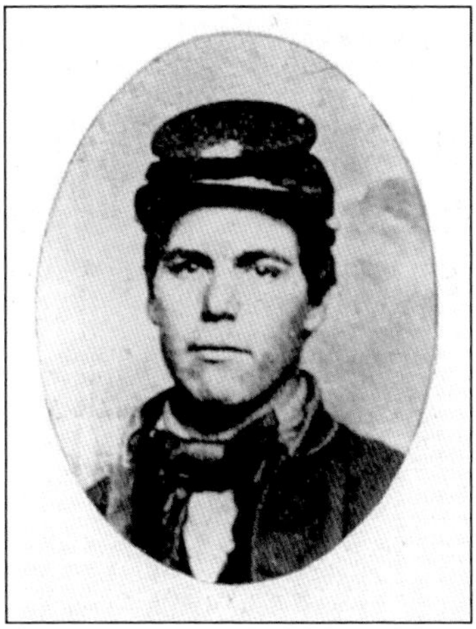

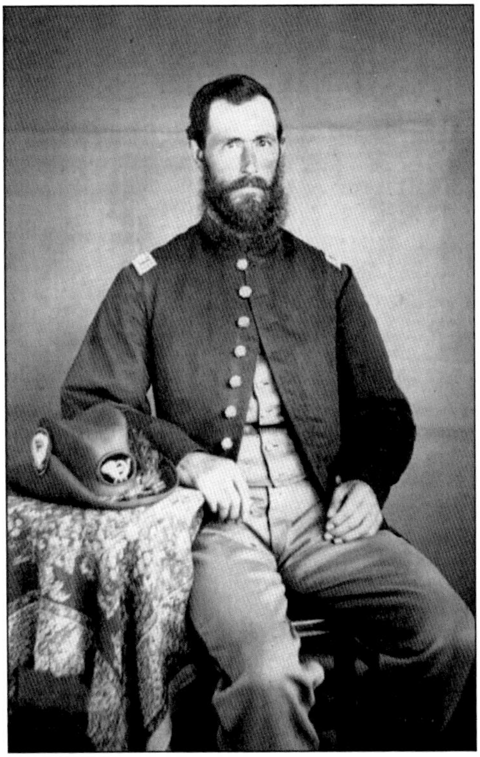

Another veteran from Platteville was 1st Lt. John Grindell, shown here in 1864 or 1865. Grindell, a cabinet maker by trade, served from May 1864 to September 1865 in (first) the 41st and (second) the 47th Wisconsin Infantry regiments. After the war, he operated a furniture store with his brother William and manufactured brick. He died on September 29, 1901.

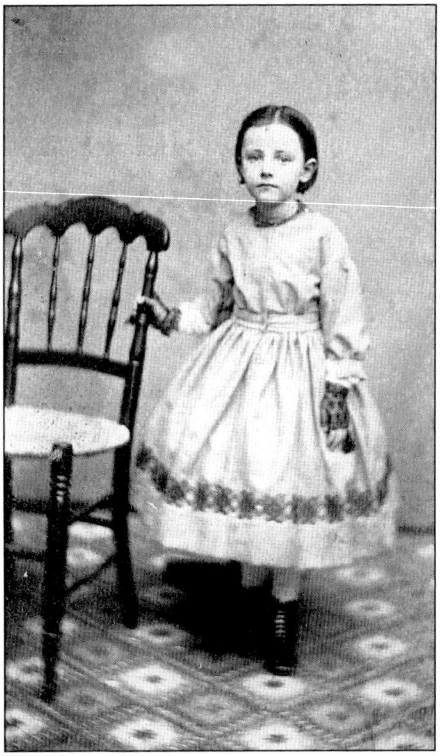

Plattevillians, like most people, were fascinated with getting their "likenesses taken." The photographs on this page were taken by Leonard Vanderbie, a Platteville photographer during the Civil War. His studio was located in the "SKY LIGHT ROOMS, above Goodell & Chase's Drug Store" on Main Street. The little girl pictured here (*c.* 1864) is believed to be Nettie Goodell, the daughter of Lemuel Goodell of the drug store.

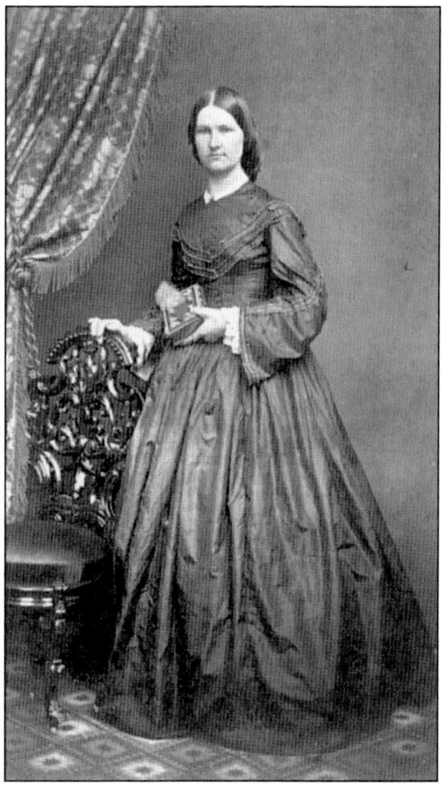

In December 1864, Vanderbie advertised that he had just returned from Chicago where he had purchased "a new fashioned reception Chair, with curtains; scenery etc., only for the purpose of taking Carte de Visite Photographs." Those new props, minus the scenery, can be seen in this photograph of an unidentified lady, *c.* 1865.

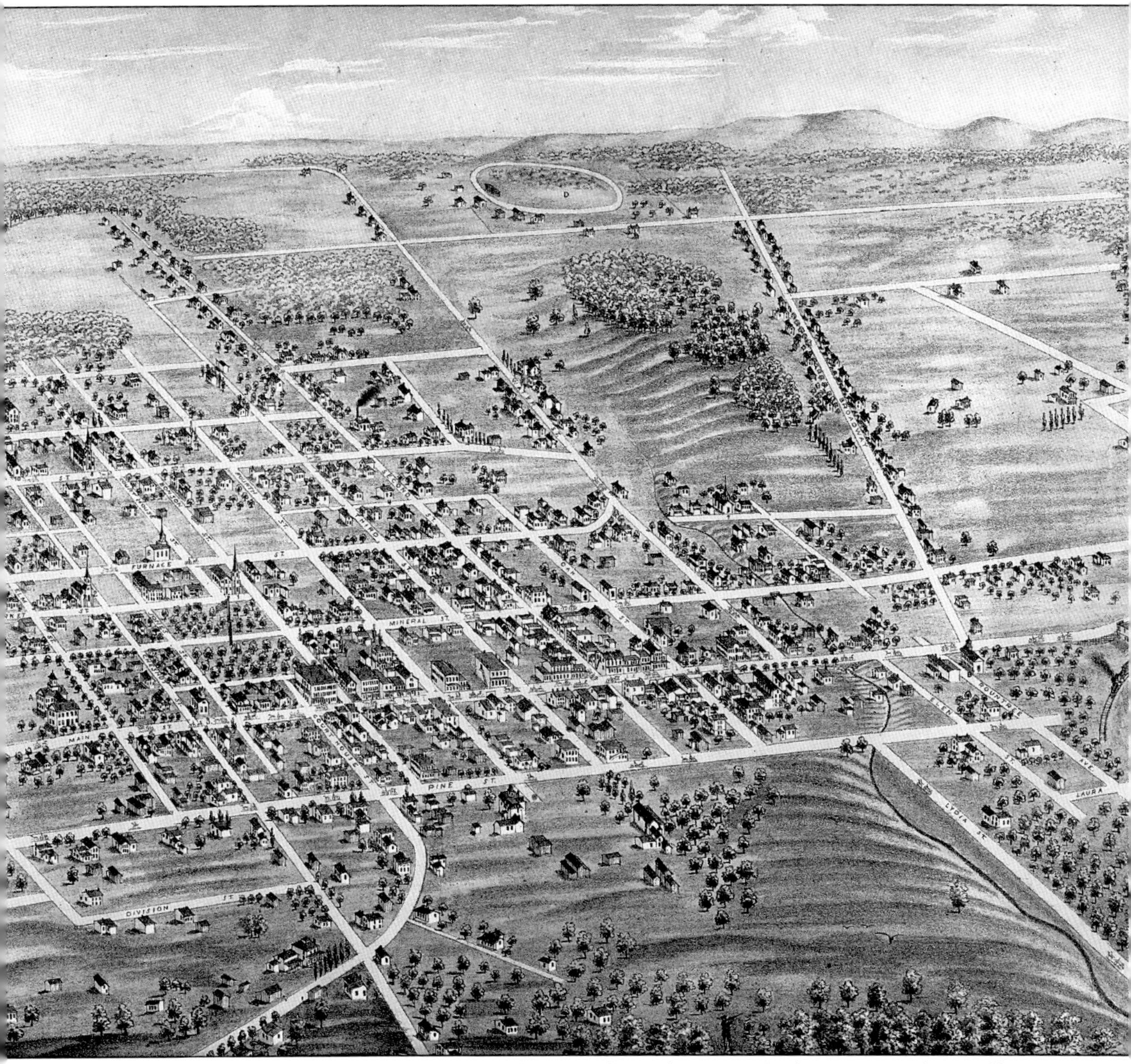

The Civil War and the years immediately following brought several changes to Platteville, many of which can be seen in this birds-eye view, *c*. 1872. Platteville's growing business district is demonstrated by the number of substantial buildings on Main Street; the lifeblood of that district, commerce, is shown by the amount of activity on Main Street and by the railroad on the right, which arrived in Platteville in 1870. The foundations of the community, its houses, churches, and schools, are sprinkled throughout the view. Most significantly, the birds-eye fails to mention or illustrate any lead mining activities, an industry that had been on the decline since 1849. Notice that Mineral Street at that time ran through City Park.

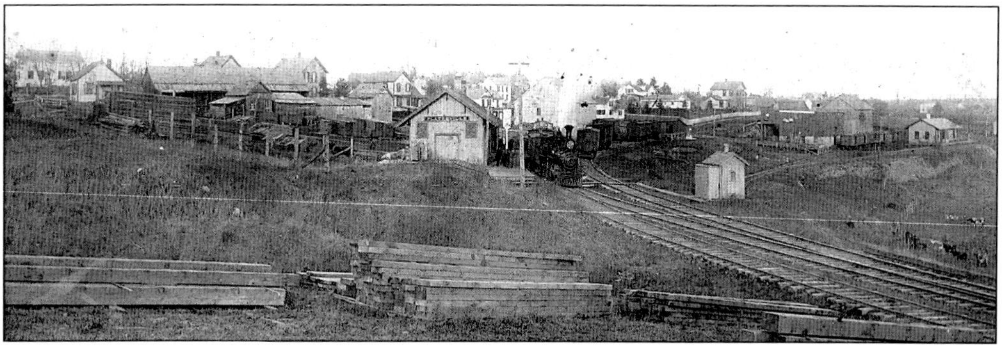

Within the first decade after the Civil War, two major events took place in Platteville. The first occurred on July 1, 1870, when the first steam engine of the Platteville & Calamine Railroad pulled into town, establishing railway service. A huge Fourth of July celebration was held in honor of this event. This photograph from 1890 shows the old Calamine Railway (by then the Chicago and Northwestern Railroad) Depot in the center and the Chicago, Milwaukee, and St. Paul Depot (far right), which had provided service since 1875. Both depots were located on the east side of town. (Courtesy of Dick Brockman.)

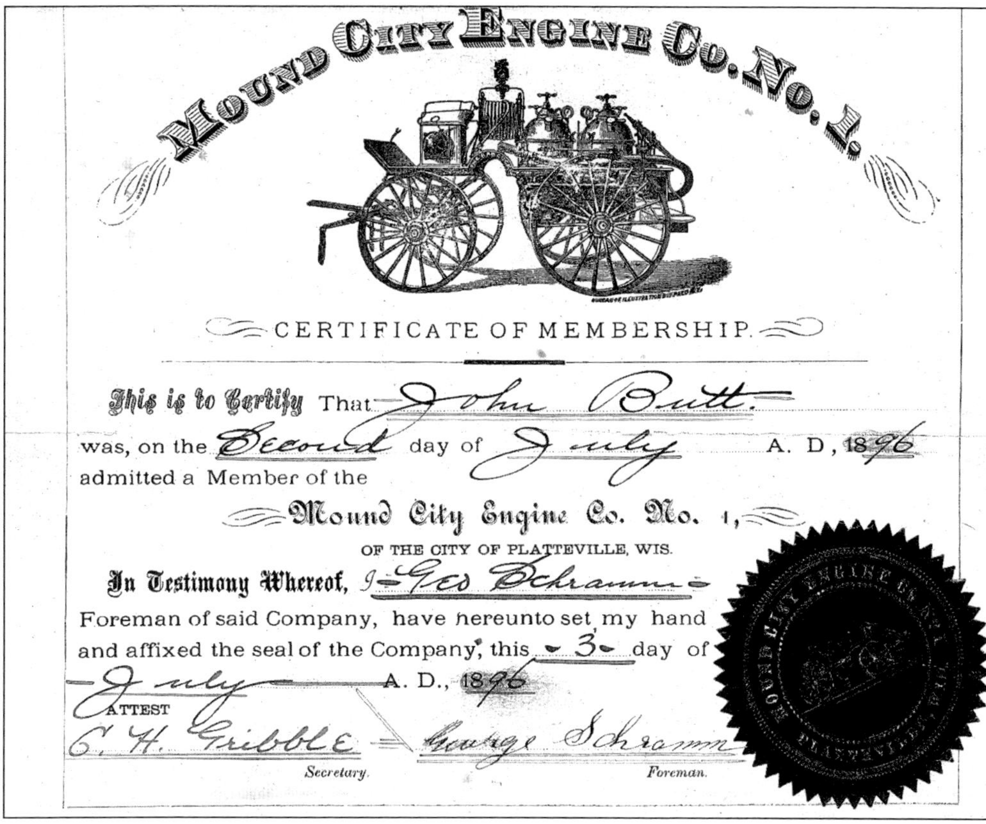

MOUND CITY ENGINE CO. NO. 1.

CERTIFICATE OF MEMBERSHIP.

This is to Certify That John Butt was, on the Second day of July A. D, 1896 admitted a Member of the

Mound City Engine Co. No. 1,

OF THE CITY OF PLATTEVILLE, WIS.

In Testimony Whereof, I Geo Schramm Foreman of said Company, have hereunto set my hand and affixed the seal of the Company, this 3 day of July A. D., 1896

ATTEST

C. H. Gribble, Secretary. George Schramm, Foreman.

The other event occurred on the morning of April 15, 1874, when a cataclysmic fire, started, it was thought, by "the explosion of a kerosenen lamp," consumed several buildings in downtown Platteville. Within a month, a hook and ladder company was formed, which was soon followed by the establishment of the Mound City Engine Company No. 1. Platteville now had a fire department. Above is an 1896 Mound City membership certificate. (Courtesy of GCHS.)

During this time, Platteville's business district expanded and began to offer a wider assortment of wares. The McKey Brothers, for instance, opened their dry goods store, shown here during the Civil War, in the spring of 1863. Located at the northeast corner of Main and Fourth Streets, they advertised that they had the best "Stock of Dry Goods Ever Offered in Platteville." This building still exists, although its facade has changed (see page 78).

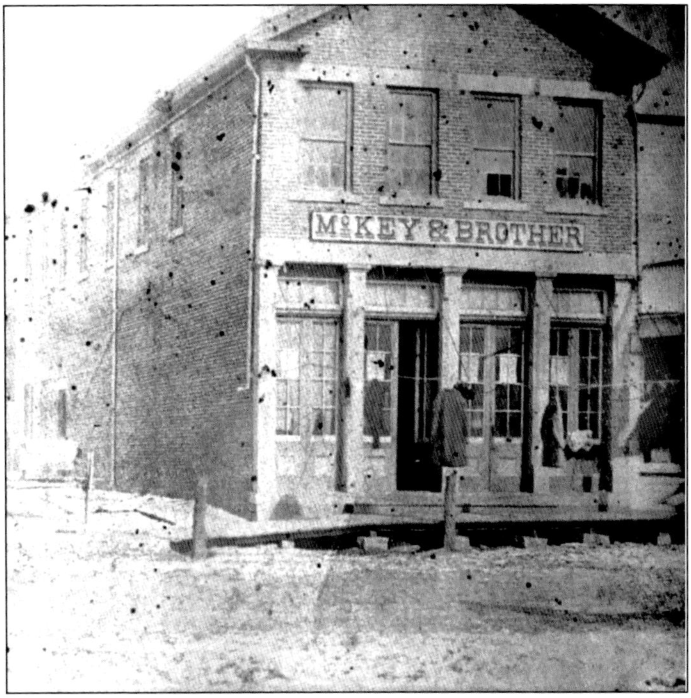

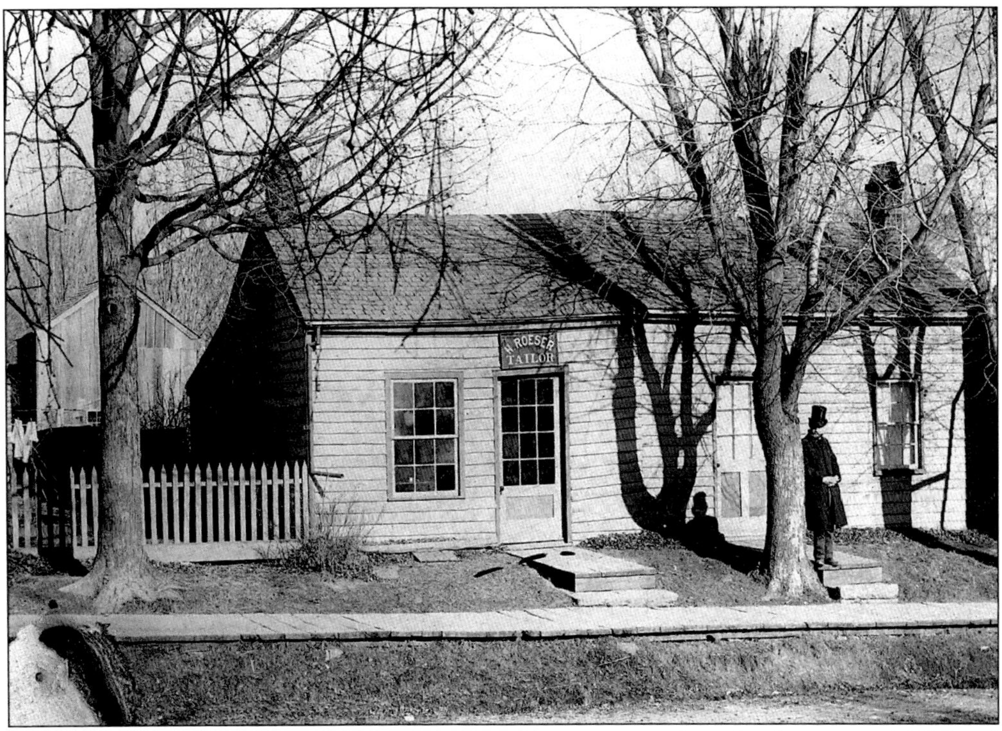

Henry Roeser, probably the man leaning against the tree, opened a tailor shop around 1870 and operated it until the early 1890s. This photograph, taken about 1875, shows his shop, located where the Bargain Nook IV is today. The trees in City Park may be seen behind the barn at left. This building was razed in 1893.

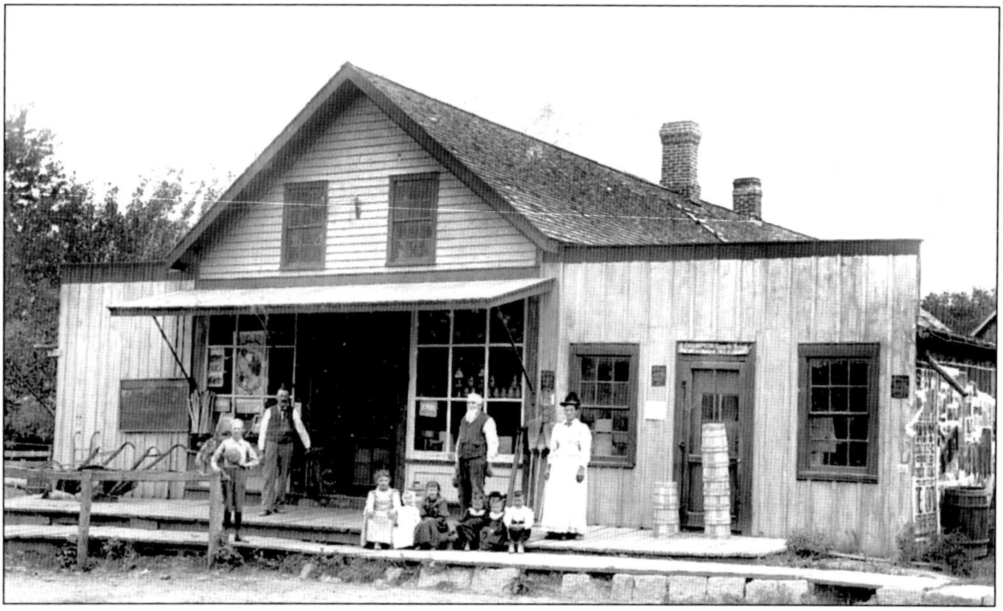

Another merchant in town was Charles Weittenhiller, the middle-aged man on the left of this image, *c.* 1885. Born in Bavaria in 1844, Charles came to Platteville in 1853. He served in the 25th Wisconsin Infantry during the Civil War. Afterwards, he took up his father's trade as a cooper and operated this store at 220 West Adams Street, near the Brick School (notice the school children). The Village Bikesmith occupies the building today.

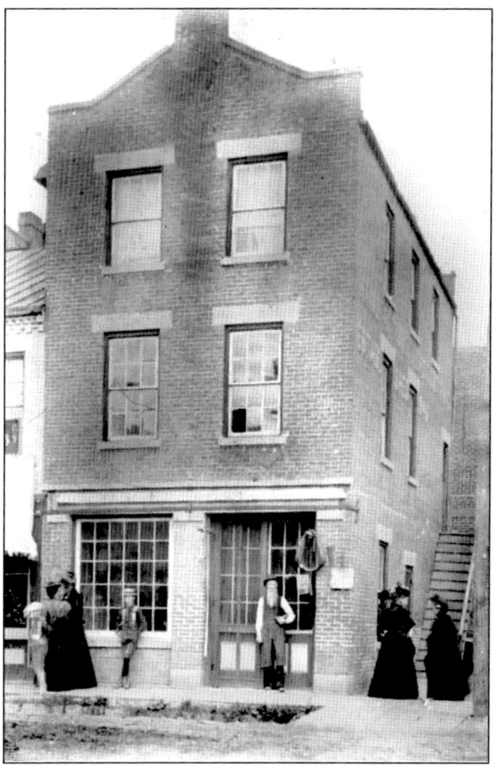

Some things remained the same, however. Here Philip Hendershot, with beard, stands in front of his harness shop, *c.* 1895, at the northwest corner of Main and Fourth Streets. Hendershot, who worked with leather all his life, came to Platteville in 1846 and had this building constructed in 1853. Mr. Hendershot died in 1910.

In 1883–84, Platteville's City Hall was built on the east side of City Park. City Hall, shown here *c*. 1891, had a theater on its north end (nearest the camera) and the fire department was located on its south end, under the belfry. (Courtesy of Dick Brockman.)

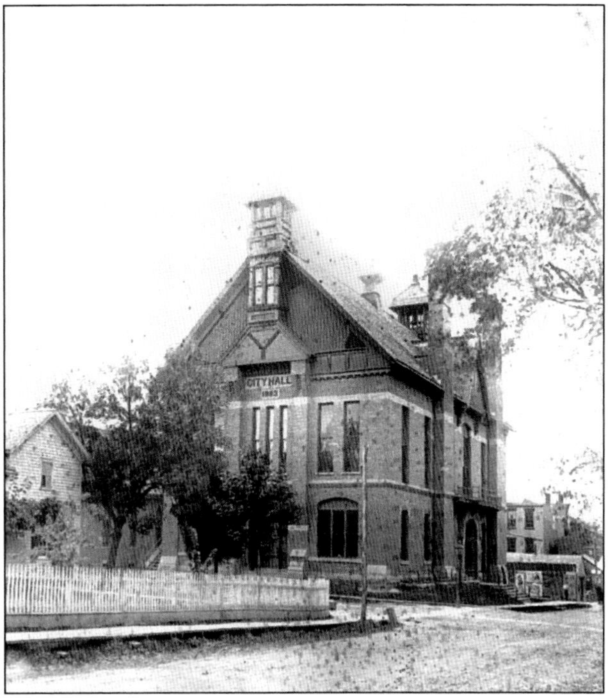

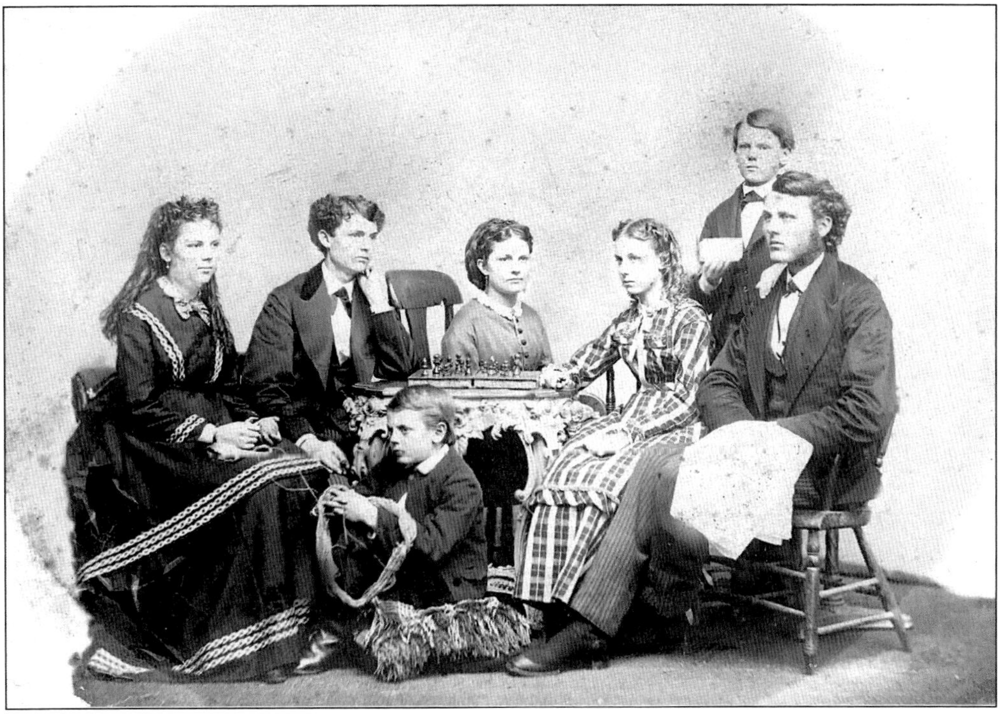

During the Civil War era, the next generation of Plattevillians began to emerge. Sometime around 1870, for example, Hanmer Robbins' children had their group portrait taken. They are, from left to right, Nettie, Tom, George, Fanny, Mary, Rod, and Frank.

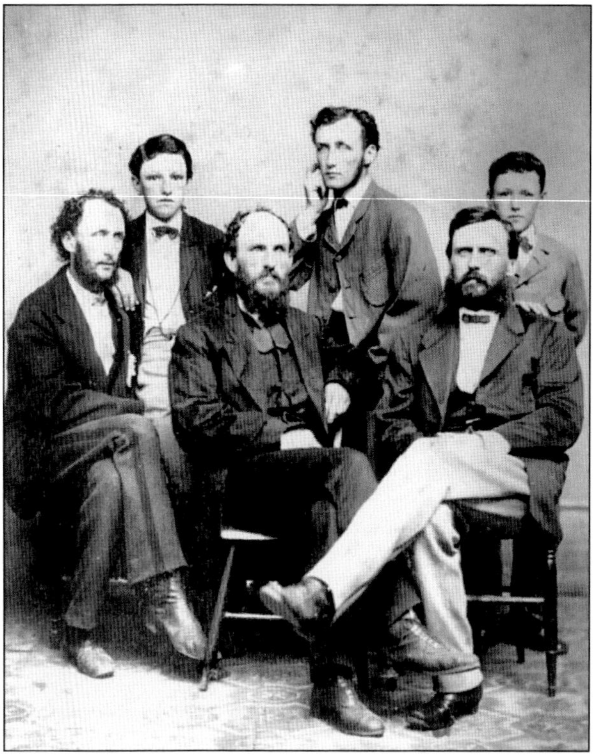

About the same time, Major Rountree's children had their group portraits taken. Shown, from left to right, are: (seated) George, Samuel, and John; (back row) Harry, Philip, and Charles.

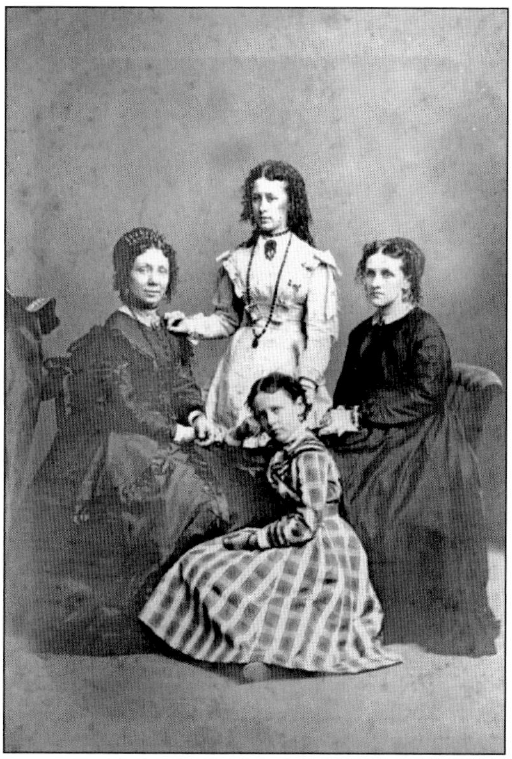

And here are the Rountree girls, from left to right, Nelly (Jewett), Lilly (standing), Laura (Smith), and Cora (Hathaway), seated on the floor.

Another member of the second generation was Mary Louise Kettler, the lady in the middle, *c.* 1885. The daughter of a town merchant August Kettler and his wife Julia, Mary would have grown up in her father's general store. She married Henry Schambow, another merchant, in 1886. They had one daughter, Clara. (See page 102 for a photograph of the Kettler family.)

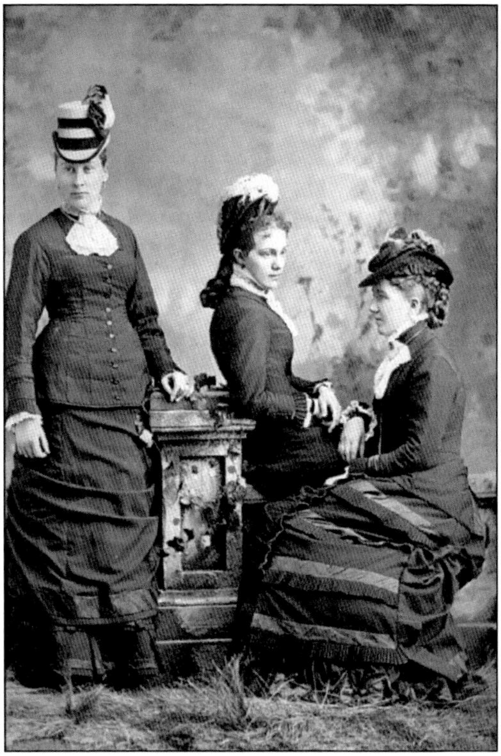

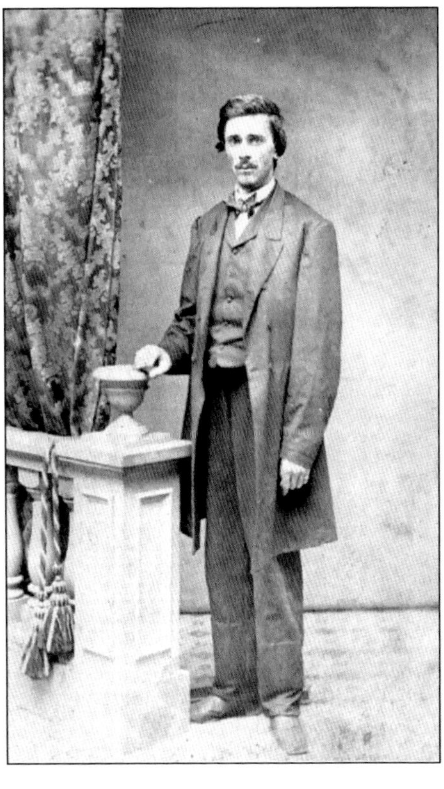

Like other towns, Platteville saw its share of newspapers come and go. The *Grant County Witness* was the first newspaper to last, it was published from 1859 to 1937. One of the individuals responsible for this longevity was Martin P. Rindlaub, shown here *c.* 1864. Originally from Gettysburg, Pennsylvania, Rindlaub traveled west to Illinois in 1858, where, as a young reporter, he saw Abraham Lincoln and Stephen Douglas debate in Freeport. In 1864, he moved to Lancaster, Wisconsin, and by 1867 he had moved to Platteville and purchased the *Grant County Witness*. (Courtesy of GCHS.)

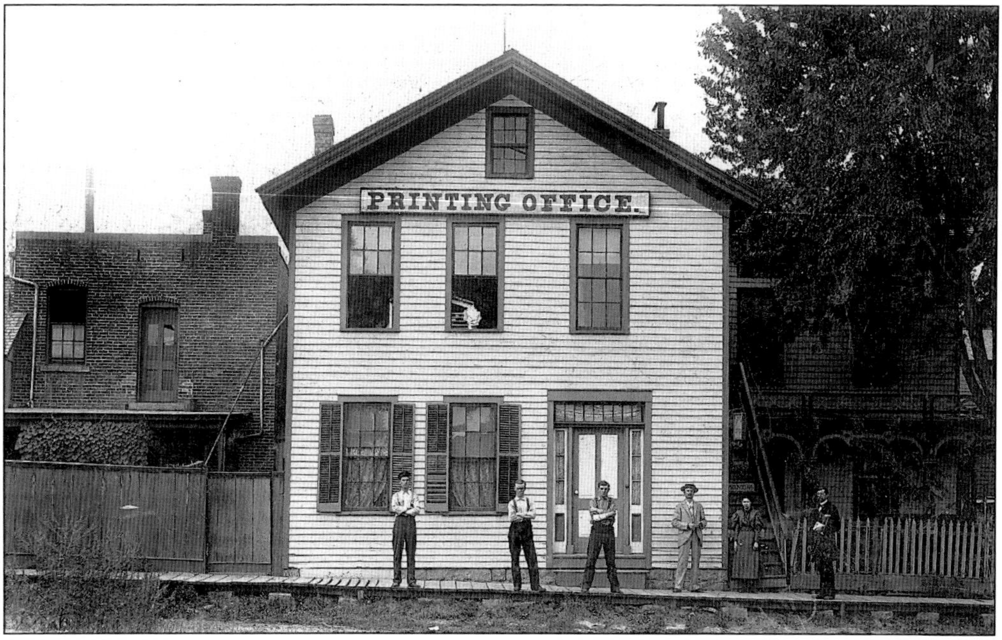

Here Mr. Rindlaub, on the far right, stands in front of the *Grant County Witness*' printing office, c. 1880. The building was located just south of the southwest corner of Main and Court Streets. Rindlaub retired as its editor in 1902.(Courtesy of Dick Brockman.)

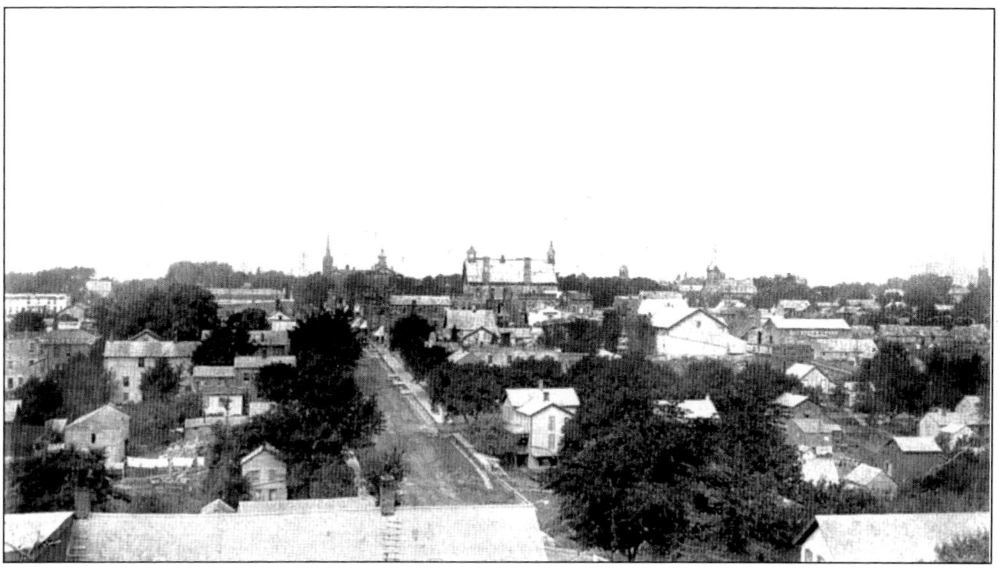

Sometime around 1885, Virgil H. Young, a photographer working at Robertson's photographic studio in Platteville, climbed to the top of the Rock School (today's Mining Museum), pointed his camera west and took this photograph of Platteville. The readily identifiable landmarks are, left to right, Methodist Episcopal Church (first steeple on left), State Normal School (belfry), City Hall, Trinity Episcopal Church (truncated steeple), Congregational Church, and St. Mary's Catholic Church (on far right).

Two

From Platteville Academy to State Normal School

"The exclusive purpose of each (Normal School) shall be the instruction and training of persons, both male and female, in the Theory and Art of teaching."

–Section 4, of Chapter 116, Laws of 1866

The origins of the University of Wisconsin-Platteville lay in the mid-19th century. The first institution of higher education in Platteville was the Platteville Academy, which operated from 1839 to 1842 as a private school and from 1842 to 1866 as a publicly supported school. It prepared students for college, business, and certified individuals as grade school teachers. At its peak, it had an enrollment of 310 students in 1857–58.

During the Civil War the state of Wisconsin recognized the need for a normal school system for educating teachers and passed the Normal School Act of 1865. On February 28, 1866, the legislature chose Platteville as the site for the state's first Normal School, partially because the Platteville Academy's Board of Trustees offered the academy as the site. The new State Normal School not only replaced the Platteville Academy, but also occupied the old academy's building.

When the Normal School opened its doors on October 9, 1866, it consisted of 5 faculty and 210 students. The students were placed into one of three divisions: Normal School for those who were academically prepared, Preparatory Class for the students who needed more academic preparation, and Model School for the students of grade school ages who were instructed by the Normal School teachers and students.

Jane Curkeet, a preparatory student, wrote the following account of student life in the new school on October 10, 1866, "Dear cousin Katie . . . if I was to tell you about Platteville or our school you could not understand it as it is so much different from any school you ever saw. . . . We have to get up at five oclock and study two hours then eat our breakfast and get ready for school. If we are not there and in our seats at $^1/_2$ past 8 we cannot go in. In the evening school is dismissed at half past four, then we have until six to eat supper and get ready to study, at nine the bell rings for us to go to bed so you see we have not much time to play."

By 1907, the Normal School, with a faculty of 26 and a student body of 459, had not only earned a reputation as an outstanding institution for the education of teachers, it had outgrown its original facility. A new main building was constructed two blocks west on Main Street and opened in September 1907.

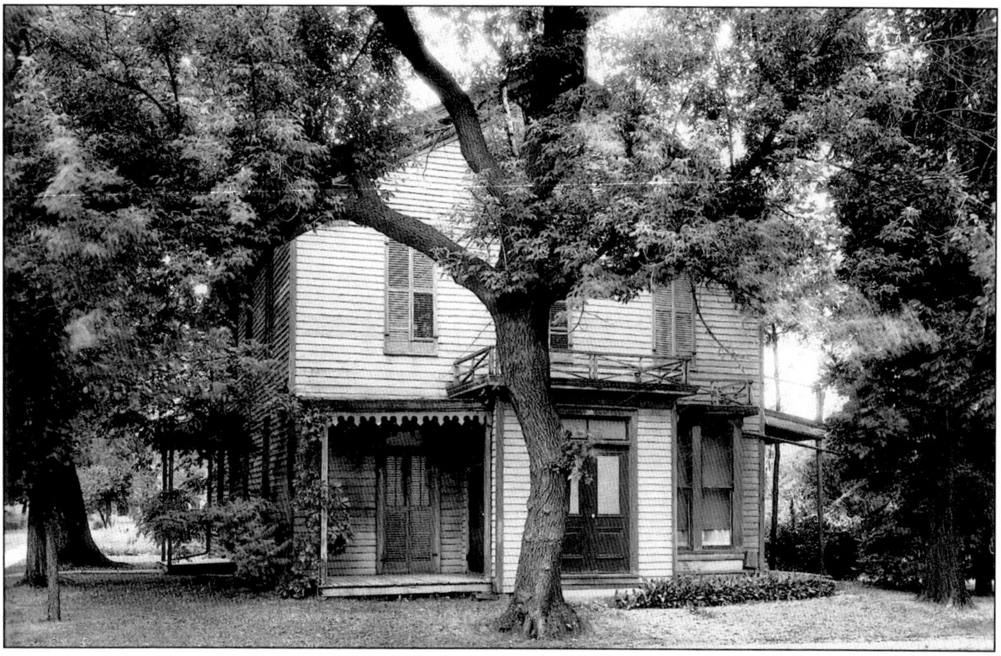

The Platteville Academy's first permanent home, from 1842 to 1853, was this Greek Revival structure at the northeast corner of Cedar and Bonson Streets. Built in 1842, the academy shared the building with the Presbyterian Church, which conducted its services on the first floor until 1846. Incidentally, the academy probably received its first books in 1843 via the Mississippi River when, evidence indicates, they were shipped "with some Merchants goods" from New York.

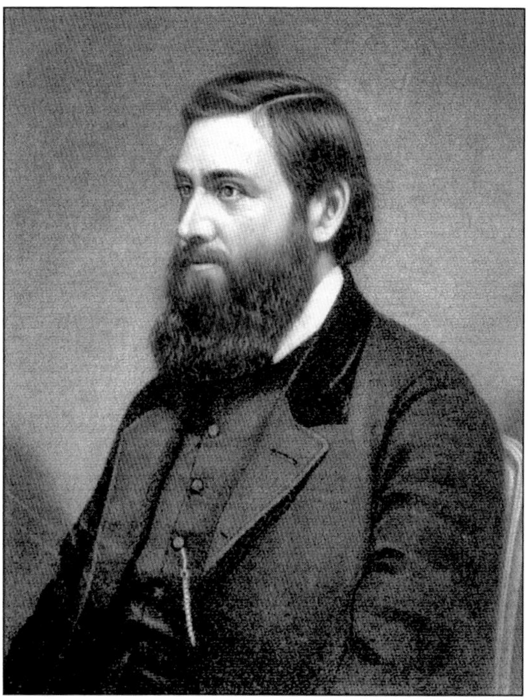

Josiah Pickard was the Platteville Academy's third and most influential principal. A native of Massachusetts, Pickard came to Wisconsin Territory in September 1846. Under his guidance, the academy increased in enrollment, opened a new building in 1853, and laid the groundwork for Wisconsin's first State Normal School, established in 1866. In 1860, Pickard left the academy to work as the state superintendent of public instruction.

In October 3, 1853, the Platteville Academy held its first classes in its new home at the northwest corner of Main and Elm Streets. That building, shown here in an 1855 drawing, was constructed with Blue Limestone. According to a student, its first floor had "recitation rooms" and "a large assembly and study hall;" the second floor had a "music room and physical Laboratory, and the third story was used as dormitory for men students." It was surmounted by a belfry with a bell that announced class changes.

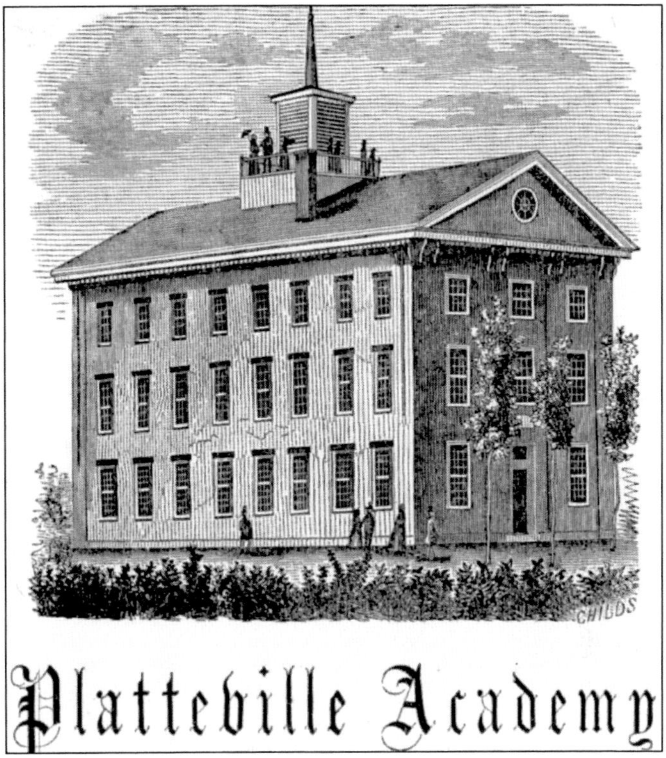

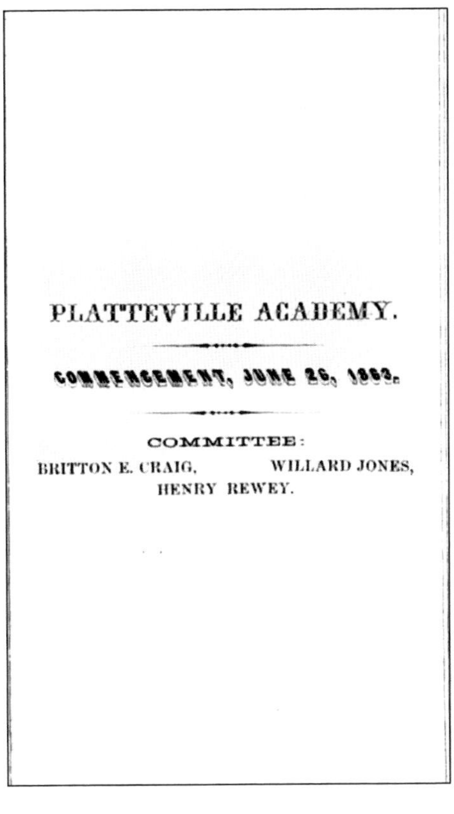

PLATTEVILLE ACADEMY.

COMMENCEMENT, JUNE 26, 1863.

COMMITTEE:

BRITTON E. CRAIG, WILLARD JONES,
HENRY REWEY.

The Platteville Academy's commencements were held each year in late June or early July. This is the front cover of the June 26, 1863, commencement program.

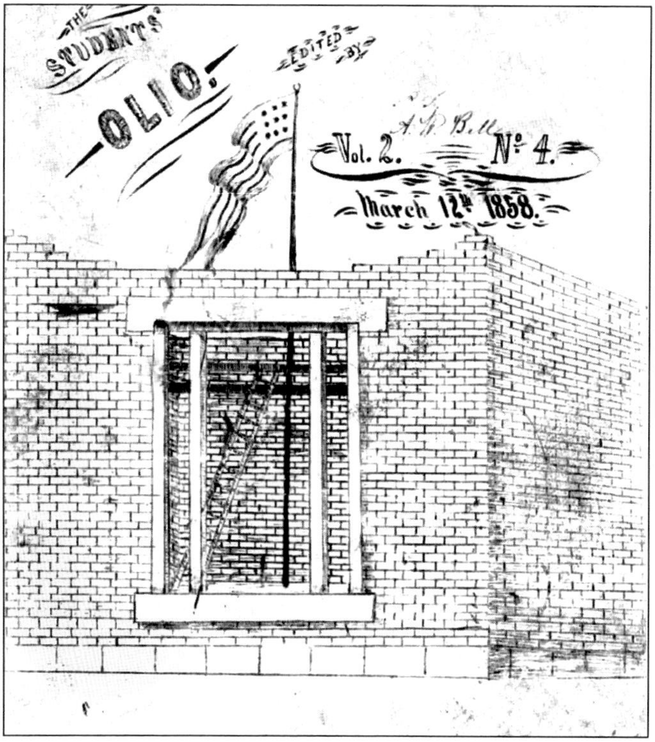

The academy students wrote their own newspaper: *The Students' Olio*. It was handwritten, because the typewriter had yet to be invented, and issued from 1857 to 1864. Shown here is the March 12, 1858, cover of the *Olio*. The illustration is probably Nicolas Messersmith's Greek Revival house, which was under construction at that time at the southeast corner of Main and Elm Streets. Nicolas, a wagon maker, and his wife Catherine had four children. The house still stands.

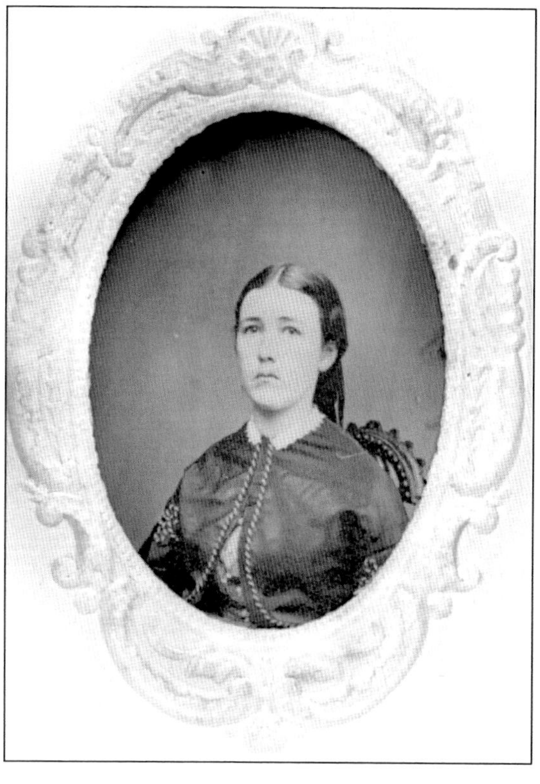

Unfortunately, few photographs of academy students have survived. Cordelia Seeley, shown here, attended the academy in the late 1850s with two of her siblings, Ellen and Rufus. The daughter of nearby Elk Grove Township (Lafayette County) farmers David and Sophia Seeley, Cordelia sat for this photograph in Platteville in late 1865 or 1866.

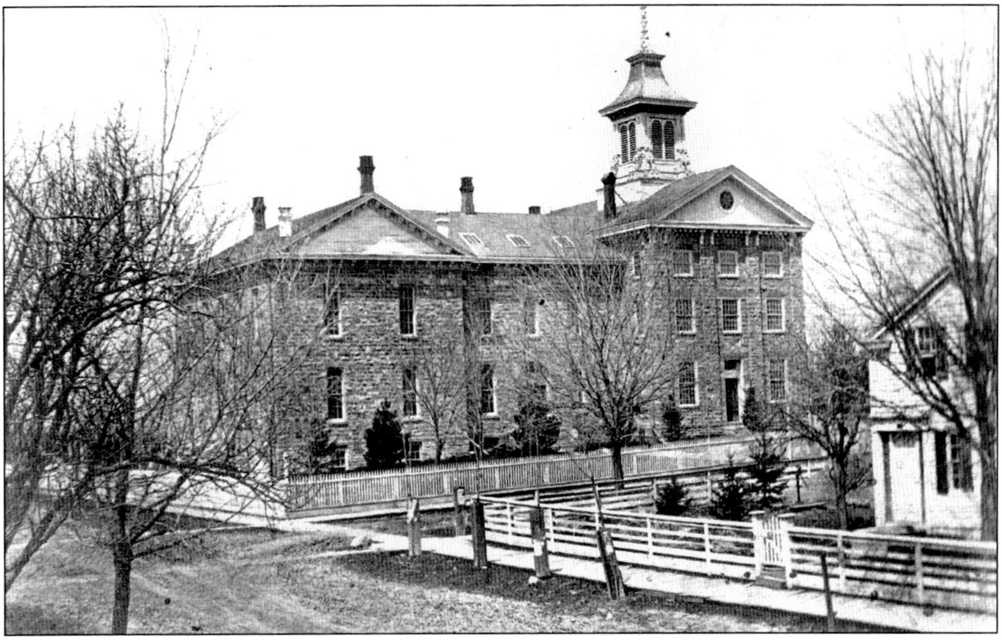

On October 9, 1866, Wisconsin's first State Normal School opened in Platteville. This photograph, c. 1875, shows how the Normal School (the old academy building) appeared after its first addition in 1867–68 had been completed. The new south wing, which cost $20,000, was dedicated on September 9, 1868. Another change occurred in 1870, when the old Academy Bell cracked; it was replaced with what became known as the old Normal Bell.

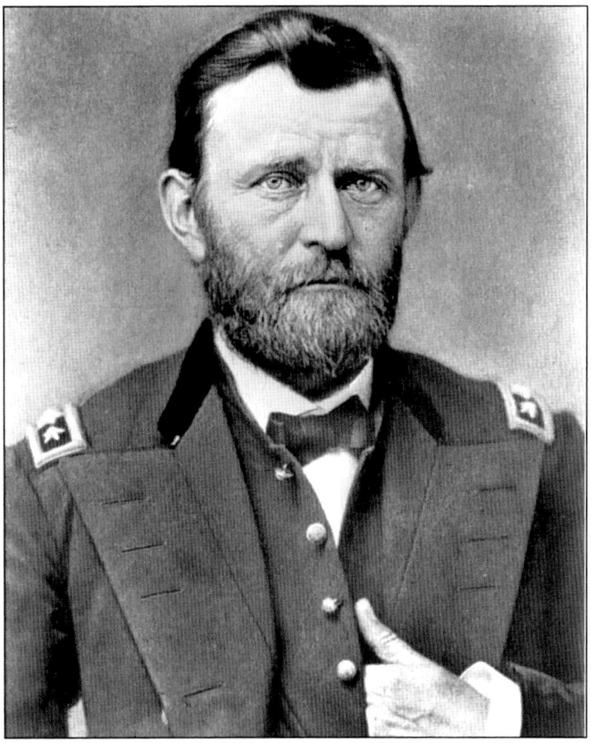

One of the attendees at the dedication in 1868 was General Ulysses S. Grant, Civil War hero and resident of nearby Galena, Illinois. Grant, who was the Republican Party's candidate for the presidency, remarked that "I did not know that an occasion of so much importance would bring you from your homes to-day, but I am glad to be with you." (Courtesy of Galena/Jo Daviess County Historical Society and Museum.)

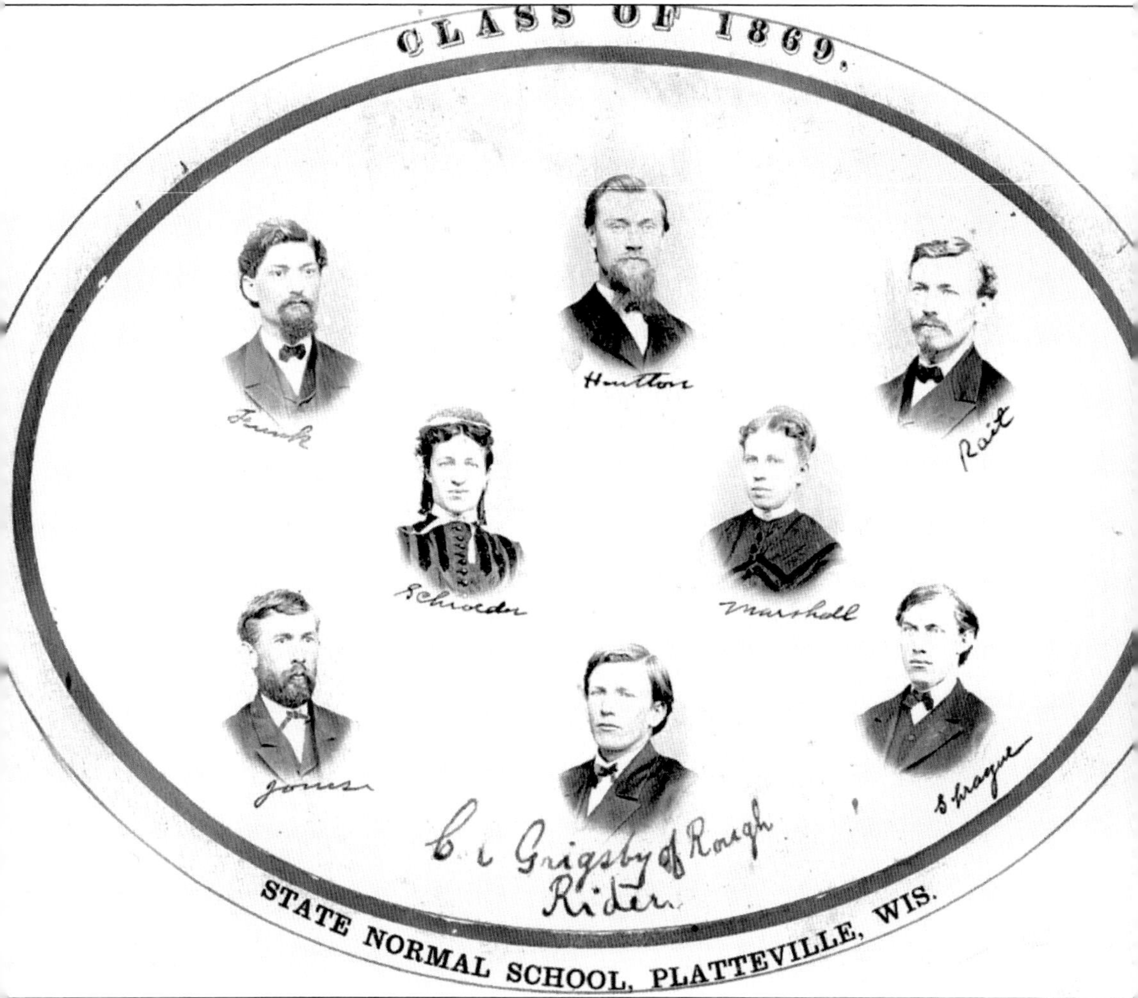

The Normal School was fortunate to have class photographs taken from the beginning. Shown here is the Class of 1869, the first class of the Normal School. The students are, from left to right: (bottom) Richard Jones, Melvin Grigsby, and Edward Sprague; (middle row) Alvana Schroeder and Ella Marshall; (top row) Lewis Funk, Andrew Hutton, and James Rait. Grigsby led an event-filled life. In addition to being a member of the first class, he also played in the Normal School's first baseball game in June 1867. During the Civil War, while serving in the 2nd Wisconsin Cavalry, he was captured and incarcerated in the infamous Andersonville Prison. In the 1880s he wrote a lively book about his war experiences, *The Smoked Yank*. And in 1898, while he was serving as South Dakota's State Attorney General, he commanded "Grigsby's Rough Riders" during the Spanish-American War.

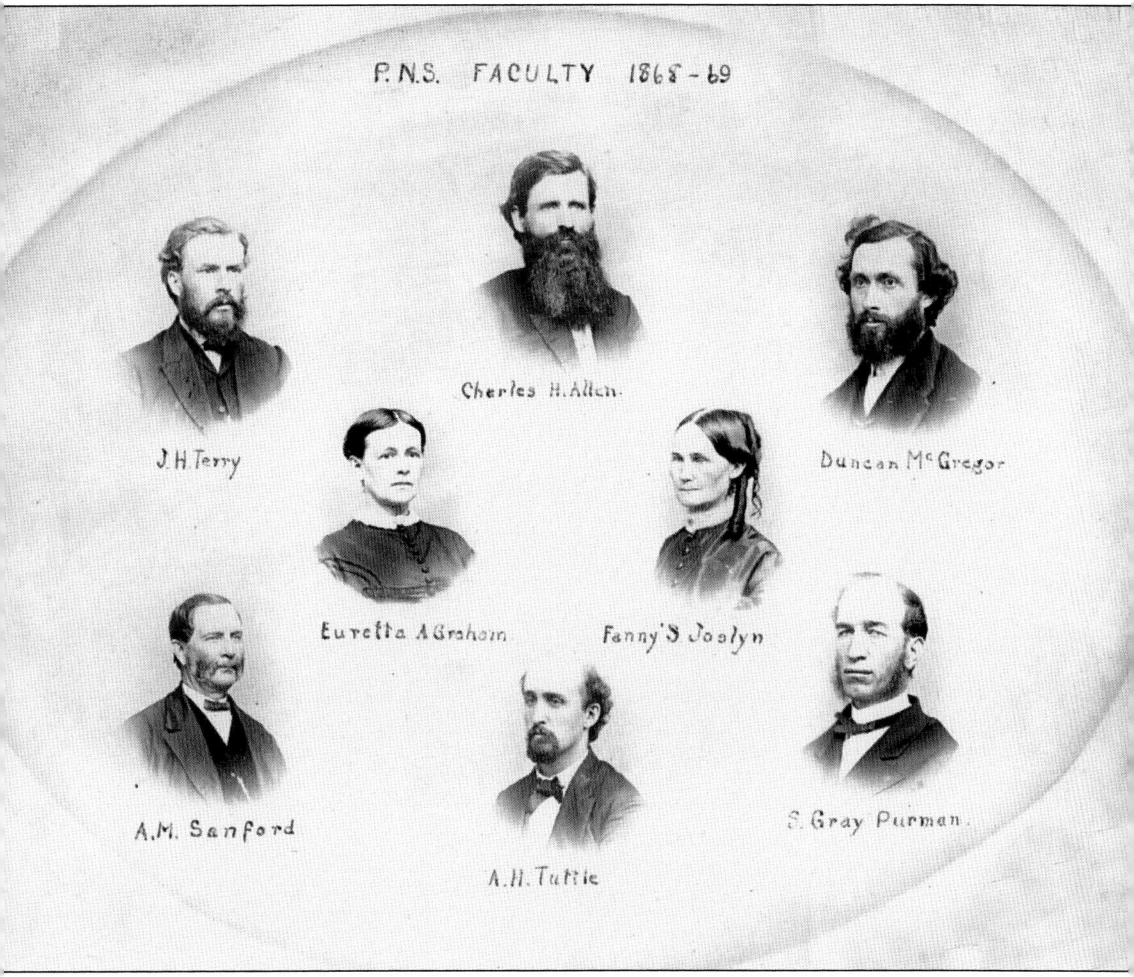

Similarly, this is a photograph of the Normal School's faculty for the 1868–69 school year. Pictured, from left to right, are: (bottom row) A.M. Sanford, vocal music; A.H. Tuttle, natural sciences; and S. Gray Purman, English; (middle row) Euretta A. Graham, Model School principal; and Fanny S. Joslyn, preceptress; (top row) J.H. Terry, principal of Academic Department; Charles Allen, first president of the school (1866–70); and Duncan McGregor, mathematics. McGregor went on to become one of the most influential administrators of the Normal School, serving as its president from 1879–94 and 1897–1904. During his tenure, two additions to the old Normal School were constructed, one in 1881–82 and the other in 1891–92, and, in the 1890s, land was purchased on the west side of town (present site of the Center for the Arts) for future expansion. He served as a member of the Board of Normal School Regents from 1905 until his death in 1921.

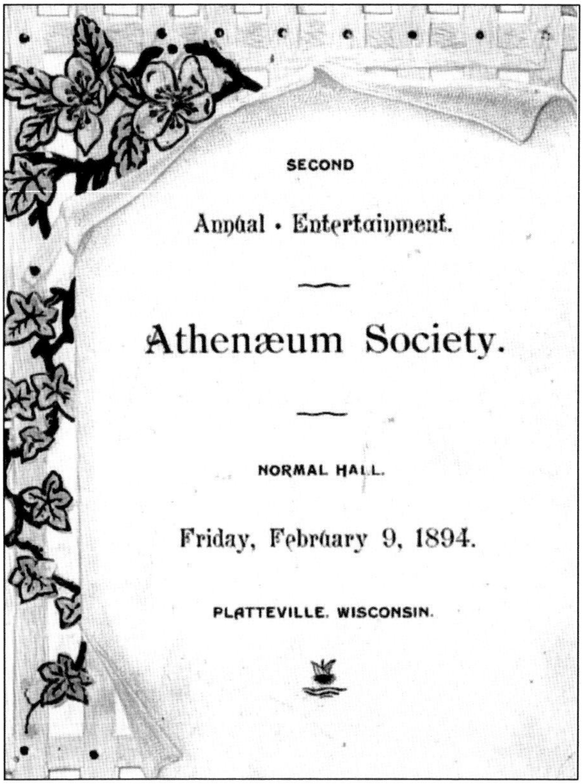

SECOND

Annual • Entertainment.

Athenæum Society.

NORMAL HALL.

Friday, February 9, 1894.

PLATTEVILLE, WISCONSIN.

Almost from the beginning, the Normal School had two student literary societies—one male, the Philadelphian Literary Society organized in 1866, and one female, Nulli Se Cundus (Second to None) Literary Society organized in 1867. Nulli Se Cundus changed its name to Athenae Society in 1868 and to Athenaeum Society by 1874. This is the cover of a program for an Athenaeum Society event sponsored in 1894.

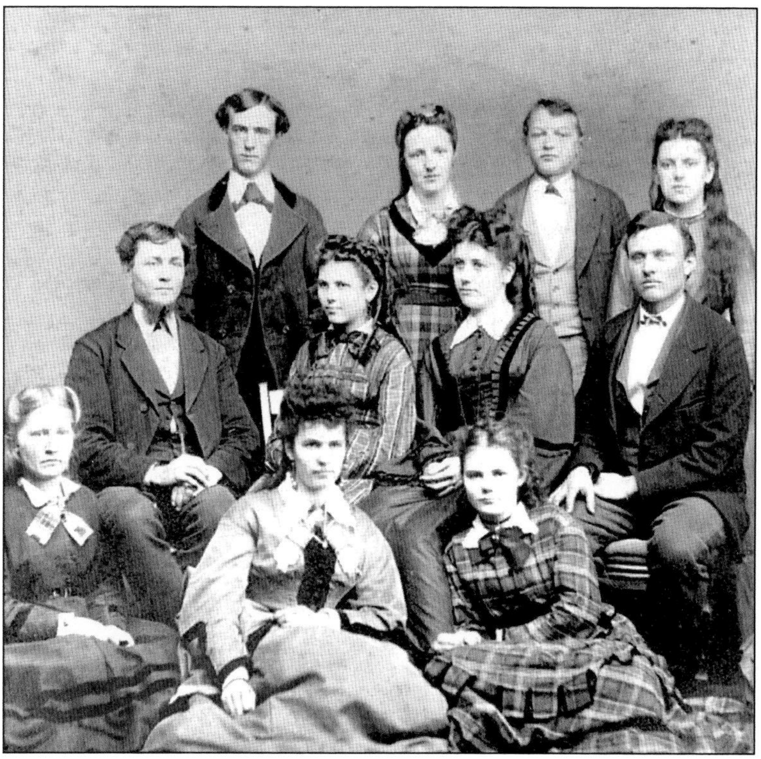

Shown here, in a typical pose for the era, is part of the Middle (Junior) Class of 1873. The students are, from left to right: (first row) Eva Grigsby (Melvin's younger sister), Via Hutchins, and Mary Barret; (middle row) Lewis Cooley, Nettie Robbins, Anna Baker, and James Oettiker; (top row) Levi Witherbee, Anna Bayley, Paul Haunus, and Maude Goodfellow.

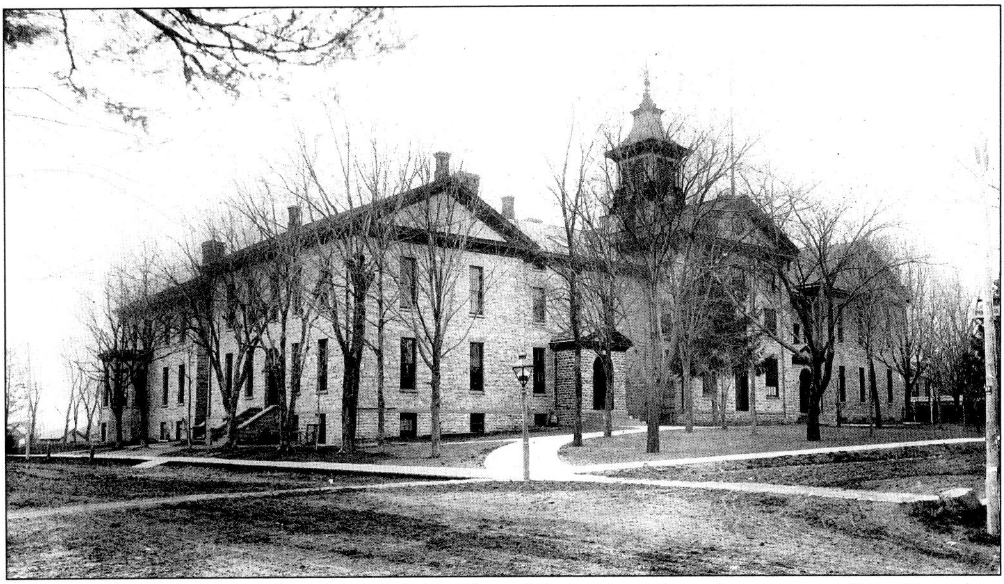

Over the next 20 years, the Normal School's building was enlarged twice, in 1881–82 and in 1891–92. This photograph, *c.* 1895, shows, from right to left, the 1881–82 addition (with bay window), the 1868 addition (with steps), the 1853 central part (with Belfry), and the 1891–92 addition on the far right. (Courtesy of the Rollo Jamison Museum, hereafter RJM.)

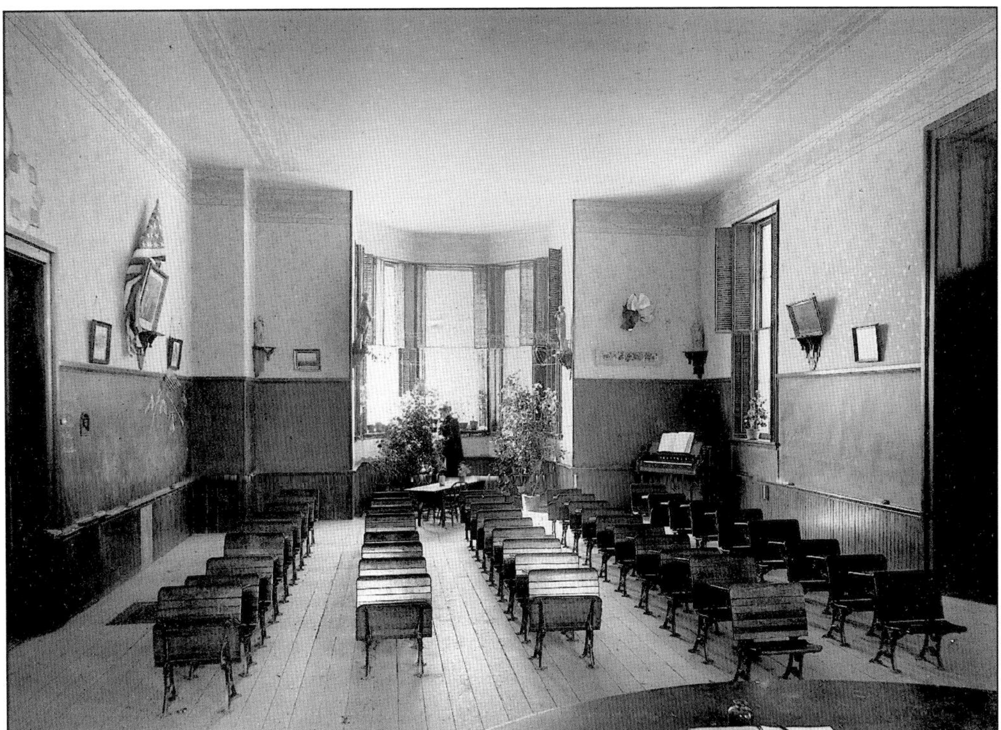

The 1881–82 enlargement added six recitation rooms and provided the Primary Department with a new kindergarten room, where the bay window is located. This is the interior of the new kindergarten room, with its bay window in 1893.

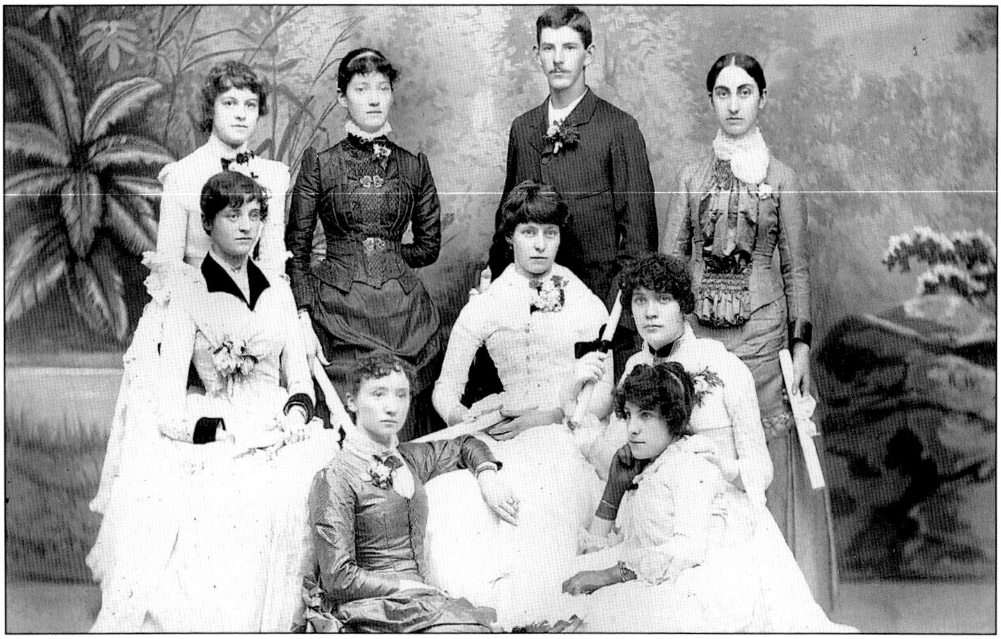

By the early 1870s, the Normal School divided its course offerings into a two-year elementary course and a four-year advanced course. Students who opted for the elementary course received a certificate that, after they completed one year of teaching, would "then have the force and effect of a five years' State Certificate." This is the Elementary Class of 1885. Notice the large, rolled certificates that they are holding.

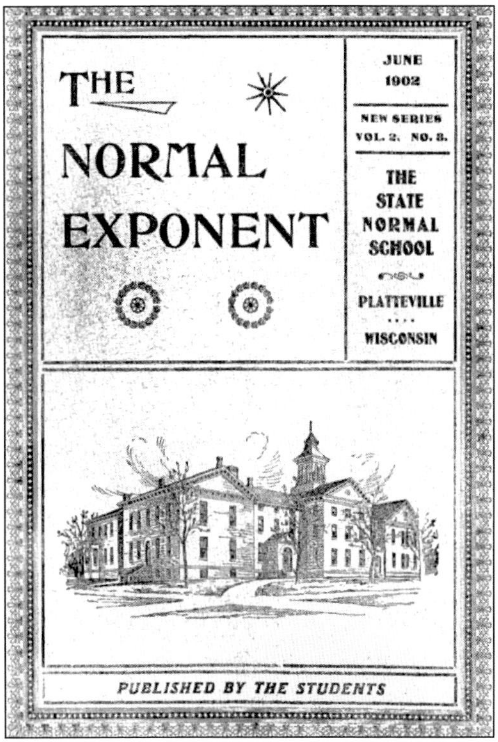

THE NORMAL EXPONENT

JUNE 1902

NEW SERIES VOL. 2. NO. 8.

THE STATE NORMAL SCHOOL

PLATTEVILLE WISCONSIN

PUBLISHED BY THE STUDENTS

In October 1889, the students began publishing a newspaper, the *Normal Exponent*. The June 1902 issue is shown here. It has remained the student newspaper ever since, except for 1892–1899, when a lack of profit halted its publication. Today it is called the *Exponent*.

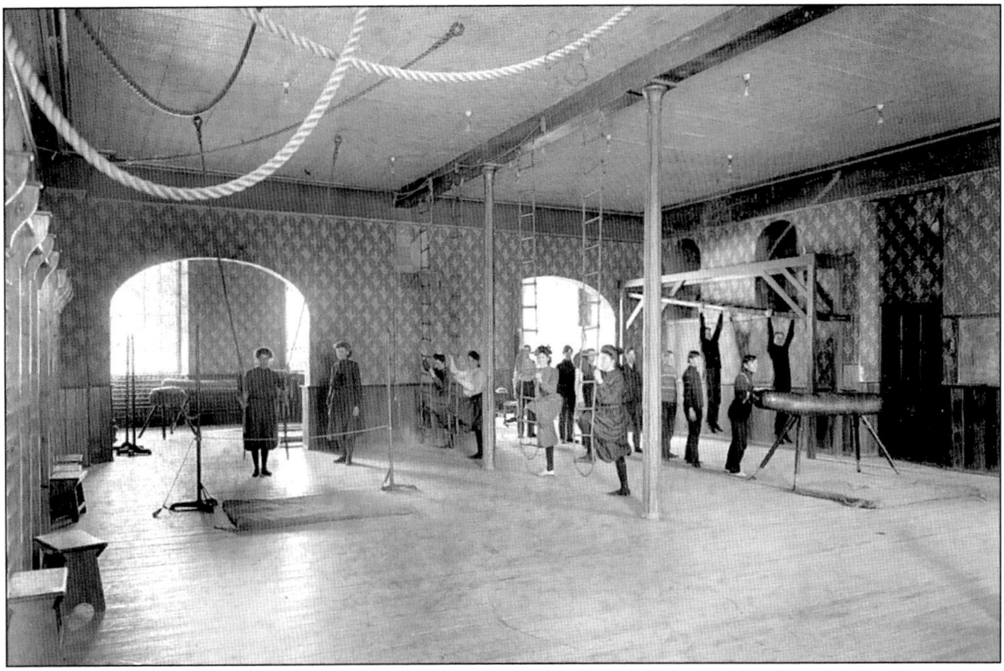

This is the third and final addition to the Normal School in 1891–92, which provided the school with a 225-seat assembly room, a gymnasium, and more classrooms. This photograph (*c.* 1896) shows the new gymnasium, complete with rope ladders, balancing beam, and chin-up bar.

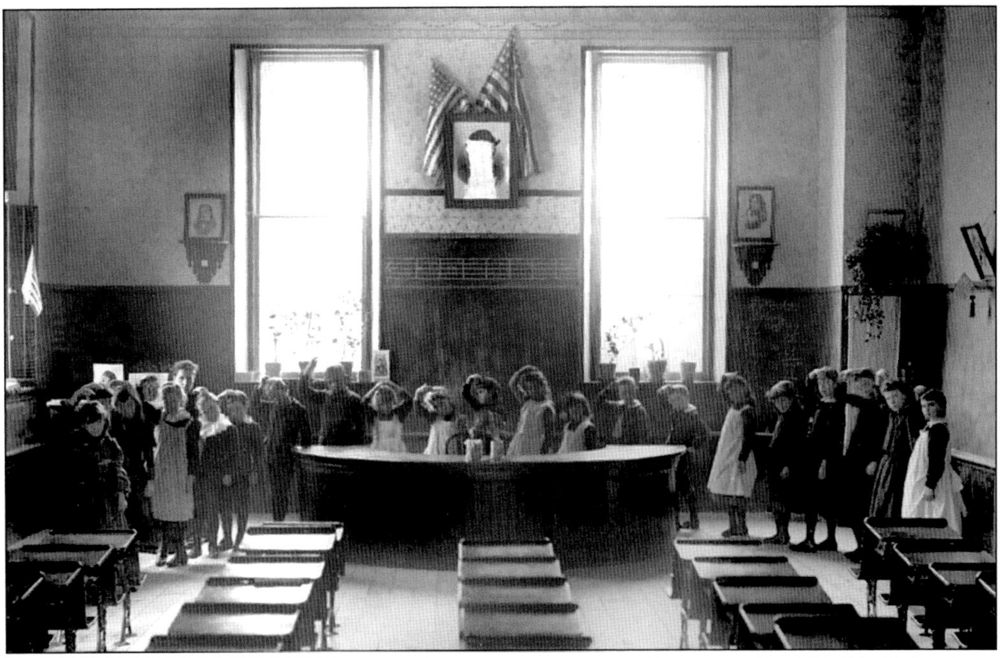

In 1893, the Normal School entered a photographic exhibit at the World Columbian Exposition in Chicago. It was entitled "Wisconsin Educational Exhibit, State Normal School, Platteville." This and the next two photographs were part of that exhibit. Here, a Model School's kindergarten class is playing a game, perhaps Simon Says.

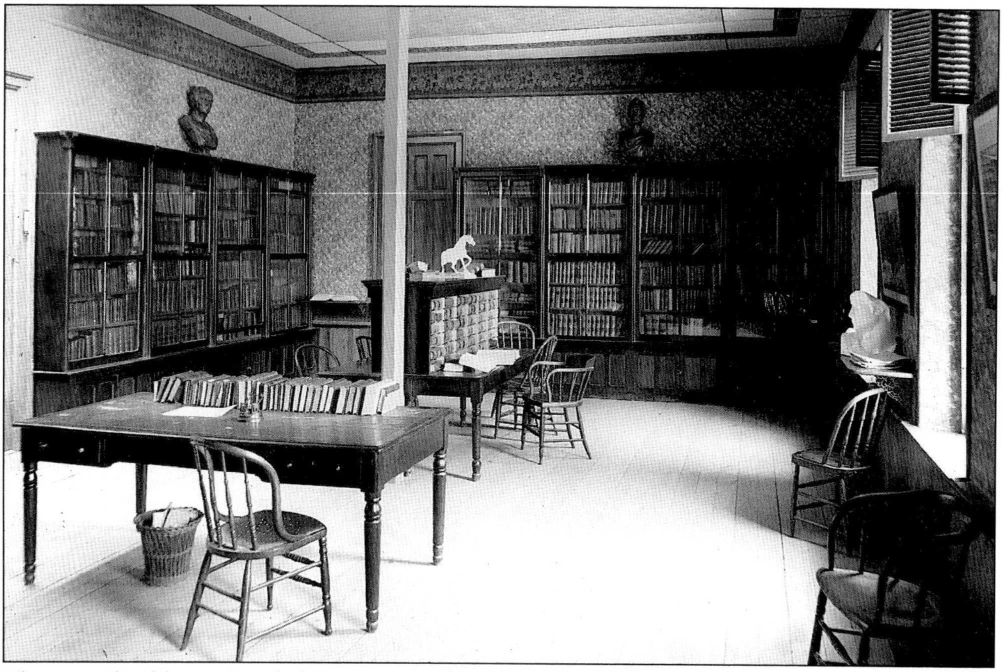

This was the library. Its shelves contained such works as Washington Irving's *Life of George Washington*, William Thackeray's *Miscellanies*, and Sherman's *Memoirs of General William T. Sherman*. Notice that the windows have shutters and the bookcases have glass doors.

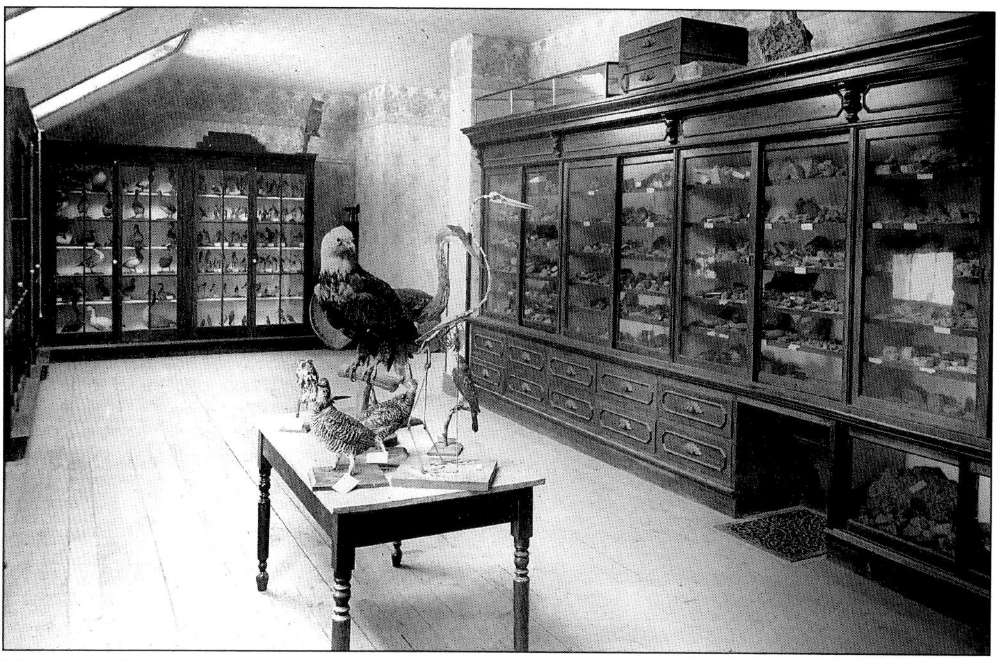

The third floor contained a natural and mineralogical collection—notice the skylights, bald eagle, and the cabinets filled with birds and rocks. According to the 1892–93 catalog, those cabinets held "two hundred and twenty-five mounted specimens of the birds of the State" and "a large geological and mineralogical collection."

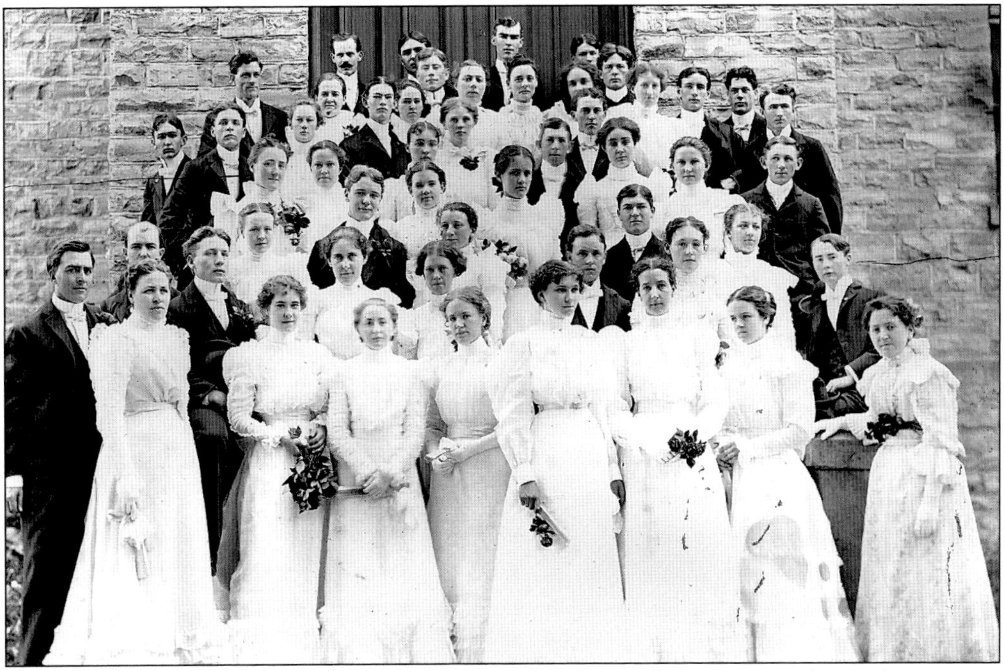

Around the turn of the century, one of the favorite spots to take a photograph was the steps on the west side of the west wing of the old Normal School. This photograph shows the Normal School Class of 1898 on those steps. The influence of famous illustrator Charles Dana Gibson and his pen-and-ink drawings on women's fashion can be seen in the long white dresses the ladies are wearing. The era of the "Gibson Girl" had arrived.

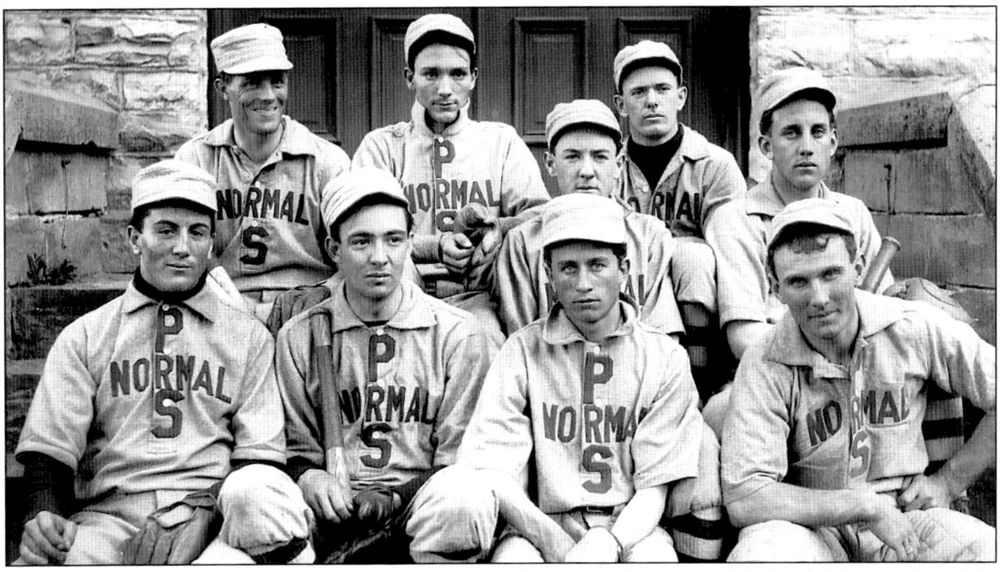

By the late 1800s, many extracurricular activities began at the Normal School. Here is the 1904 Normal "Base Ball" team—all nine of them. Baseball was the first organized sport played by the Normal School. On June 8, 1867, the Normal School played the "Darlington Base Ball Club" at Strawberry Diggings in Lafayette County. As reported in the local press, midway through the contest "the game was stopped for a pic nic dinner." Darlington won 16 to 15.

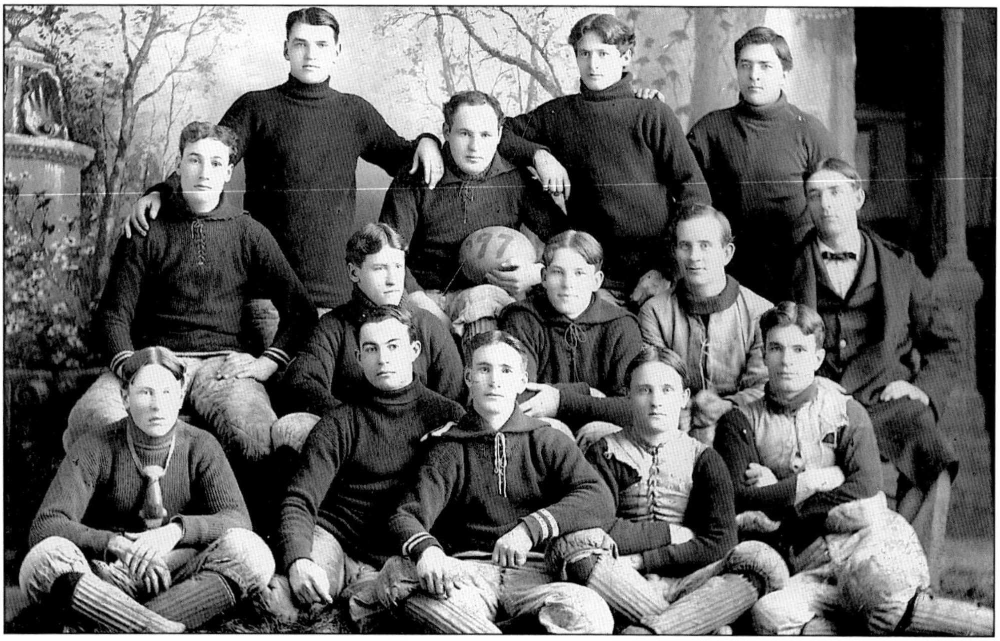

Football got its start at the Normal School in 1894. In its early years, the football team played teams from other villages, high schools, and colleges. The 1897 team, shown here, suffered two losses, one to the Darlington Athletics and the other to Whitewater Normal. Notice the players' lack of padding, helmets, and other protective gear.

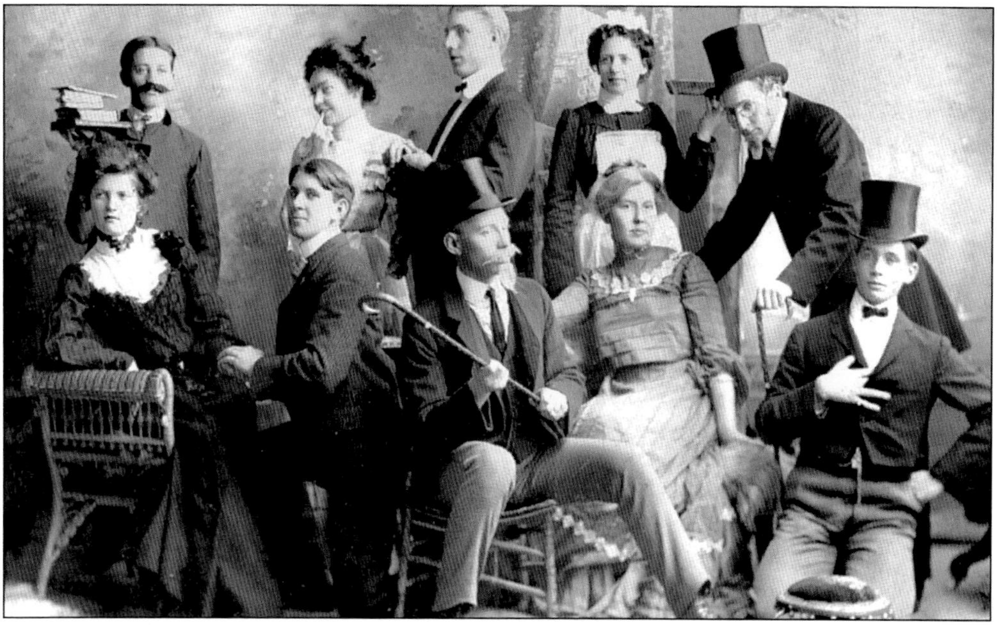

The Normal School also started to present plays around this time. Pictured here is the cast of the play, *A Night Off or A Page From Balzac*, presented on December 20, 1902, in Platteville's City Hall theater. The cast is, from left to right: (front row) Kitty Perry, George Dobson, John Burkholder, Lucille Jeardeau, and Edwin Tredinnick; (back row) Robert Cundy, Rilla Chisholm, Oscar Lee, Anna Stagner, and Scott Bailey.

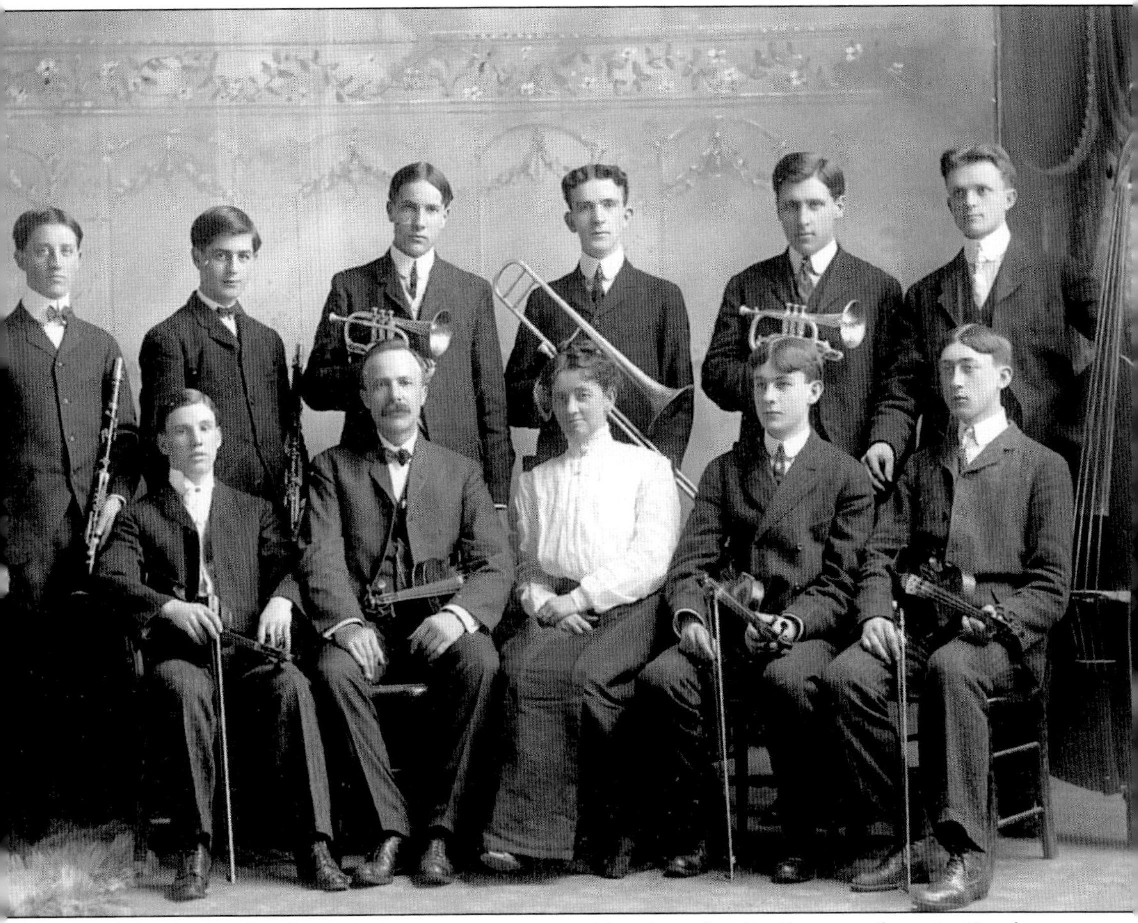

In 1903, the Normal School Orchestra was organized by the school's director of music, Frank Churchill, the middle-aged man seated second from left. Above is a photograph of the 1905 Normal School Orchestra. Professor Churchill and his assistant, Clara Grindell (on his left), also worked with the Training School students (the new name for the Model School), creating what became known as the Training School Orchestra. In the process, they collaborated to write songs for the children to play. They eventually formed the Churchill-Grindell Company and published their songs in a series of nationally-recognized children's song books. The orchestra members are, from left to right: (front row) Elmer Eastman, Churchill, Grindell, Will MacKay, and Richard McGregor; (top row) Robert Cundy, Ivan Breylinger, Floyd Churchill, Donald Grindell, John Curkeet, and Charles Fawcett.

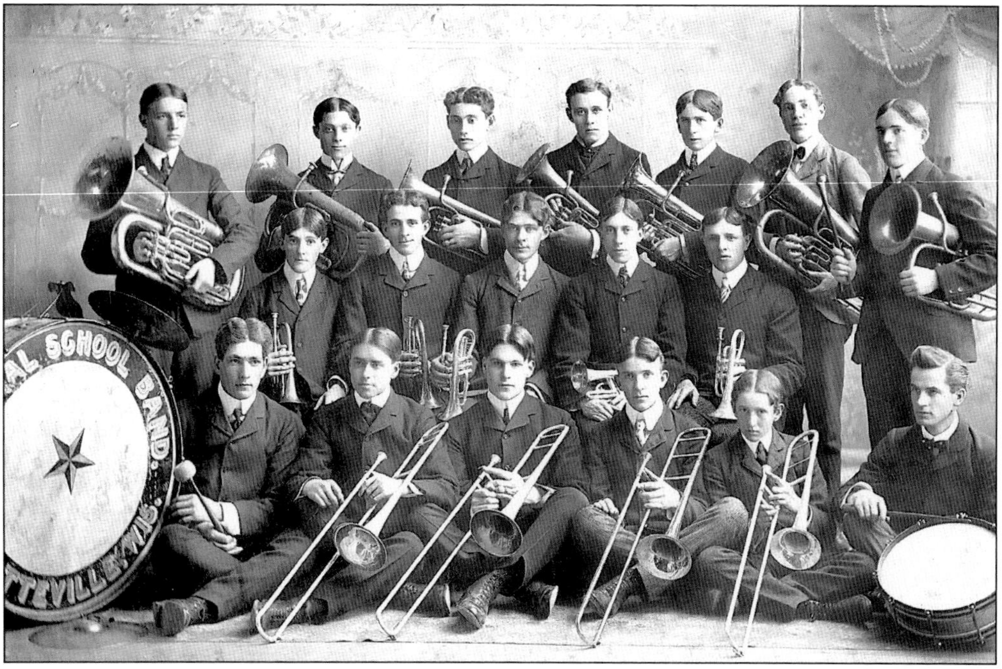

Four years earlier, in 1899, Platteville had been the first Normal School to organize a music band. This is the 1899 Platteville Normal School Band. The band played for a couple prominent people right at the start. In October 1899, the band played for President William McKinley, and, in 1900, it played for the governor of New York, Theodore Roosevelt.

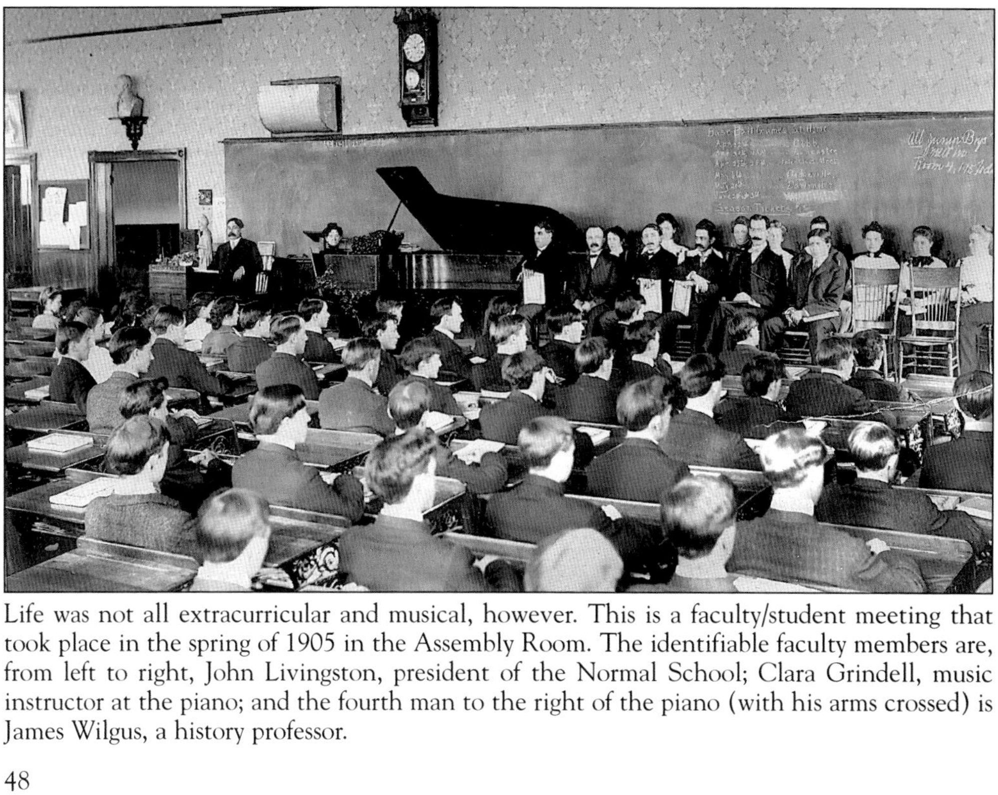

Life was not all extracurricular and musical, however. This is a faculty/student meeting that took place in the spring of 1905 in the Assembly Room. The identifiable faculty members are, from left to right, John Livingston, president of the Normal School; Clara Grindell, music instructor at the piano; and the fourth man to the right of the piano (with his arms crossed) is James Wilgus, a history professor.

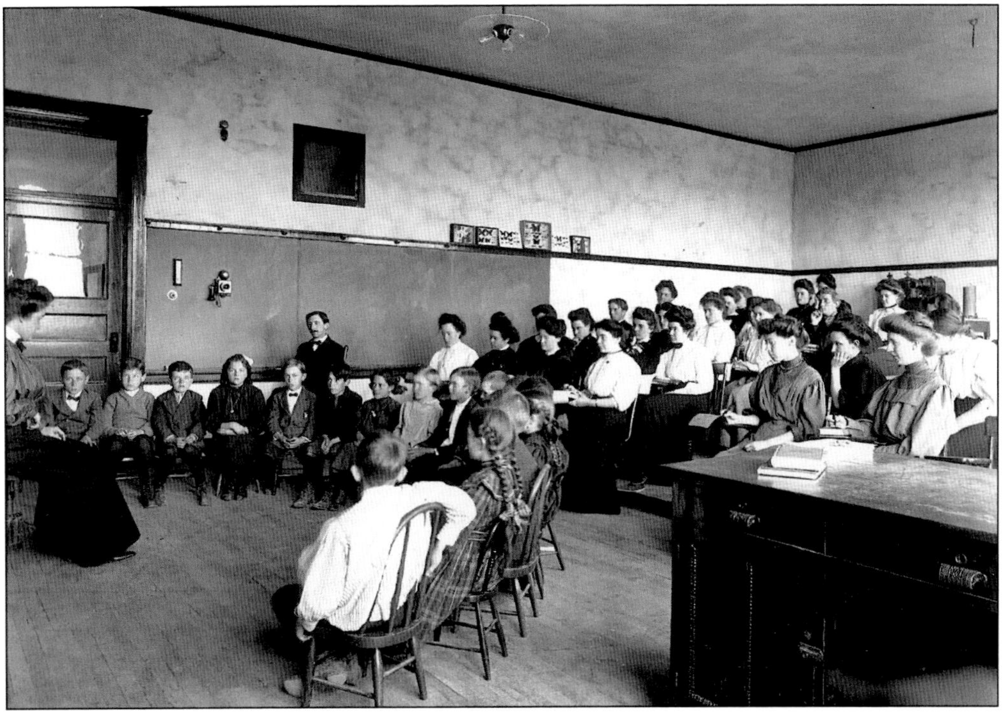

By this time the old Model School (for grade school students) was renamed the Training School. Here is one of the Training School classes in progress, c. 1905. Seated at the far left is Miss Jessie Todd, principal and critic of the intermediate grades; and the man seated in front of the blackboard is Mr. Thomas Gentle, the Director of the Training School. The Training School was eventually called the Laboratory School. It closed in 1973.

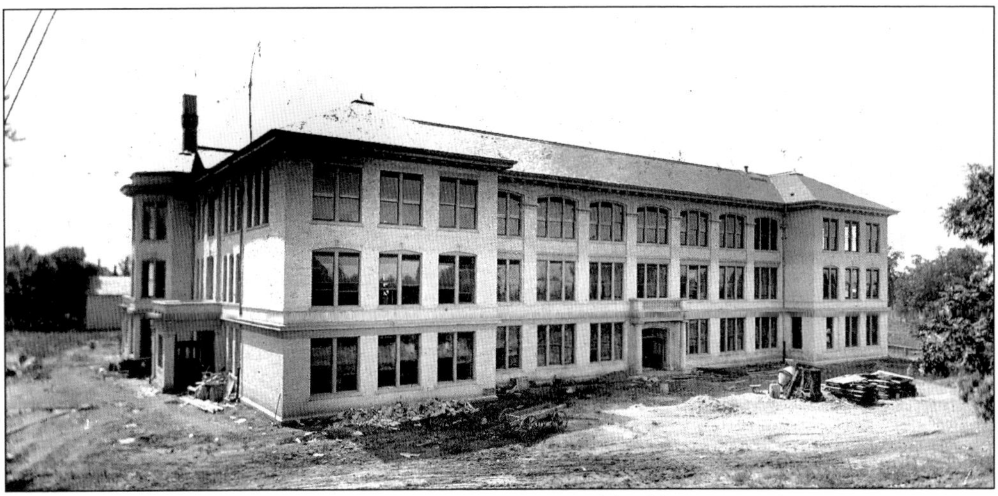

By 1907, the Normal School, having outgrown its original building, started constructing its new Main Building, shown here. At a total cost of $175,000, the building included "Large Libraries and Modern Laboratories, Manual Training Room, Fine Gymnasium, Drawing Department, Training School for Practice Teaching, Kindergarten Department, Vocal Music, Bands, and Orchestra." The building eventually became known as "old Main." It was razed in 1981. The Center for the Arts replaced it. (Courtesy of the author.)

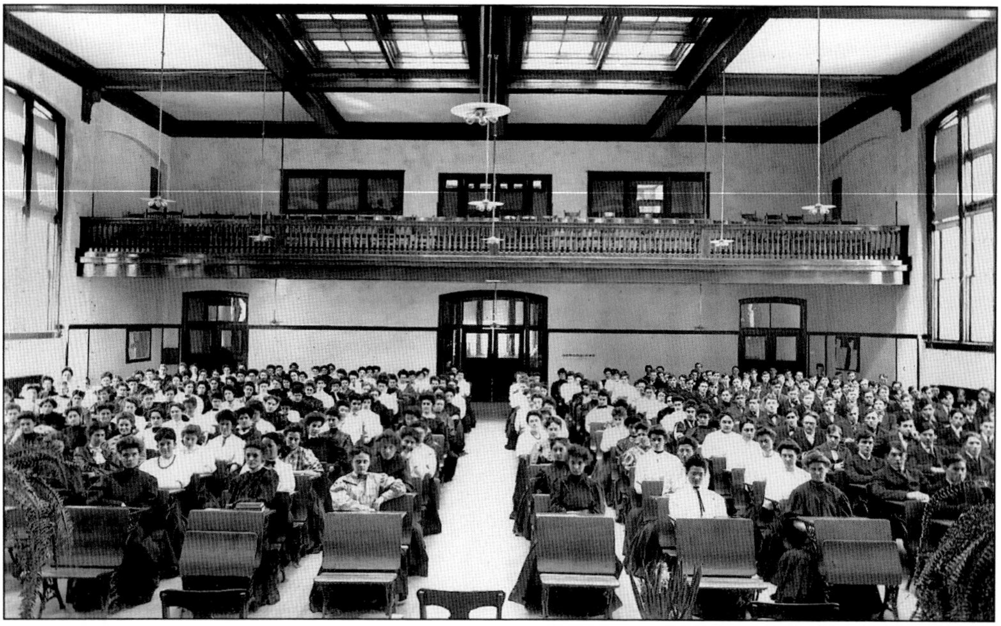

The Main Building's central meeting place was its Assembly Hall, shown here in 1907 or 1908. Notice that the women and men were seated separately. Assembly Hall was used for graduations, plays, and community events. Assembly Hall's third floor location, positioned between two interior courtyards, allowed it to receive natural light through skylights and side windows.

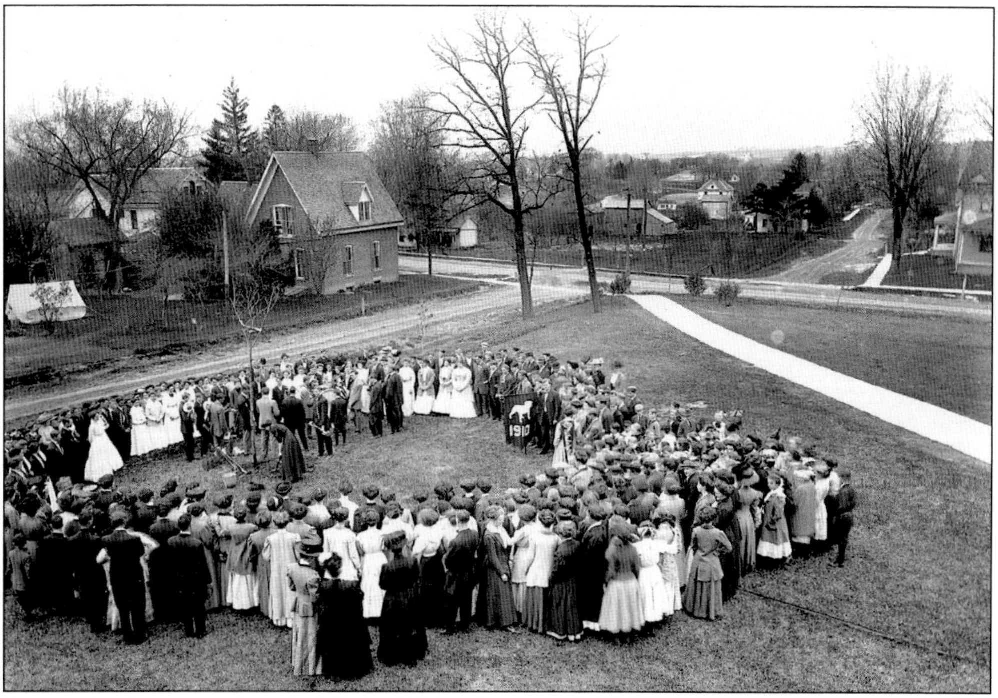

During the first years that the Normal School occupied the Main Building, planting a tree on Arbor Day was an annual event, complete with music, singing, and proclamations. Here the Class of 1910 is planting their "Senior Tree," an Elm tree, on the north lawn of the Main Building.

Three

Platteville Comes of Age

"The present situation in mining matters in Southwest Wisconsin far surpasses the expectations of the most enthusiastic. That Platteville and the surrounding territory are experiencing a sort of a 'boom,' no one can deny."

–*Platteville Witness and Mining Times*, February 21, 1906

On January 3, 1900, Dr. Wilson Cunningham, Platteville's legendary medical doctor, noted in his diary, "Arrived in Platteville my new home." The Platteville that he called home was in transition—it was leaving its pioneering era and quickly being transformed into a modern city. The two forces driving this change were economic and technological. Economically, zinc ore mining was on the rise in Southwest Wisconsin. The opening of the Enterprise (1899) and Empire (1902) Mines on the east side of town made Platteville a significant mining center again.

At the same time, Platteville was the recipient of a number of technological improvements. In July 1891, for example, electric lighting arrived when the Platteville Electric Light and Power Company began stringing power lines along Main and Second Streets. In 1896, the city's first water tower was constructed and water mains began to be laid. From 1899 onward, most of the new sidewalks were constructed with cement, instead of wood planks, and in 1900 the Platteville, Rewey & Ellenboro Telephone Company was incorporated.

These improvements were soon followed by other developments. In 1902, Dr. Cunningham became one of the first Plattevillians to own an automobile; in 1906 the city of Platteville started installing its first sewer system; and in 1910 the city paved Main and Second Streets with brick. All of this improved the quality of life. For the first time, a business or home could expect indoor plumbing, running water, electric lighting, telephone service, and, another significant improvement, coal-fired central heat.

It was during this time period, moreover, that Platteville shed its older look and began to assume its modern appearance. In 1907, the Normal School moved a couple blocks west, permanently anchoring the west side of town; in 1929 a new Art Deco Civic Memorial Building replaced the old City Hall; the city's first swimming pool opened in 1934; and several of the buildings associated with Main Street were constructed during this time.

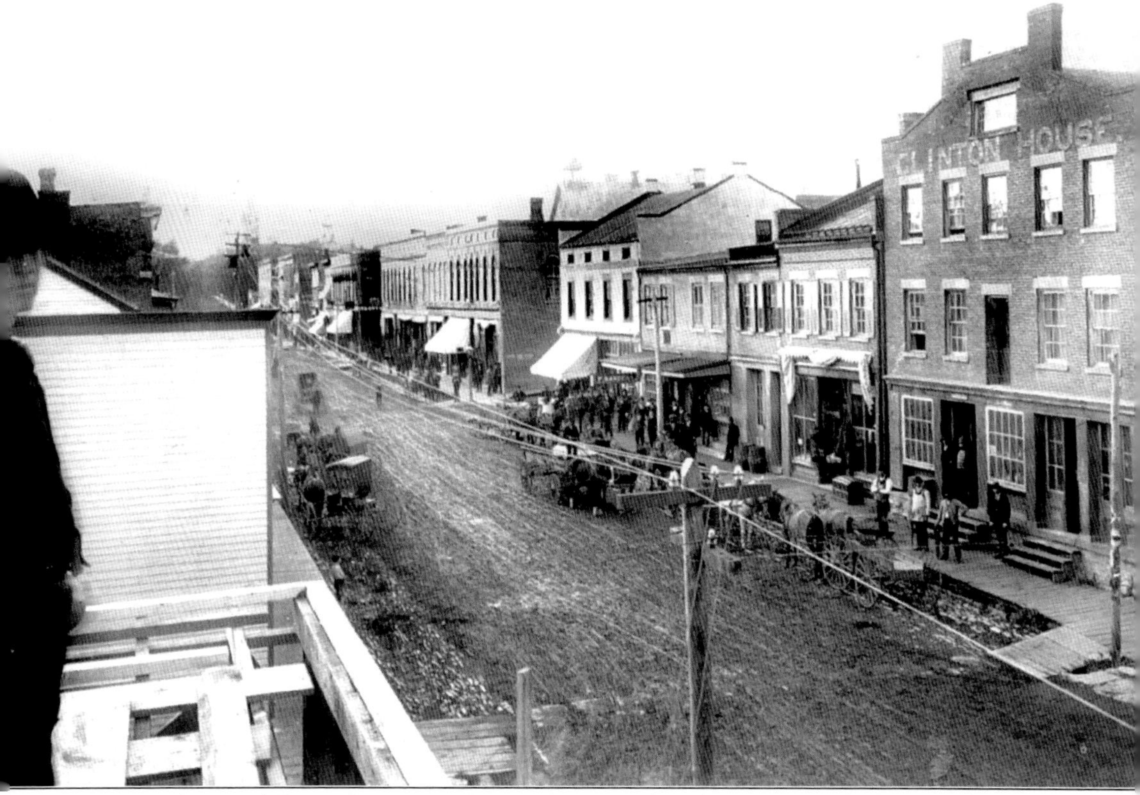

In and around December 1891, George Perry, and perhaps a second photographer, took six of the next seven photographs. The photographs captured how Main Street appeared when changes began to take place. This photograph, taken from the roof of the Columbia Hotel, located at Main and Oak Streets, shows the newly installed electric power lines running west on Main Street. The building on the far right was the Clinton House, an old general store building constructed in the 1840s. Around 1915, it became the home of Platteville's GEM Theatre. Perry's story itself is remarkable. Born in Platteville in 1858 and educated at the Normal School, an accident had left him a paraplegic. Undaunted, he became a photographer. Specializing in outdoor photography, he traveled throughout Southwest Wisconsin taking photographs. George Perry died on November 19, 1893, at the young age of 35.

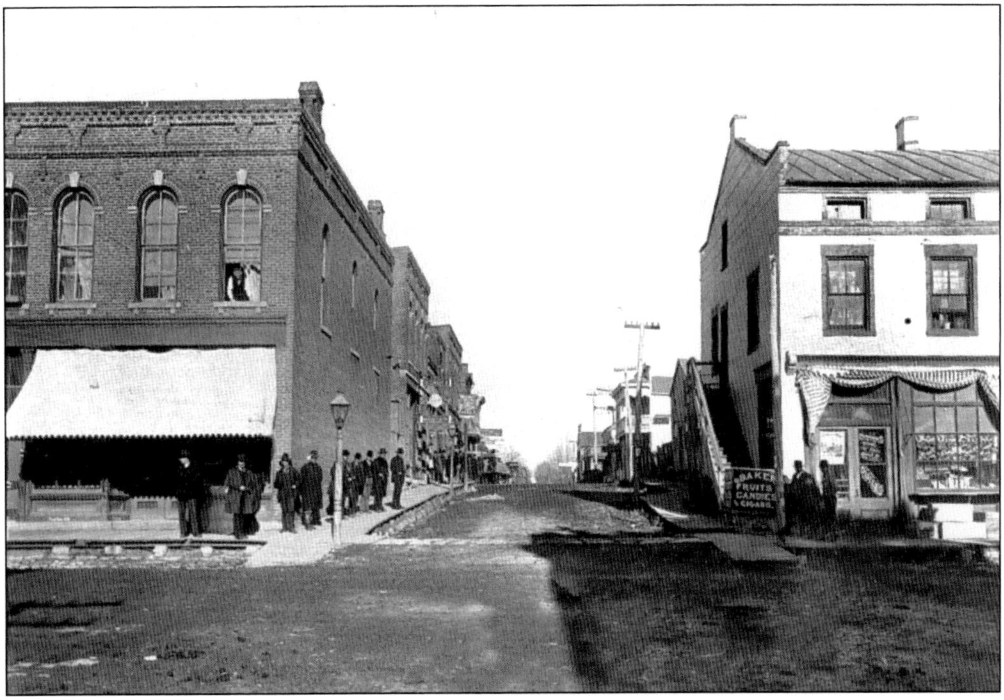

Here is Second Street in December 1891. The white building in the center of the previous image is on the right. Notice the wooden-planked sidewalks and the free-standing street light on the left. Again, the photographer captured the newly installed power lines.

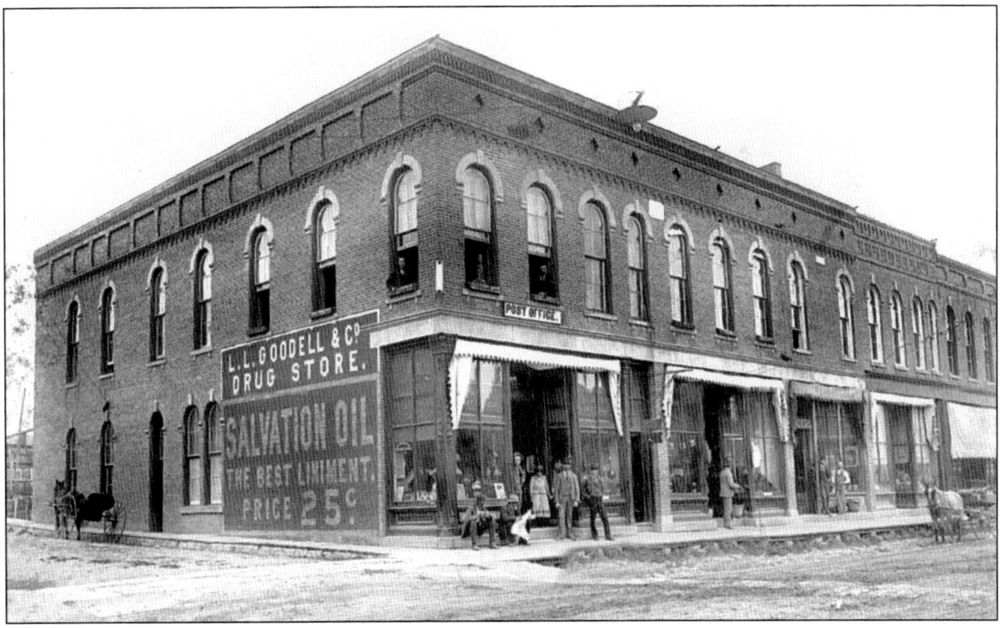

Moving another block west, here is the Goodell Drug Store at the northeast corner of Main and Third Streets, taken in 1891. Lemuel Goodell was one of Platteville's original druggists, operating a drug store in Platteville since the 1850s. Notice the post office located above Goodell's and the suspended electric street light.

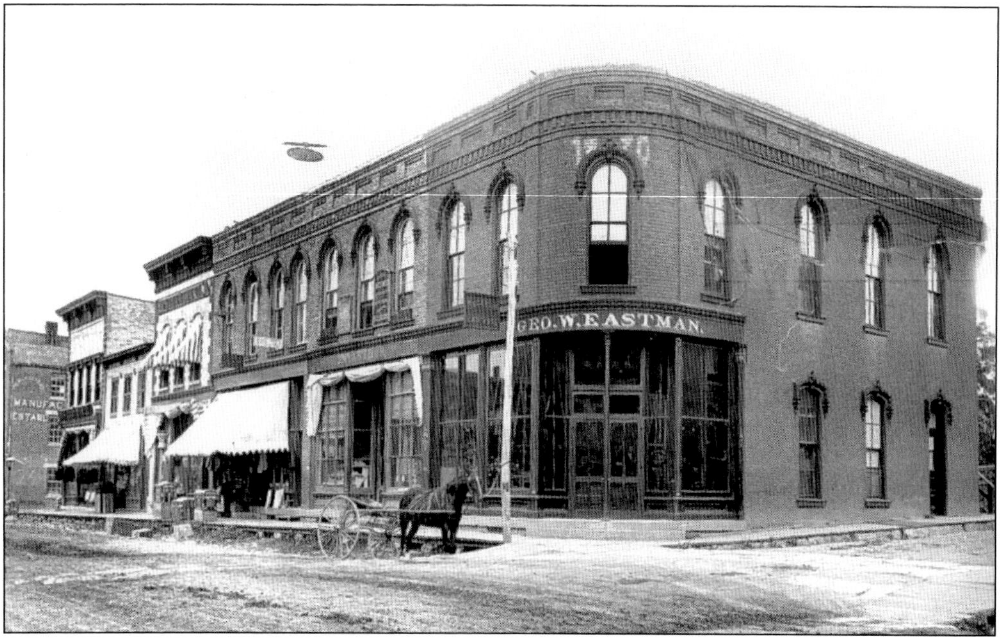

Repositioning his camera 90 degrees, the photographer then took this photograph of the George Eastman Bank, located on the northwest corner of Main and Third Streets. An early physician in Platteville (Dr. Eastman came to Platteville from Maine in 1850), Eastman organized this bank in 1884. In 1891, it became the First National Bank. Eastman served as its president until his death in 1900. (Courtesy of GCHS.)

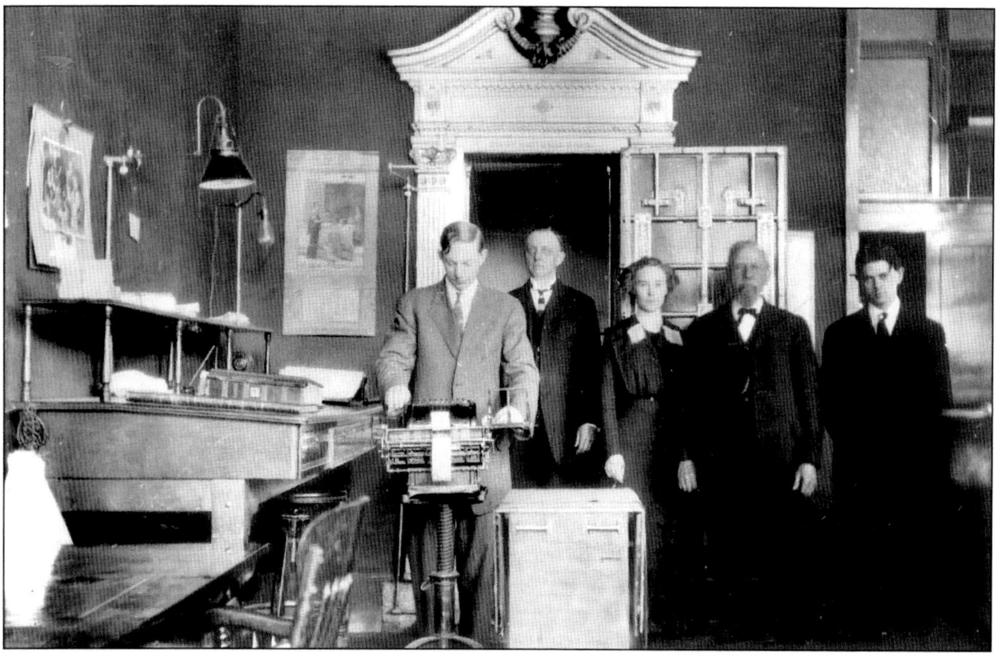

This is an interior image of the First National Bank in 1913. Shown from left to right are Frank Whitcher; Oliver E. Gray, cashier; Lillian Ruggles; Eibe Riege, president; and Charles Alexander, assistant cashier.

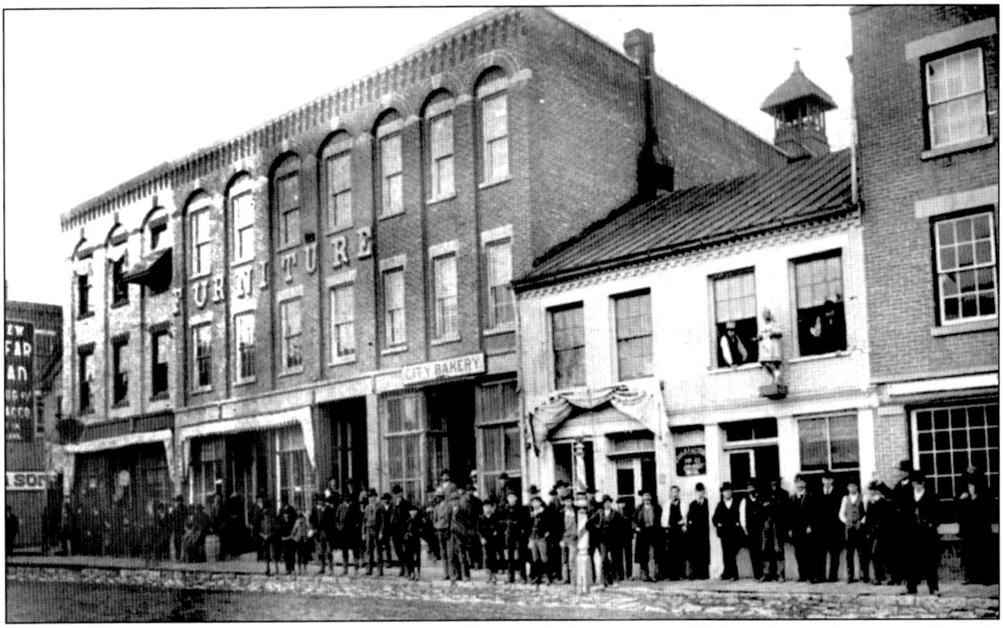

Moving west on Main Street, the photographer took this image of Main Street between Fourth and Bonson Streets. Shown , from right to left, are Jotham M. Smith's Hardware, the Grindell Brothers' Furniture Store, a cigar factory (with cigar store Indian), and Phillip Hendershot's Harness Shop. (Courtesy of GCHS.)

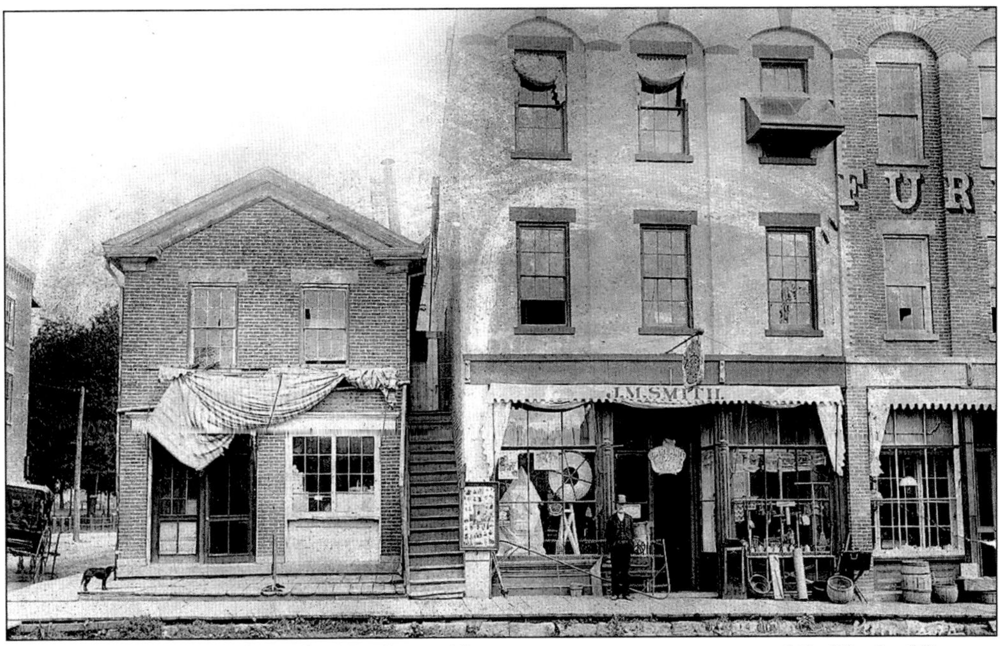

This is another view of Smith's Hardware (for an interior image, see page 64). The building on the left was once a little grocery store. The stairs led up to James L. Nye's photography shop on the third floor. Notice that Nye was advertising some of his work on the board to the right of the stairs, and that he has installed a glass shield (protruding from the third story window) to assist him in developing prints.

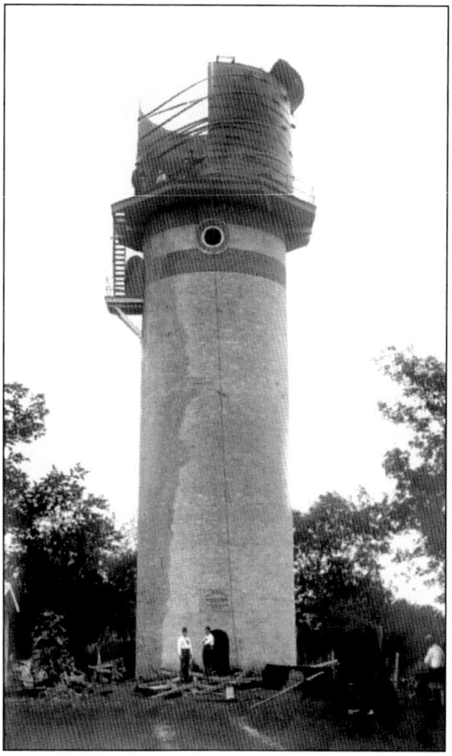

In October 1895, the city awarded the contract for water works to a Chicago firm, Fairbanks, Morse & Company. By the spring and summer of 1896, that company started laying water mains on Main Street and had built this water tower, located at the west end of Furnace Street. (Courtesy of RJM.)

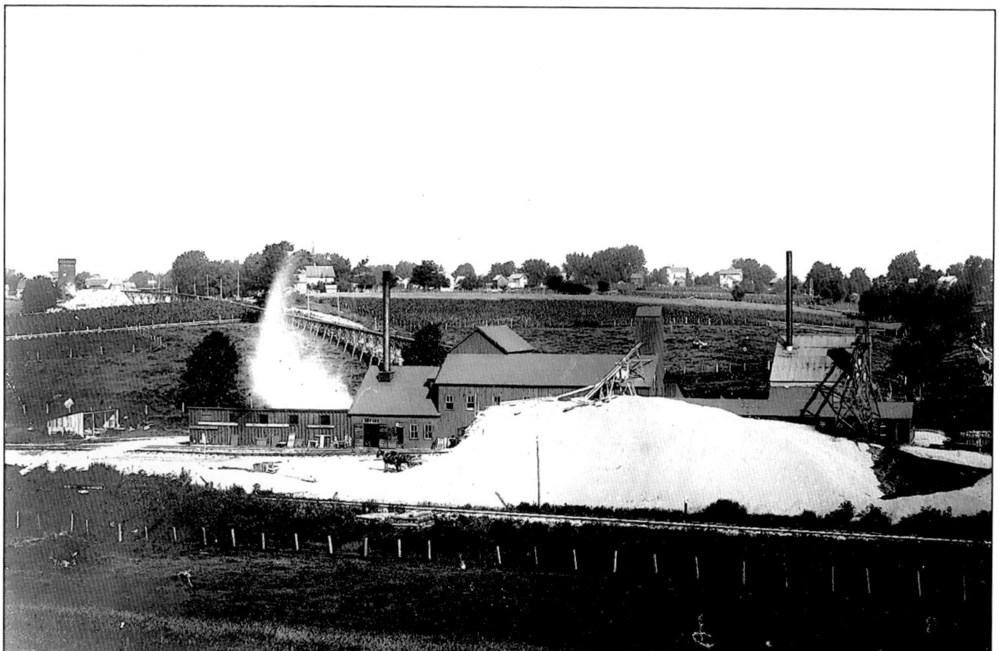

Economically, Platteville got a huge boost when it became an important mining center again at the turn of the century, this time of zinc ore. Here is a photograph of the Empire Mine, located on the east side of town, *c.* 1905. Notice the rising sulphurous acid fumes from the roaster. Roasting was necessary to separate the zinc from iron. (Courtesy of RJM.)

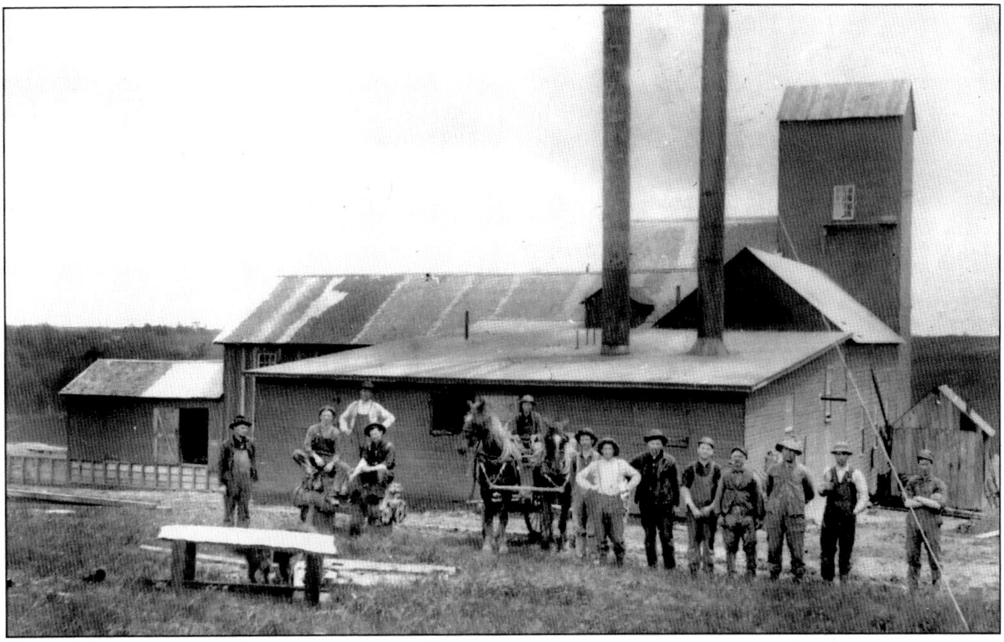

Unlike lead mining (which was usually a one or two man operation), zinc mining was conducted by large corporations that could finance the cost of deep mining and processing. But, like lead mining, zinc mining was labor intensive. Here is a group of zinc miners (*c.* 1910) at the Klar-Piquette Mine, located in section 29 of Platteville Township, about three miles southwest of Platteville.

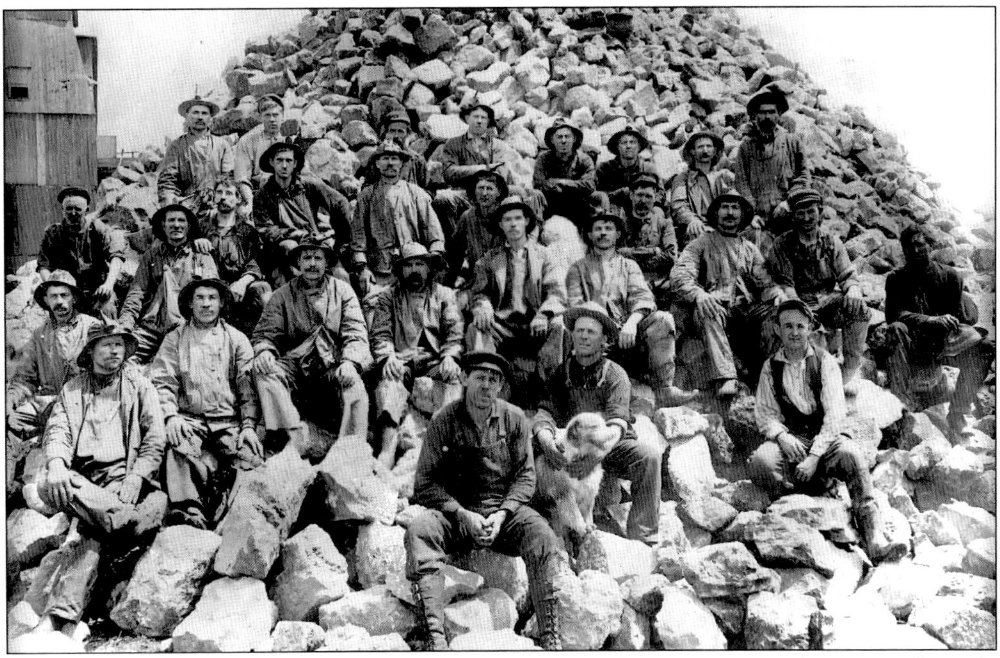

Here, the crew at the Empire Mine sit on a pile of coarse tailings, *c.* 1910. Tailings were the rock, soil, and other waste products separated from the zinc ore. Tailings were used in local construction. Many of the foundations and bricks of Platteville's houses were made from tailings.

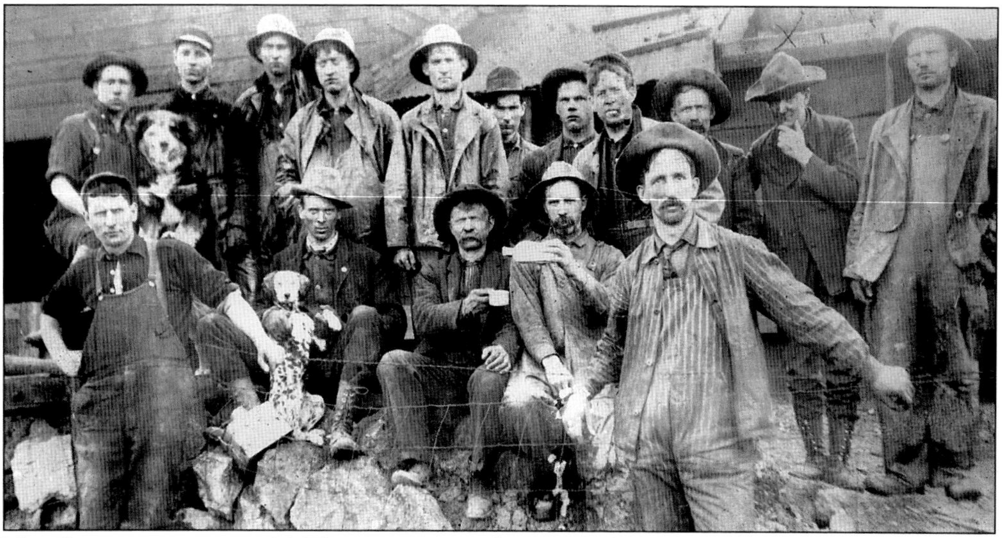

Not all mines were successful. This is an image of miners at the Weigle Mine, located in section 36 of Platteville Township, c. 1908. The Weigle mine closed in 1910 after only two years of operation. Zinc ore mining in Platteville and the surrounding area reached peak production during World War I, with the need for zinc ore in the production of brass. High production costs and declining prices eventually ended all mining activity in Southwest Wisconsin. (Courtesy of RJM.)

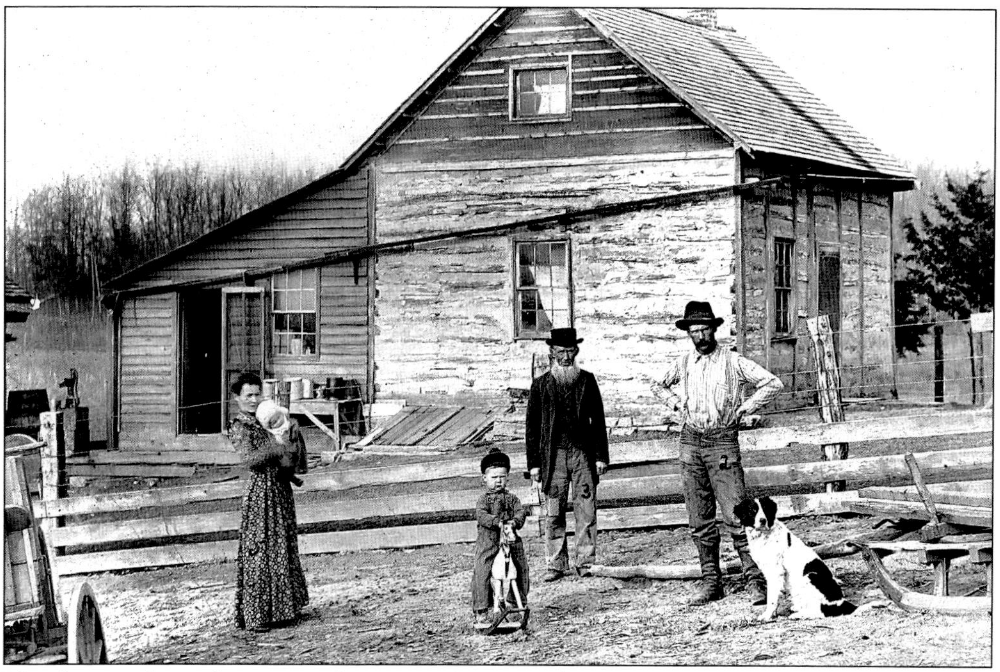

The farmers from the surrounding area also contributed to the economic development of Platteville. This photograph, taken in 1902 or 1903, shows a pioneer-era log cabin still in use in Beetown Township. In front of the cabin, which was probably constructed in the 1850s, stands George Jamison and family. Shown, from left to right, are Stella, wife, with baby Stella; Rollo, son; Grandpa James Jamison; George Jamison, father; and Old Pal. This is the Rollo of the Rollo Jamison Museum.

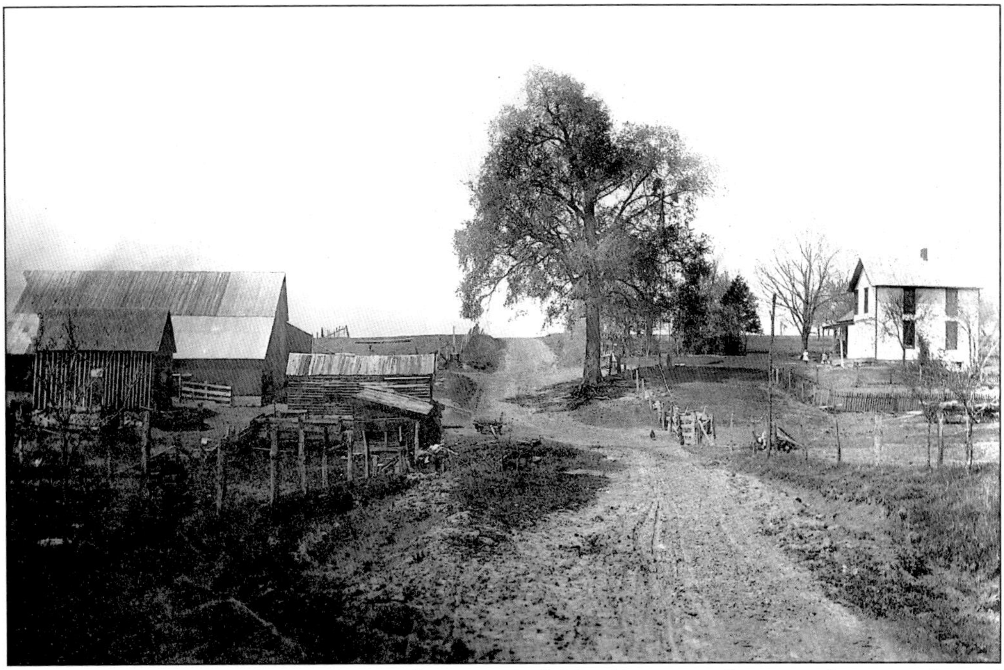

Here is the Thomas and Mary Butson farm, *c.* 1915. The Butsons, who were sheep, cattle, and crop farmers, built the house around 1878. Thomas passed away in 1898 and Mary died in 1923. The farm is located north of Platteville in Lima Township at 1724 Butson Road, and has been in the Butson family since 1848. The road still divides the farm. (Courtesy of GCHS.)

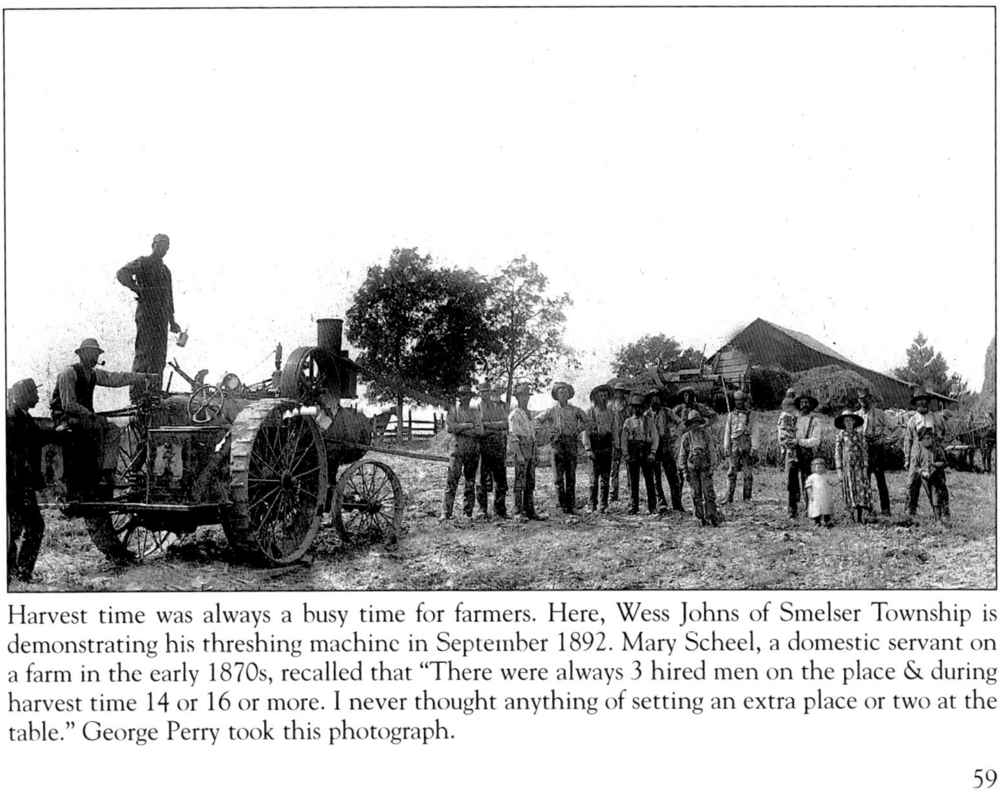

Harvest time was always a busy time for farmers. Here, Wess Johns of Smelser Township is demonstrating his threshing machine in September 1892. Mary Scheel, a domestic servant on a farm in the early 1870s, recalled that "There were always 3 hired men on the place & during harvest time 14 or 16 or more. I never thought anything of setting an extra place or two at the table." George Perry took this photograph.

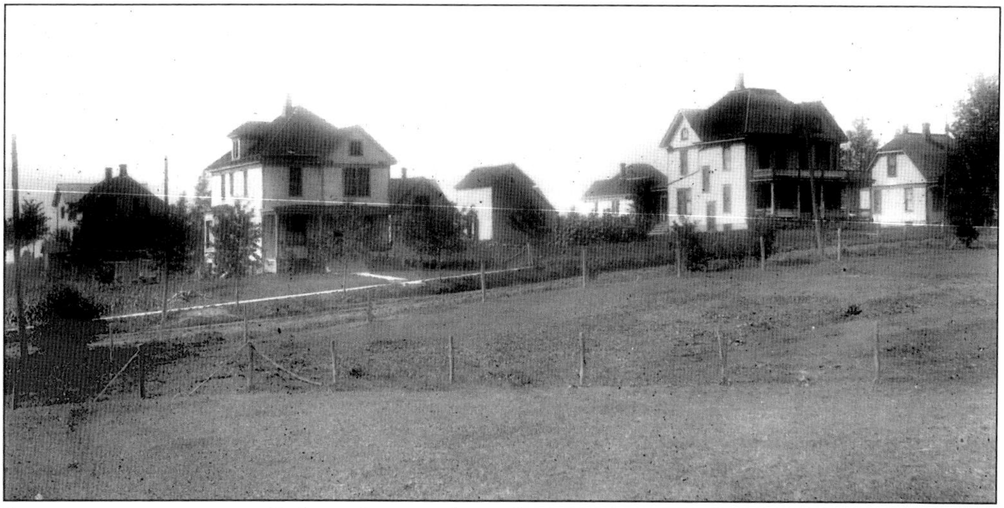

Economic activity naturally brought growth, and new houses were rising in new subdivisions. One such house was Samuel Poller's house at 350 South Hickory Street, constructed in 1906–07, in the new Jones Addition. Samuel, a painter by trade, lived here with his wife Millie and their daughter Lenice. Notice that the Poller house, which is the prominent house on the left, has a sidewalk running in front of it and freshly planted trees. The one drawback, however, was that Hickory was still a dirt street. This and the next three photographs were probably taken in the summer of 1907.

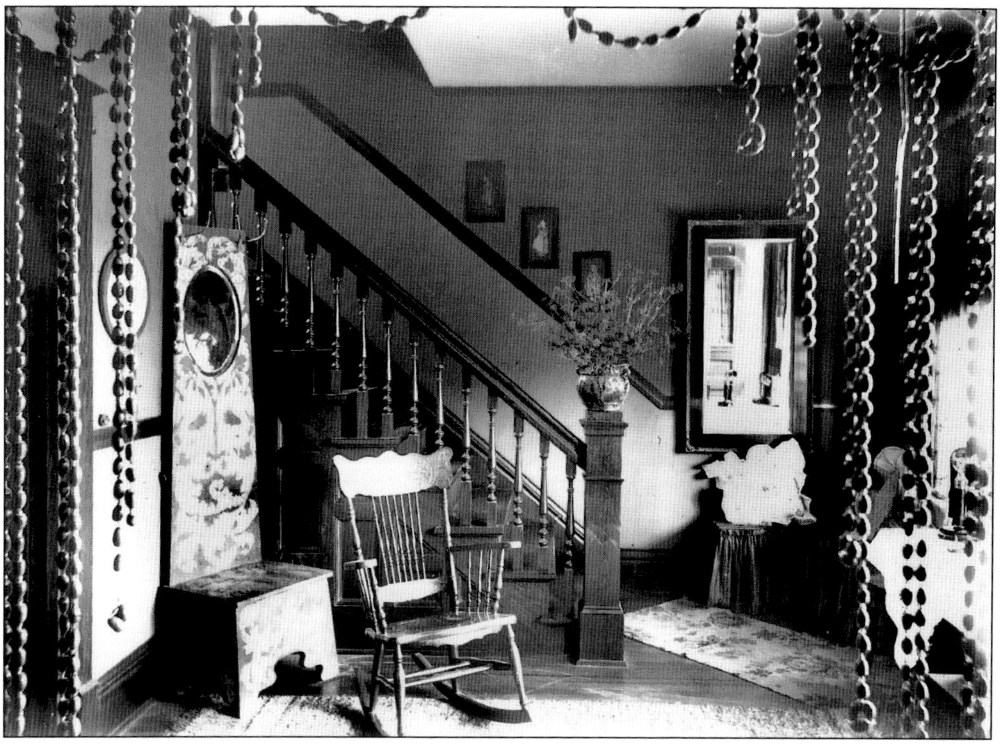

Here is the front entranceway of the house. Notice the plant resting on the newel post. Greenery was in vogue at this time.

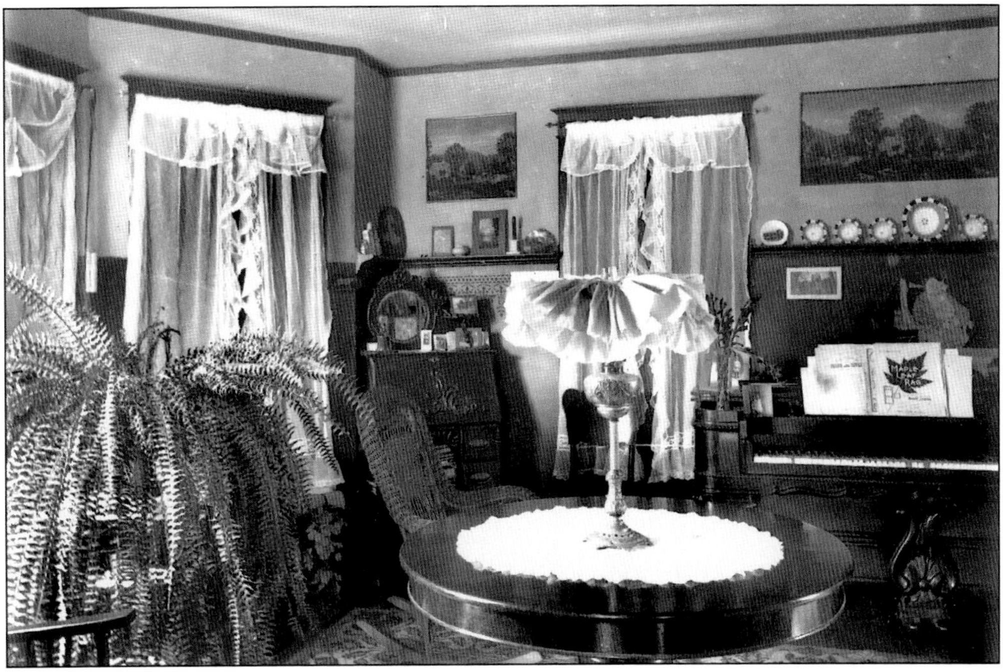

This was their dining room/parlor, complete with kerosene lamp, bay window, and Scott Joplin's Maple Leaf Rag (on the piano). Lenice, who was very musical, surely played this piano.

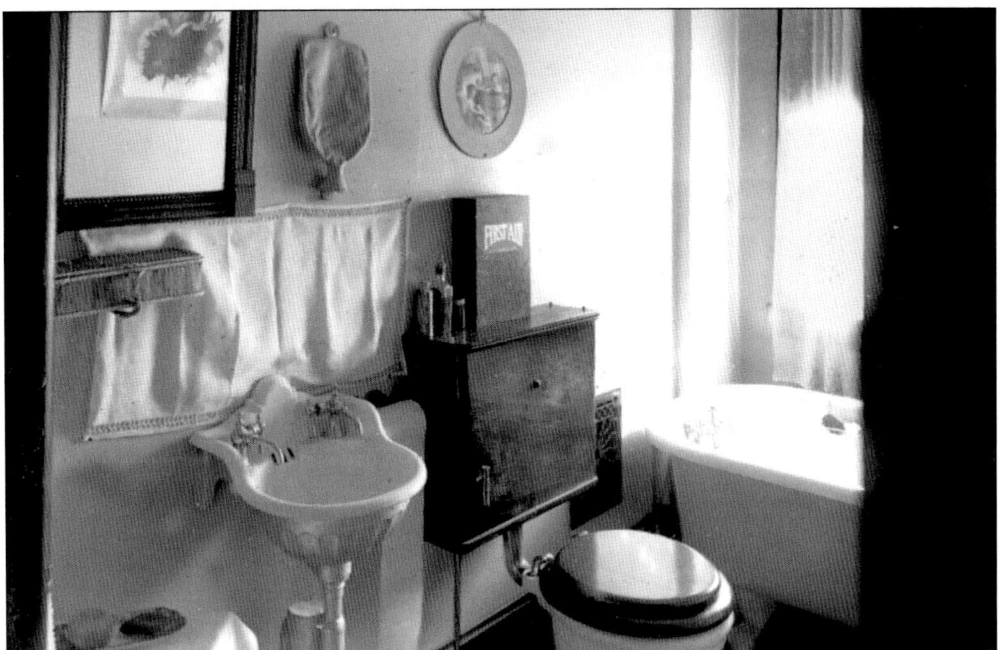

And here is their bathroom. Notice the heat register to the right of the toilet. The Jones Addition would have been one of the first sections of the city to be connected to the new city sewer system. For the Pollers, who had previously lived in an older house, indoor plumbing, central heat, and cement sidewalks were significant improvements.

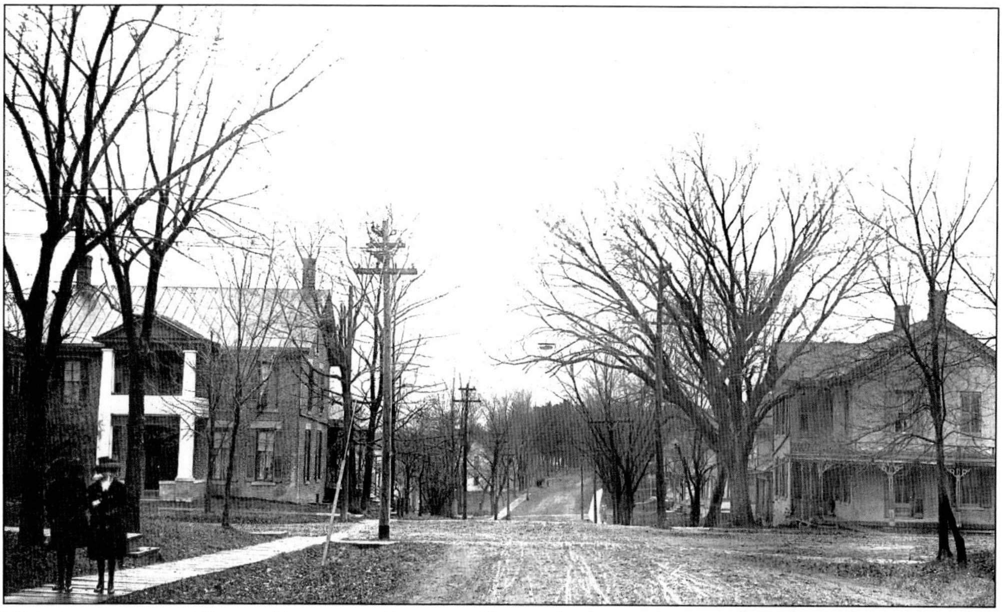

This is not to say Platteville was without problems. As late as 1925, the *Platteville Witness* still complained about the annual oiling of the streets (meant to reduce dust), because a fair amount of the oil ended up being tracked into houses, "ruining hundreds of dollars worth of rugs and carpets." This image, looking south at the intersection of Chestnut and Pine Streets (*c.* 1910), shows a typical Platteville street before paving. Notice the wooden sidewalk on the left. The First English Lutheran Church has replaced the house on the right and the house on the left still stands.

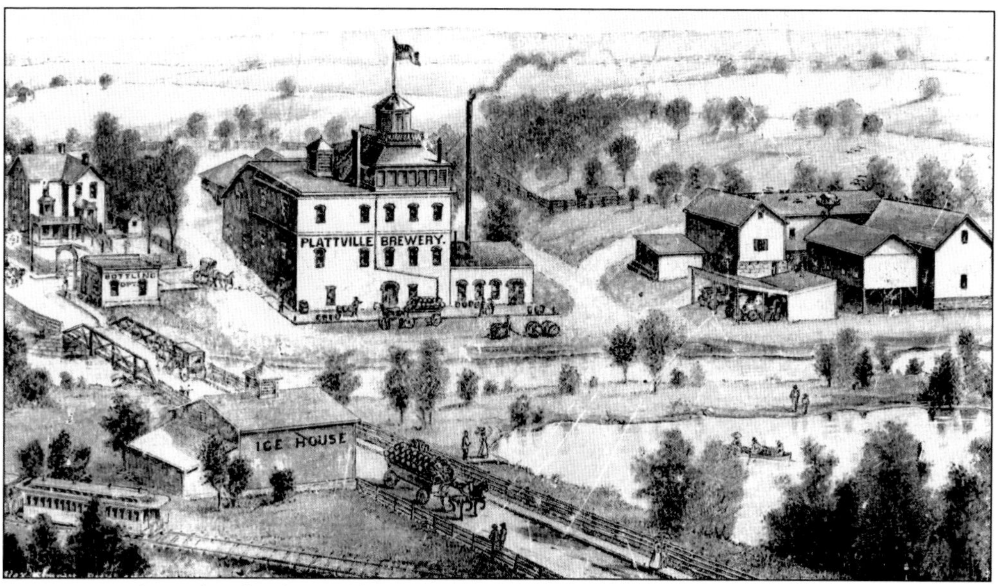

At its most basic level, Platteville was essentially a mom and pop, small business kind of town. Here is an illustration of the Platteville Brewery, *c.* 1890. Established in 1868 by Dennis Centliver, the brewery's main building, in the foreground, was constructed in 1872. By the time Fritz Hoppe purchased it in 1890, the brewery was producing 35,000 barrels of beer per year. Today the Swiss Valley Farms Dairy occupies the building.

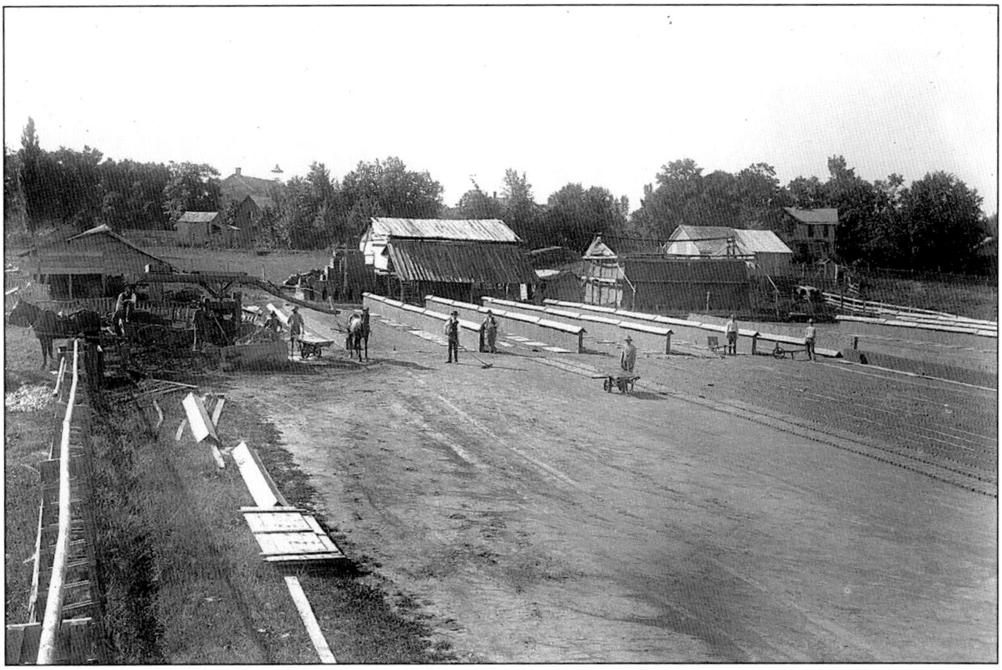

For their part, the Grindell brothers, William and John, established the Platteville Brick Yard in 1874. The brick yard, shown here in 1891, was located just north of the intersection of Lewis and Elm Streets, and produced 750,000 bricks per year. (Photograph courtesy of GCHS.)

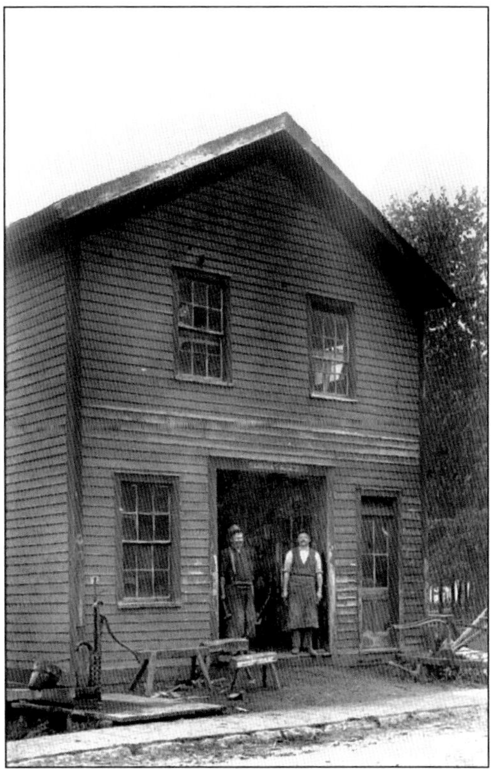

This is the Libert & Tiedemann Blacksmith Shop, c. 1895. Located at the northeast corner of Pine and Third Streets, Carl Tiedemann and Fred Libert remained partners from 1889 to 1897. This building is gone.

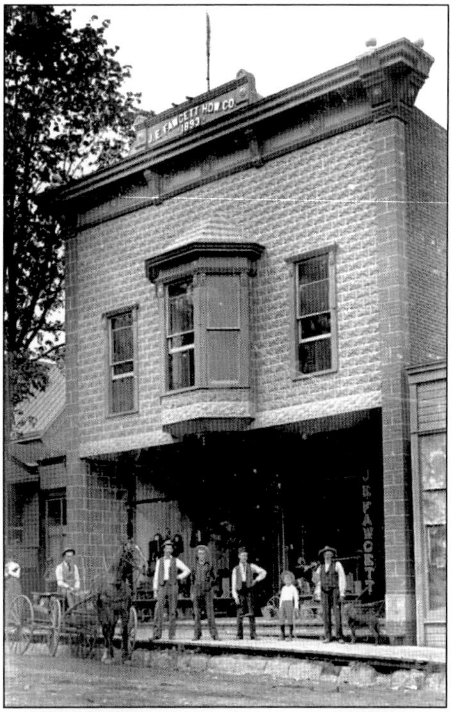

Platteville had its share of hardware stores. This is James Fawcett's store, c. 1895, located at 120 West Main (Bargain Nook IV). Fawcett had this building constructed in 1893. He specialized in stoves, cutlery, general hardware, and guns. A tinkerer at heart, Fawcett made many of the telephones used by Homer Beebe's telephone company (see page 106). (Courtesy of Dick Brockman.)

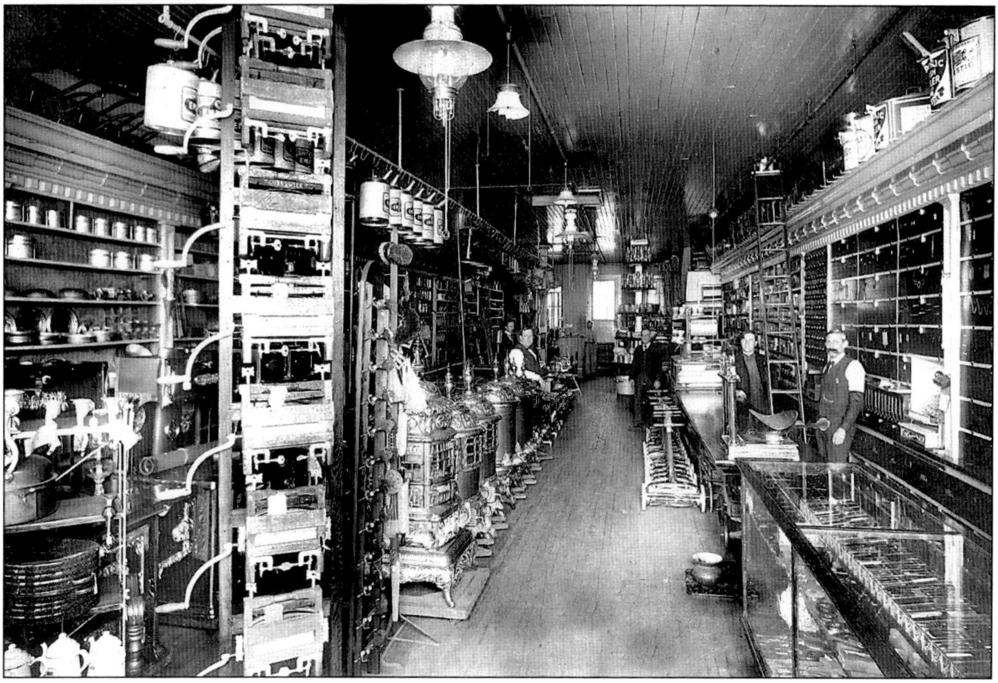

Two blocks east, at 60 West Main Street, was the Smith Hardware, shown here c. 1910. Established by Jotham Smith in 1879, Willard Smith took over the family business when his father died in 1909. The Smith Hardware specialized in Garland Stoves. Notice that Willard has a good supply of ringers for washing clothes (on the rack at left), and stoves and manual lawn mowers in the center aisle. (Courtesy of Dick Brockman.)

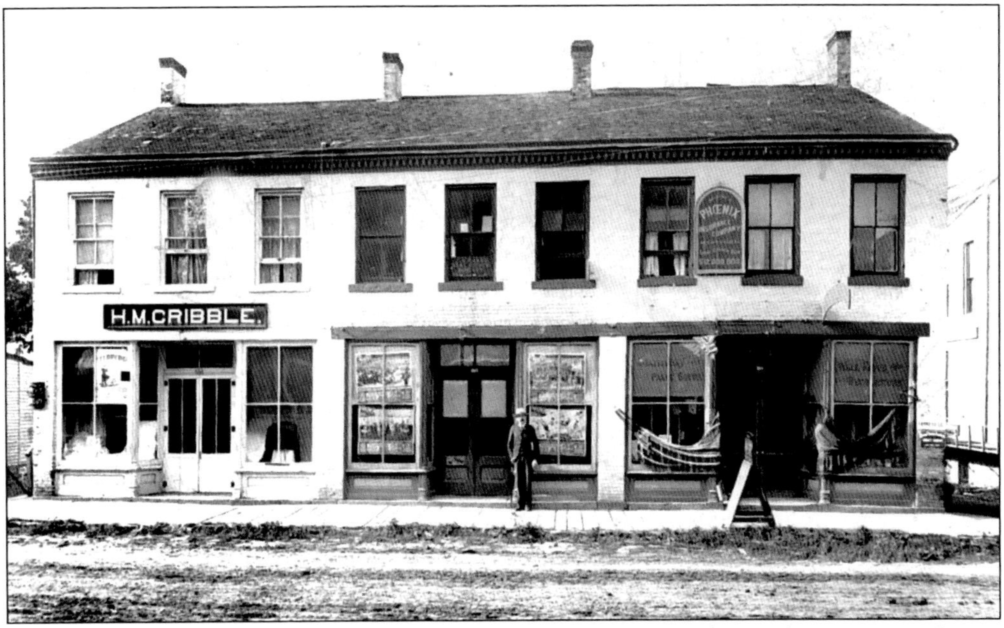

Henry Gribble, for his part, operated a general store for decades at the southeast corner of Main and Third Streets. This photograph was taken in August 1898, when "The John Robinson Greatest of All American Shows," came to town. A few weeks after this photograph was taken this building was torn down.

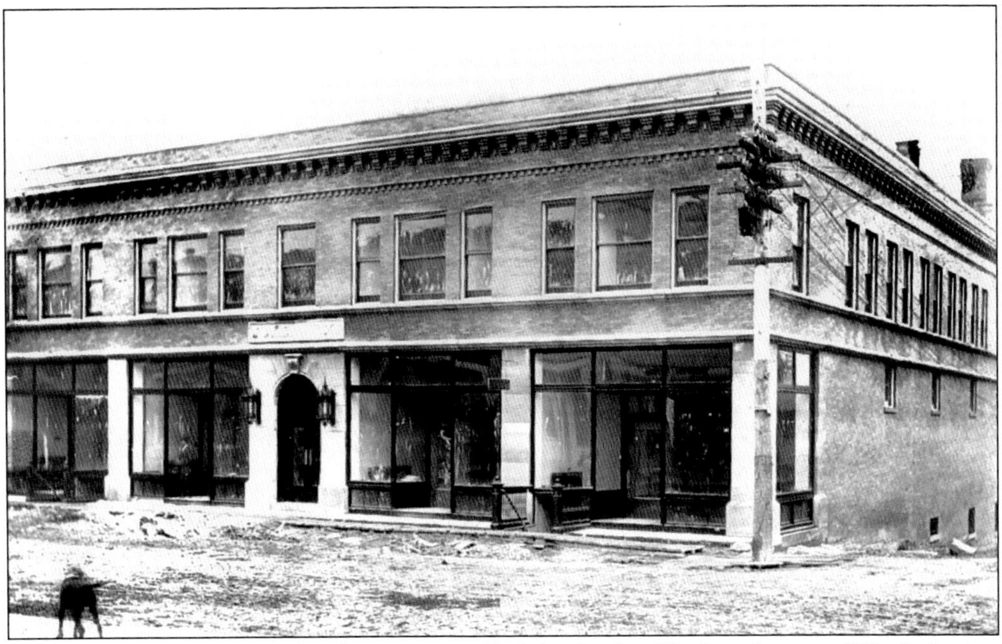

The new Bayley Block replaced it. It was called the Bayley Block in honor of Elijah Bayley, an early Platteville merchant who had constructed the building in the previous image. Besides being the home to various small businesses, Dr. Wilson Cunningham located his first hospital in the new building. This photograph was taken in the spring of 1899, just before the cement sidewalk was laid and the building occupied. (Courtesy of Dick Brockman.)

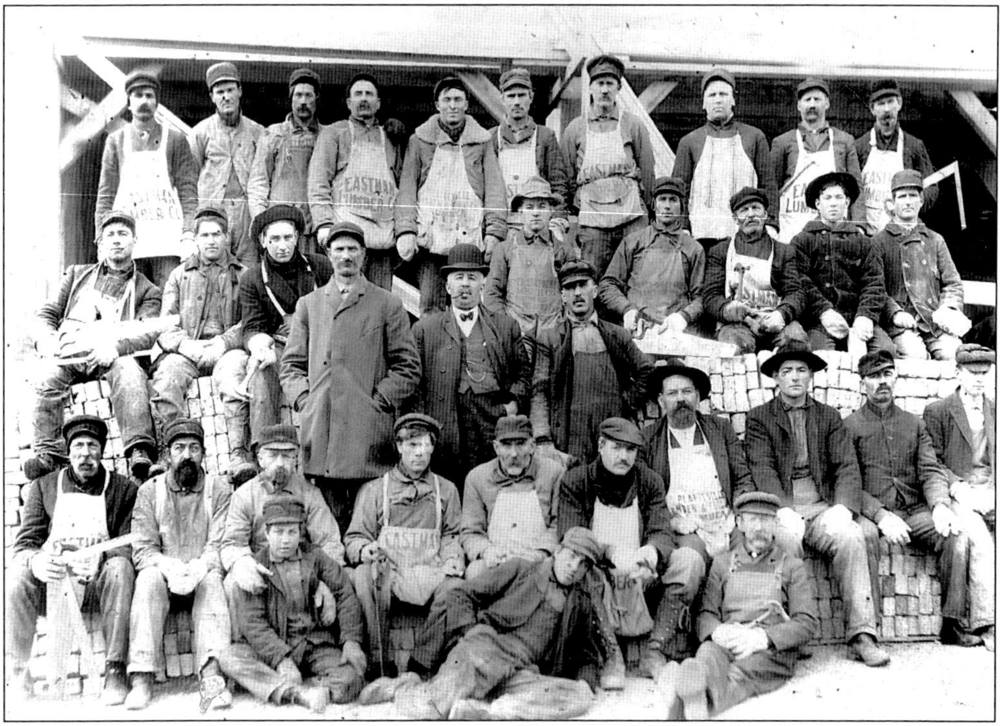

This is the crew, c. 1900, of the Eastman Lumber Company. Nadab Eastman, a farmer from Smelser Township, began this company, which was located on the east side of Platteville, in 1892. He eventually established lumber yards in several area towns.

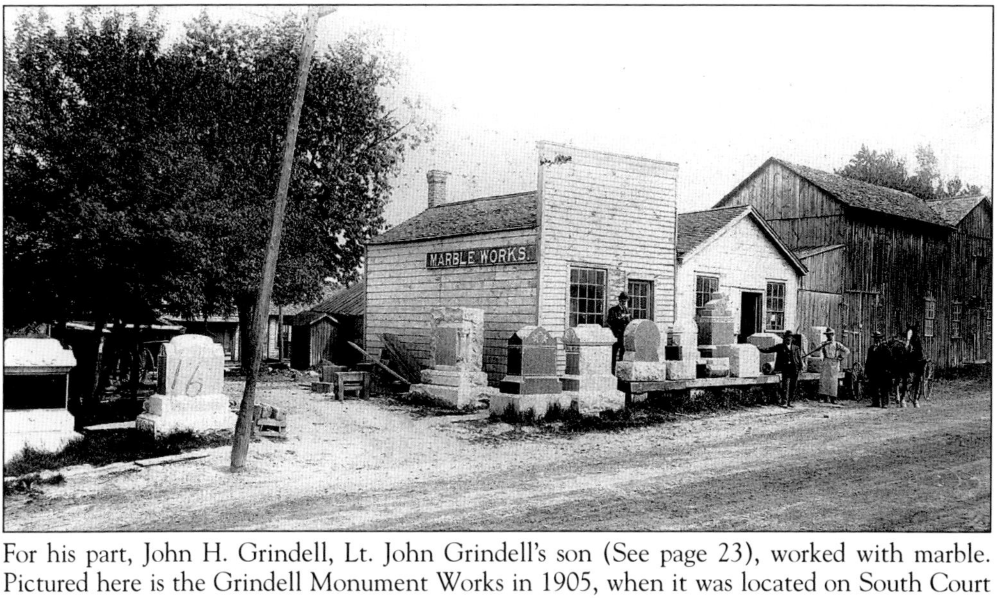

For his part, John H. Grindell, Lt. John Grindell's son (See page 23), worked with marble. Pictured here is the Grindell Monument Works in 1905, when it was located on South Court Street, just north of today's post office. Standing in this image are, from left to right, Roy Grindell, son; John H. Grindell, father; Jesse Thomas, stone cutter; and Rufus Seely with his horse "old Dot." Sadly, Rufus was trading in "old Dot" for a monument for his wife Julia and daughter Eleanor, both of whom had died in March.

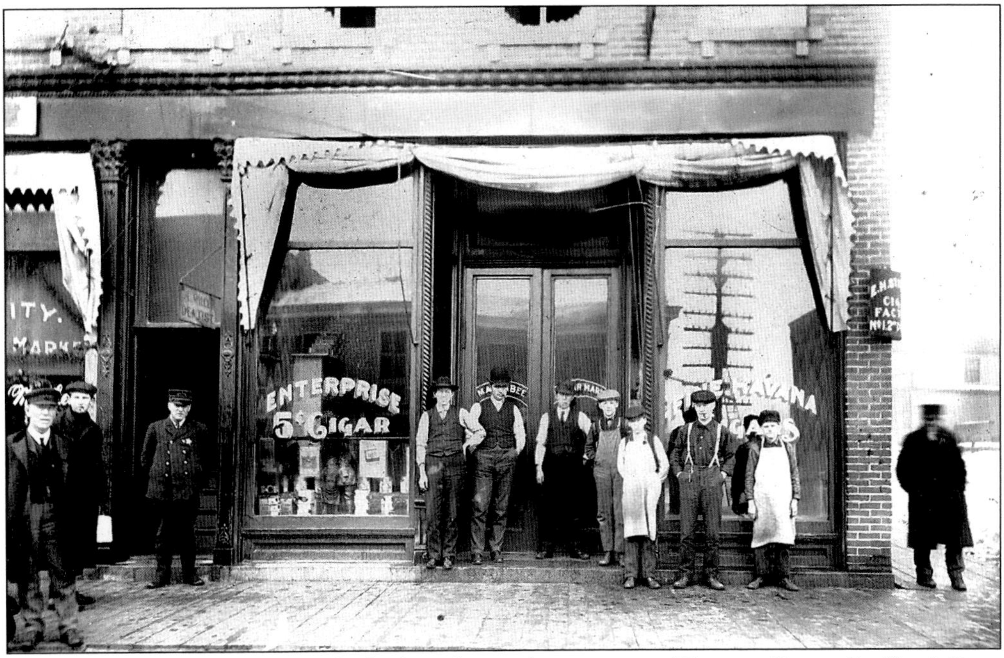

And, like most towns, Platteville had its share of cigar stores. This was Ernest Steffens' Cigar Factory, c. 1904, located at the northwest corner of Main and Second Streets. Mr. Steffens also sold ice cream and had beer on tap. The saying went that a person could enter Steffens' store, buy a beer, and claim to have never been on Second Street, where all of the bars were located.

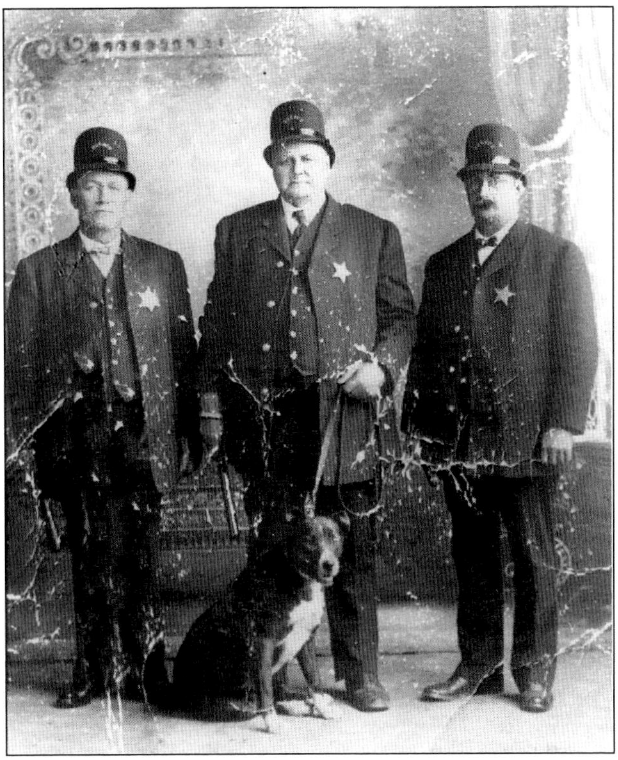

Official Platteville was also coming of age at this time. This is the Platteville Police Department, with all three officers, c. 1906. Shown, from left to right, are Zed Drapper, George Long, and Cyril Huntington.

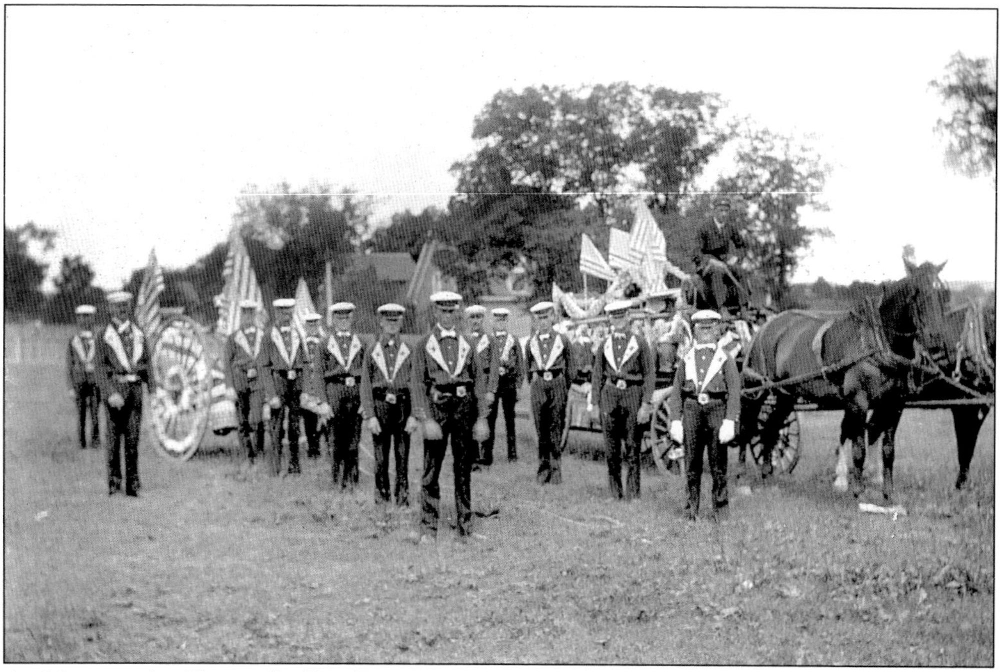

And here is the Platteville Fire Department, c. 1910. In the left distance is the hose cart. (Courtesy of Dick Brockman.)

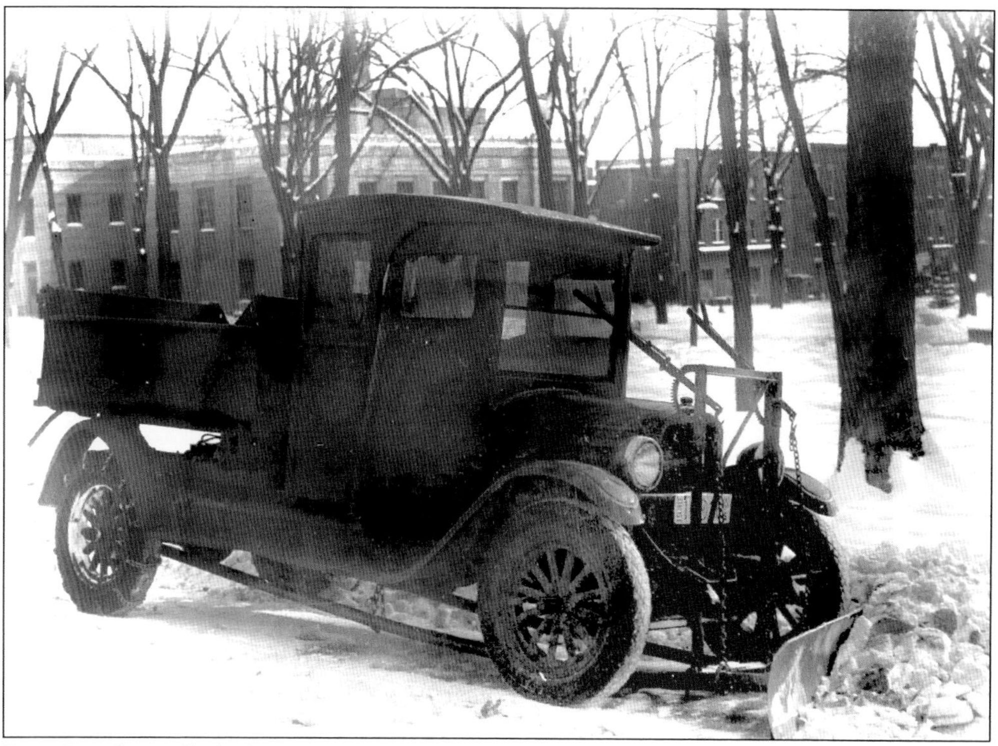

By 1930, Platteville had even put into service its first snowplow truck, shown here parked on the north side of City Park.

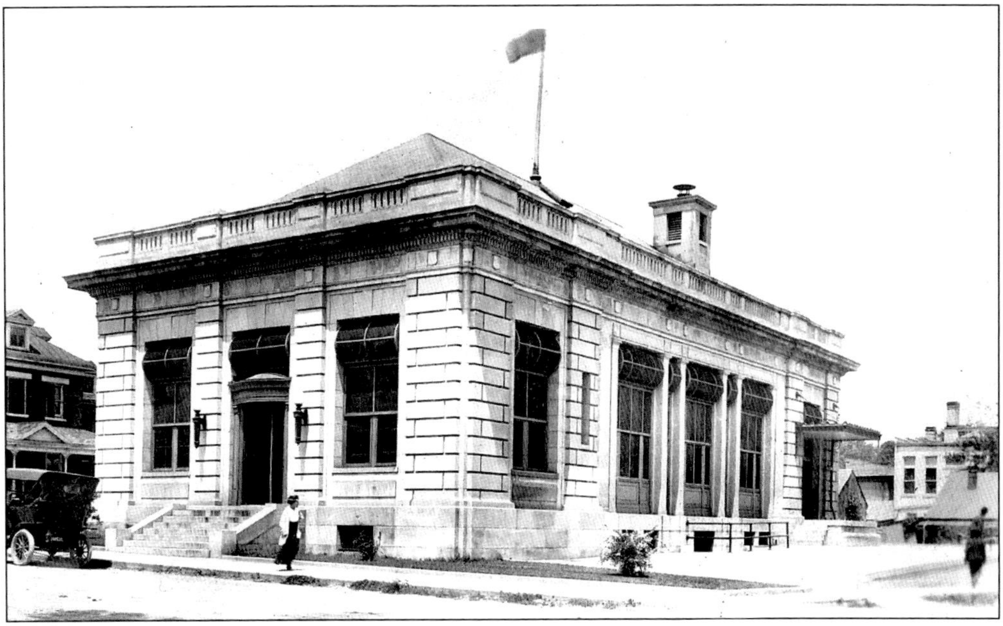

In February 1911, after being located in several different buildings since 1829, Platteville's Post Office finally moved into a permanent home at the northeast corner of Pine and Court Streets, shown here c. 1912. According to the *Platteville Journal*, the new post office's lobby contained "windows and doors trimmed in quarter sawed white oak, dark green wainscoting, terrazo tile with dark red marble border floor." There was also a "retiring room for ladies."

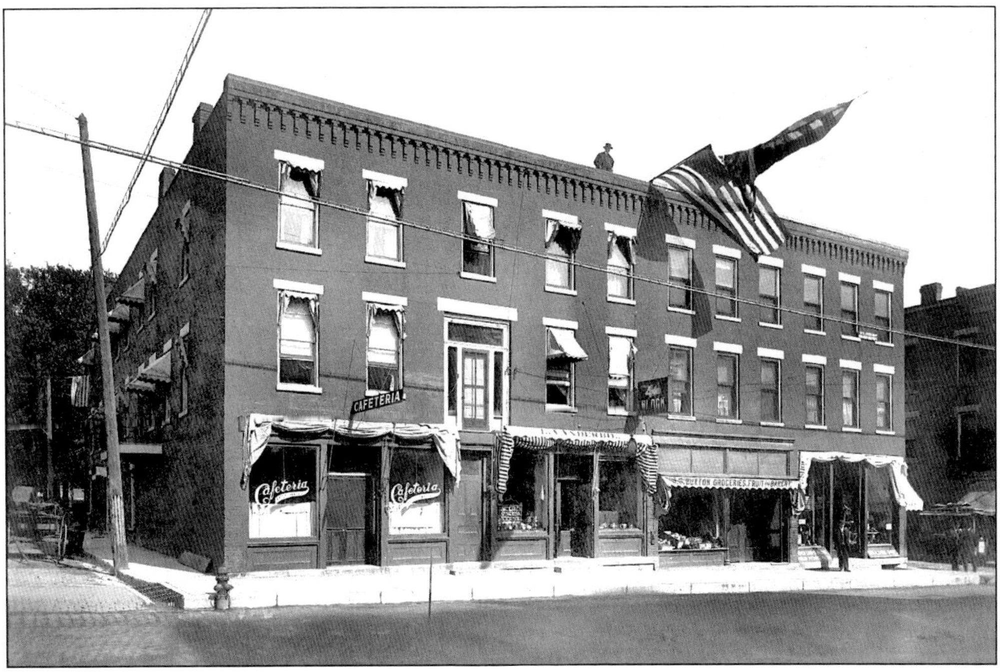

Within a decade after World War I ended, Platteville had two tragic fires that permanently altered downtown. The first occurred at the Forehand Block (located on Main Street) on the afternoon of February 8, 1919. What began as a seemingly small, containable fire quickly turned deadly.

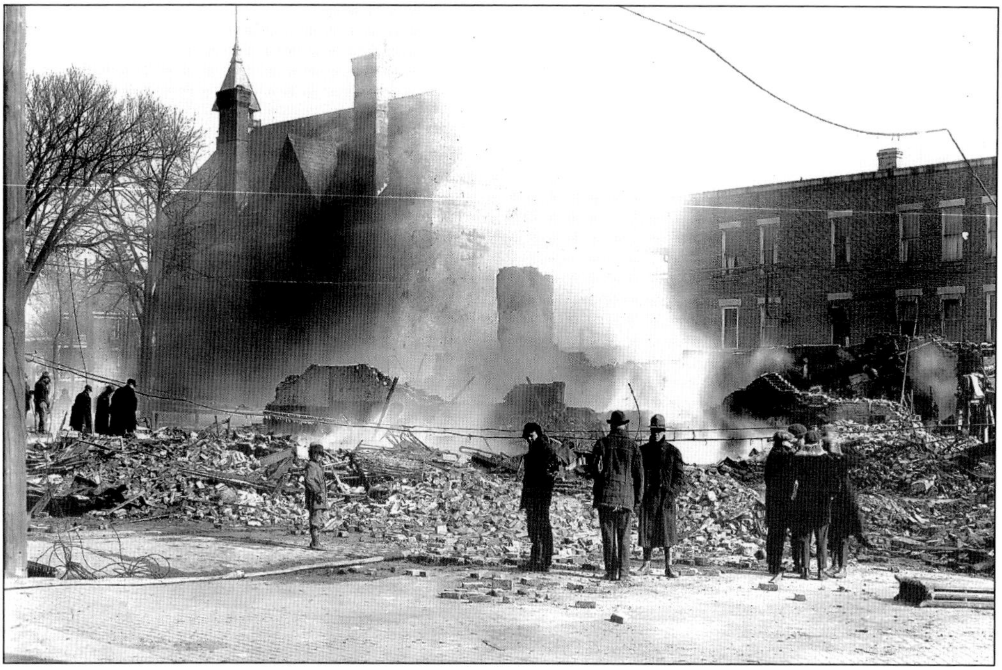

As store owners and area residents ran in and out of the building, retrieving valuables, the building unexpectedly exploded and came crashing down, killing eight people, three of them volunteer firemen. Today, the IOCO gas station is at this location. (Courtesy of GCHS.)

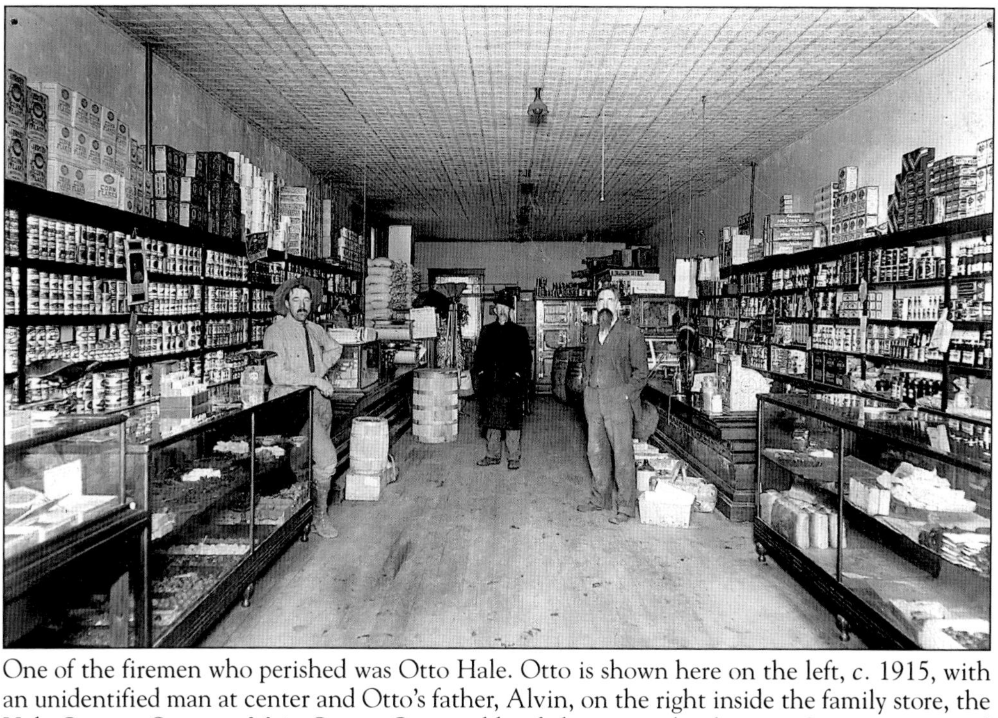

One of the firemen who perished was Otto Hale. Otto is shown here on the left, *c.* 1915, with an unidentified man at center and Otto's father, Alvin, on the right inside the family store, the Hale Grocery Store on Main Street. Otto and his father were also farmers. Otto was survived by his wife Margaret and their son Frank.

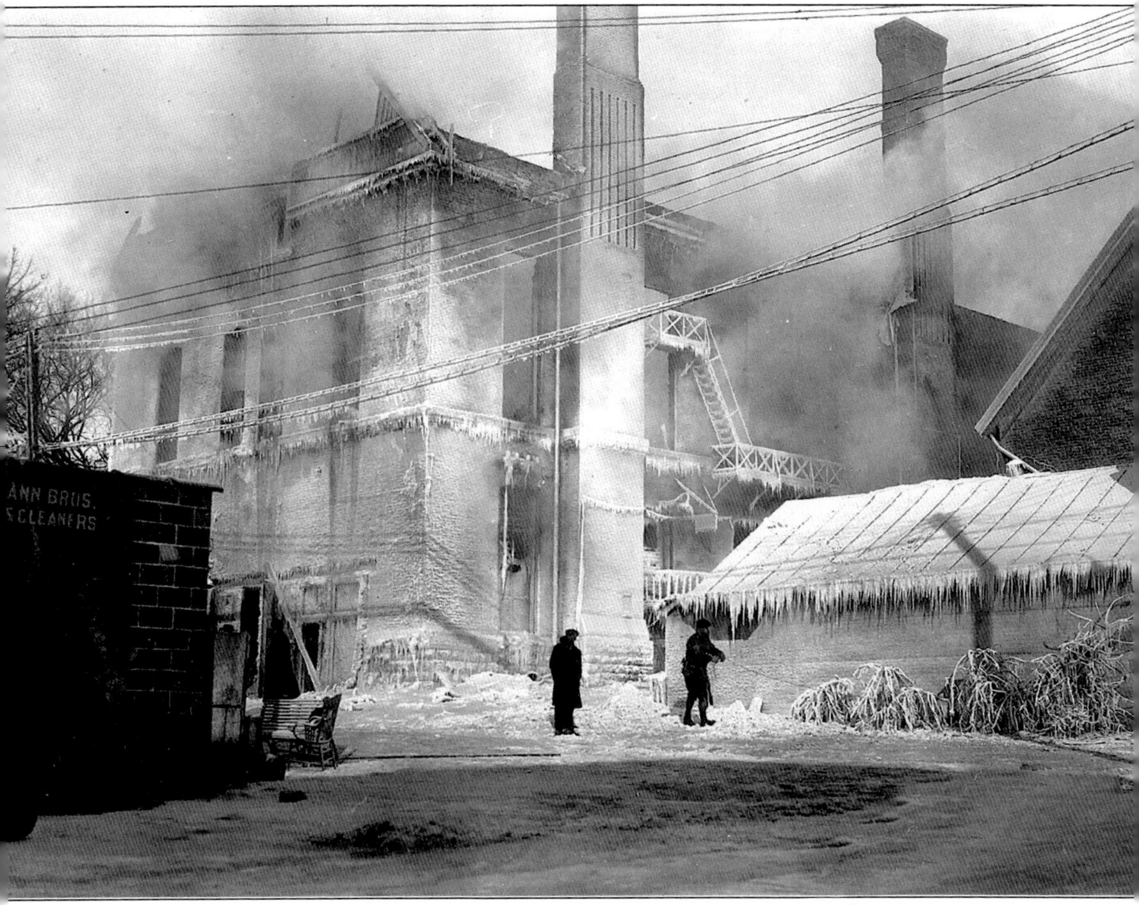

The second fire occurred on the evening of December 13, 1926, at City Hall and completely destroyed the building. This time there were no fatalities. The valiant firemen did, however, save the First English Lutheran Church (the gable of its roof is on the far right). This photograph was taken the next morning and shows the area covered by ice from the water poured onto it by the firemen. Temperatures had dipped as low as 20 degrees below zero that evening. Remarkably, this fire touched off a proverbial David and Goliath struggle. Soon after the City Hall fire, the city drew up plans for a new, larger City Hall building, one that required the site of the First English Lutheran Church building. Neither side could agree on a price and the city actually initiated condemnation proceedings against the church before an agreement was finally reached.

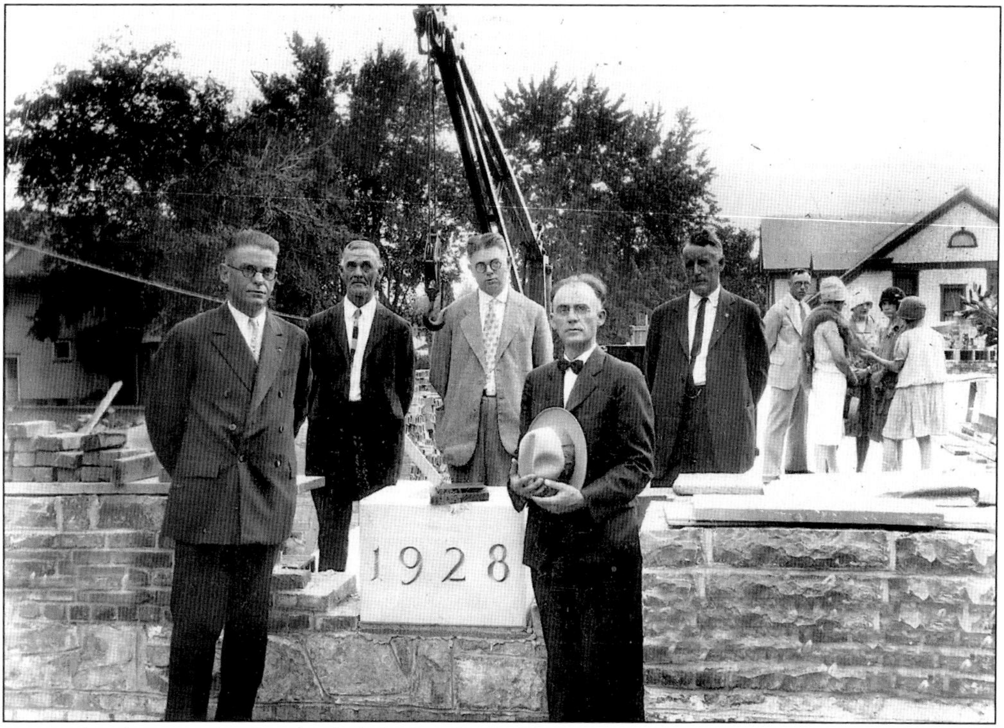

Hence, by the time the dust settled, both sides held cornerstone ceremonies just a month apart. This is the cornerstone ceremony held by the First English Lutherans on September 9, 1928. Rev. Russell R. Doering is on the right, holding his hat.

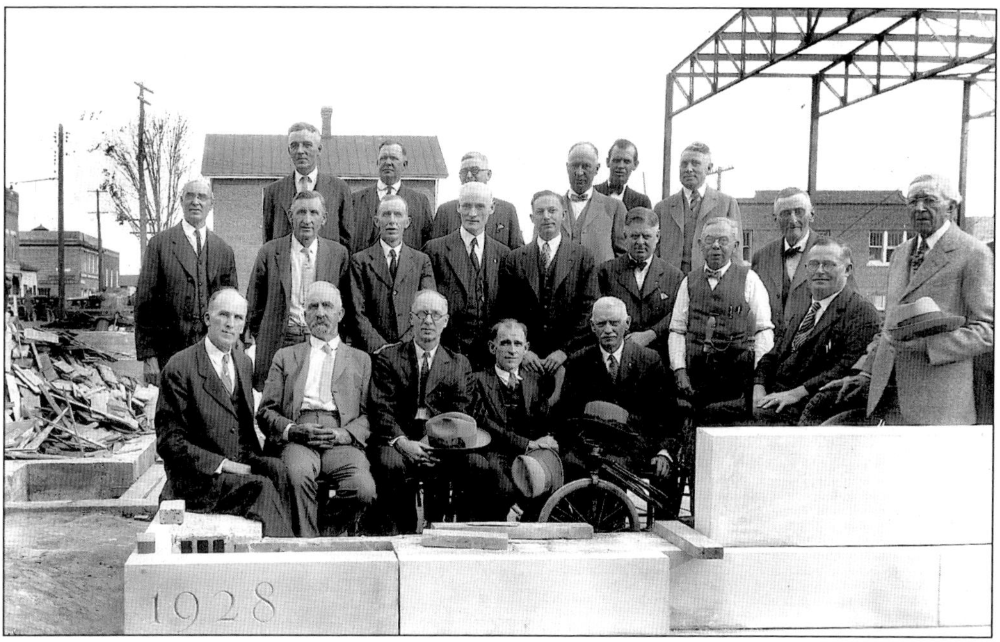

And here is the cornerstone ceremony held by the city for its new Municipal Building, on October 11, 1928.

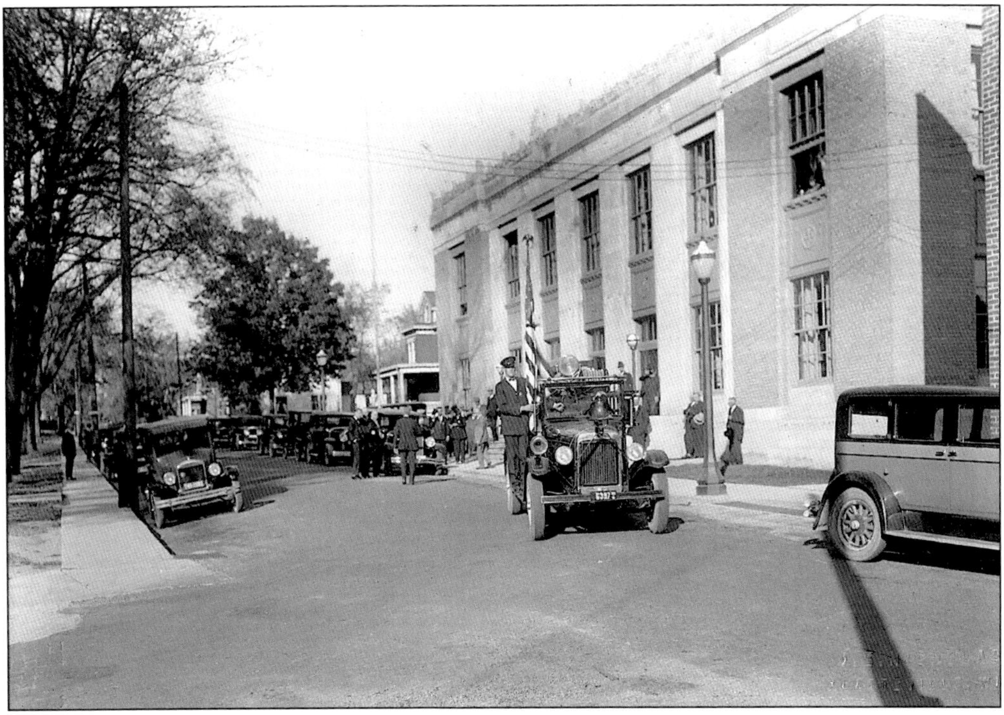

Officially called the Civic Memorial Building in honor of Platteville's "Soldiers, Sailors, Marines and Volunteer Firemen," Platteville's new Municipal Building was officially dedicated on September 20, 1929. Here, a fire truck from Platteville's Fire Department starts a parade in front of it.

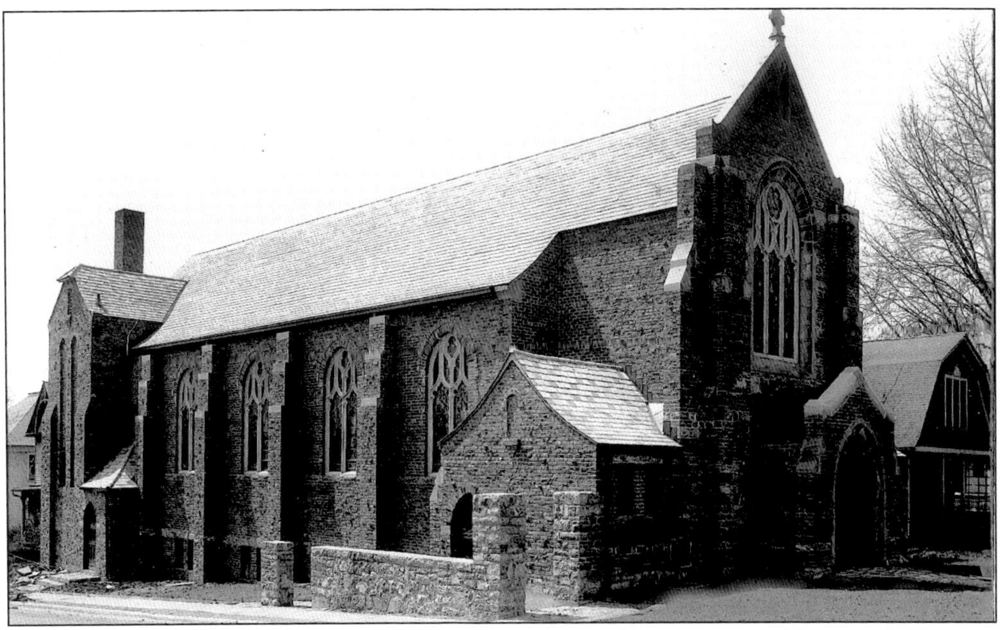

The First English Lutheran Church relocated to the southwest corner of Pine and Chestnut Streets, and constructed this church building. Their new church was dedicated on May 5, 1929.

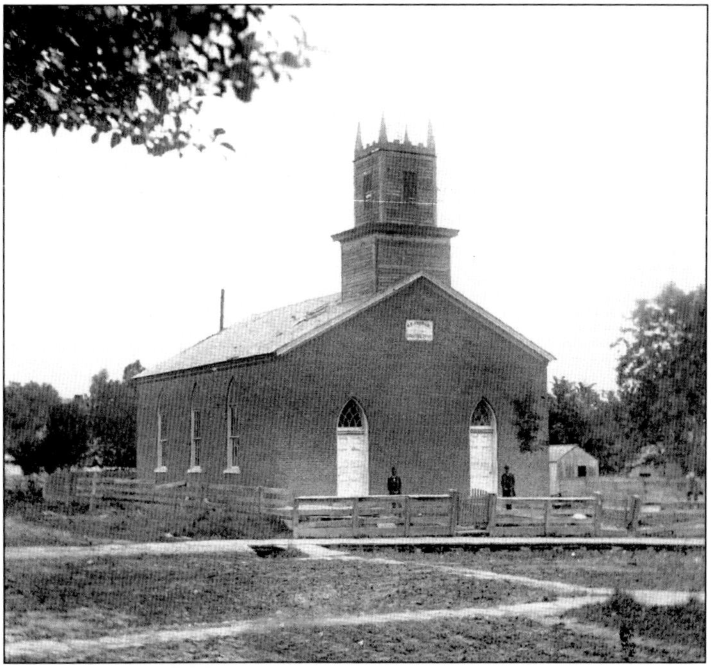

Platteville's other churches had less dramatic, but no less important, cornerstone ceremonies. One of Platteville's oldest denominations, the Methodist Episcopalians (*c.* 1832), or Methodists, constructed this brick church in 1845–46. Located at the northeast corner of Main and Chestnut Streets, this photograph of the church was taken around 1865.

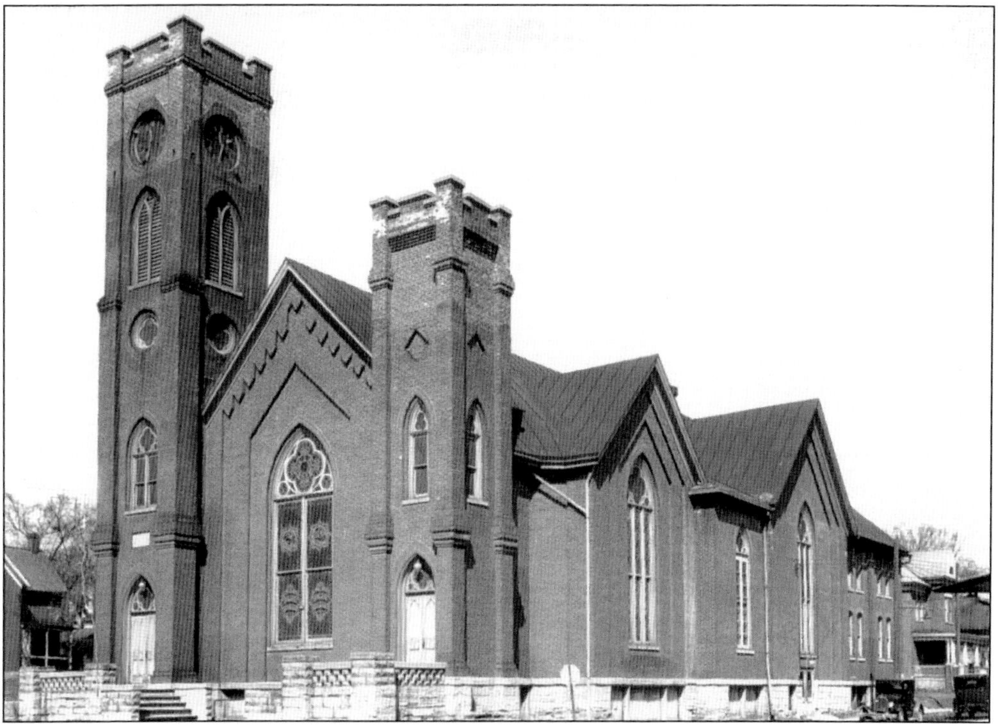

When the Methodists decided to expand in 1877, they razed their old brick church and replaced it with this beautiful Gothic structure, shown here *c.* 1925. It was dedicated on Thanksgiving Day, 1878. The castle parapets, seen here, were relatively new, having been built in 1921. They replaced the church's original spires. This church was razed in 1971 and replaced by the First National Bank.

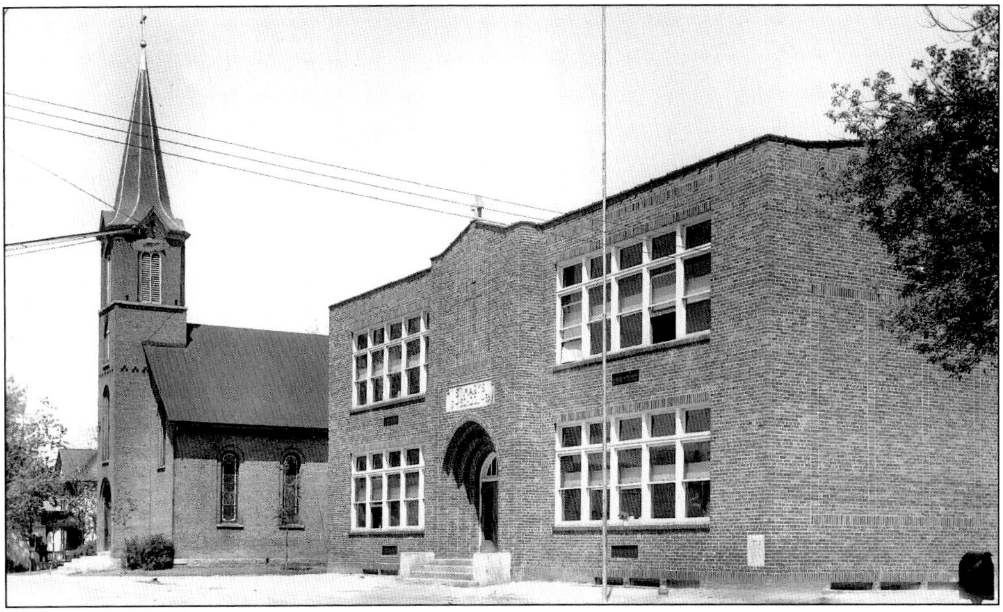

The Catholics also had an early presence in Platteville, holding their first service around 1842. The cornerstone ceremony for St. Mary's Church, on the left, was held May 31, 1870; it was dedicated on November 21, 1871. This church building, located on Cedar Street, was replaced with a newer building in the 1960s. St. Mary's School, in the foreground, was constructed in 1935. This image was taken *c.* 1940.

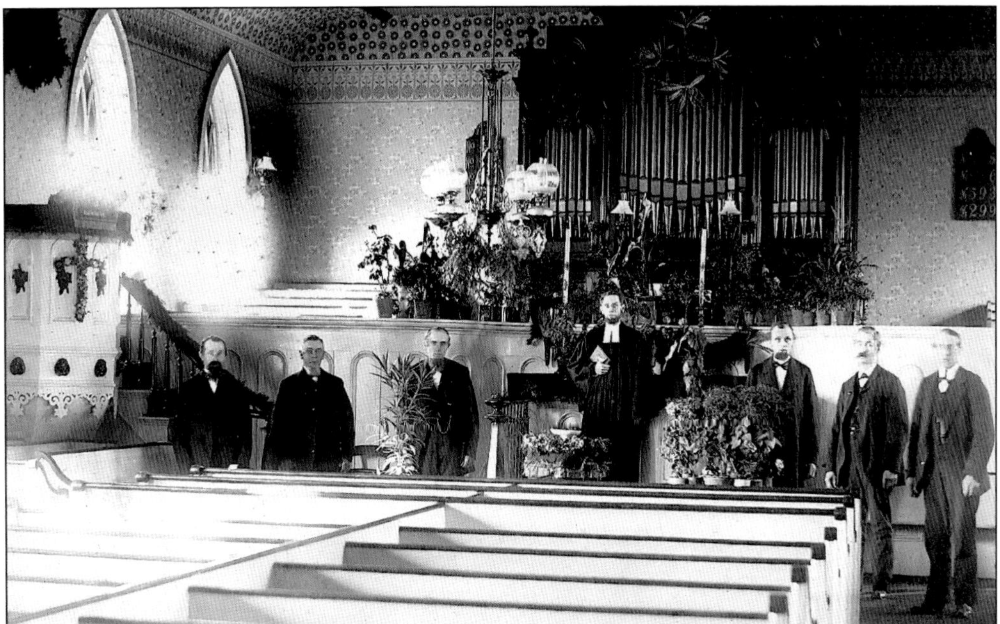

For their part, some of Platteville's German immigrants established the German Evangelical Lutheran Church in 1855. This photograph, *c.* 1890, shows the interior of their brick church, which was located at Furnace and Lutheran Streets. Today the Free Methodist Church occupies the building.

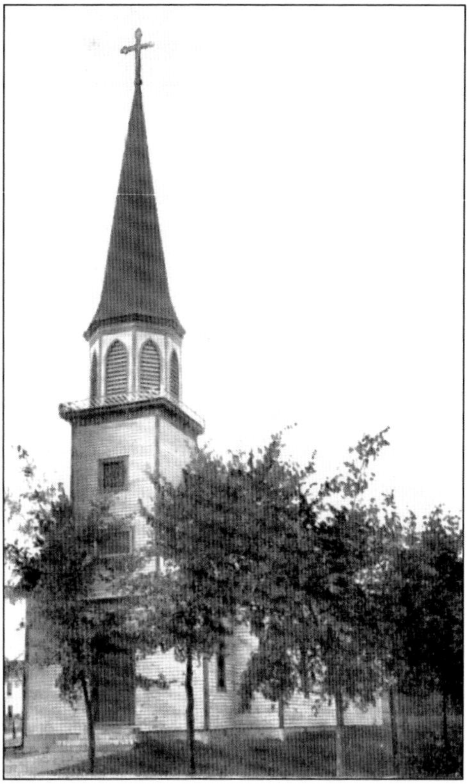

In 1876, a group of Lutherans broke away from the previous church and, that same year, constructed their own Lutheran church, one block east, at the corner of Furnace and Broadway Streets. They called their church St. Paul's Evangelical Lutheran Church. This image was taken *c.* 1910.

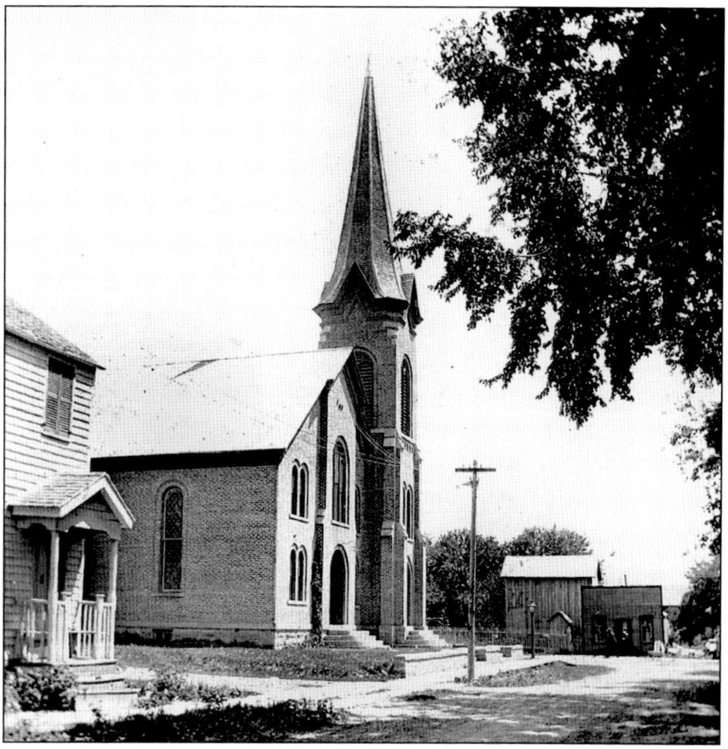

Another early denomination was the Congregational Church. Initially organized in 1839 as a Presbyterian church, it held its first services on the first floor of the Academy building (See page 34) in the early 1840s. By 1849, it had changed to a Congregational church and relocated to the north side of City Park. This image, *c.* 1900, shows their third church, which was dedicated on July 19, 1869. (Courtesy of GCHS.)

Trinity Episcopal Church, shown here *c.* 1930, was designed by George Nathan of Janesville, who was also the architect of the Congregational Church. Located at the northwest corner of Chestnut and Market Streets, Trinity Church is a good example of a Gothic Revival architecture. The Episcopalians, who were organized as a mission parish in 1862, constructed this church in 1863 and 1864.

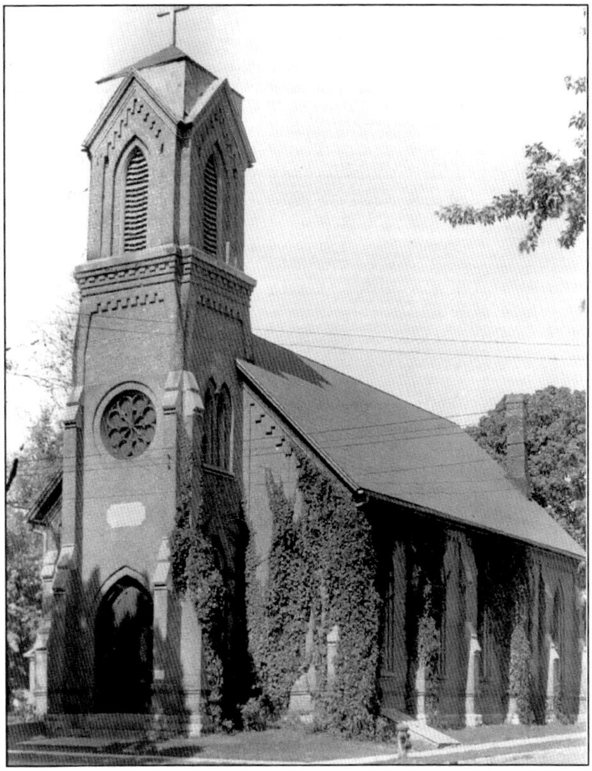

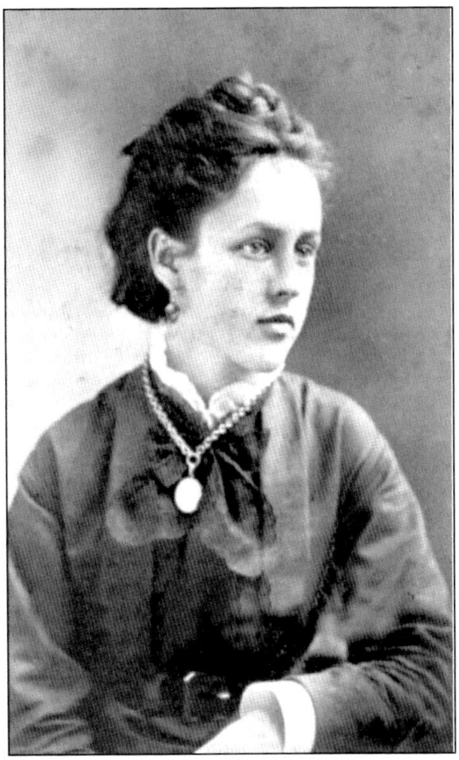

One of Platteville's celebrated weddings took place at Trinity Church on October 5, 1882, when Cora Rountree (Major Rountree's youngest daughter) married Charles Hathaway of New York City. The newspaper commented that, "The richness and tastefulness of the dress for the bride and her six bridesmaids made a suitable setting for the beauty and grace of the bride and her attendants." This photograph of Cora was taken around the time of her wedding.

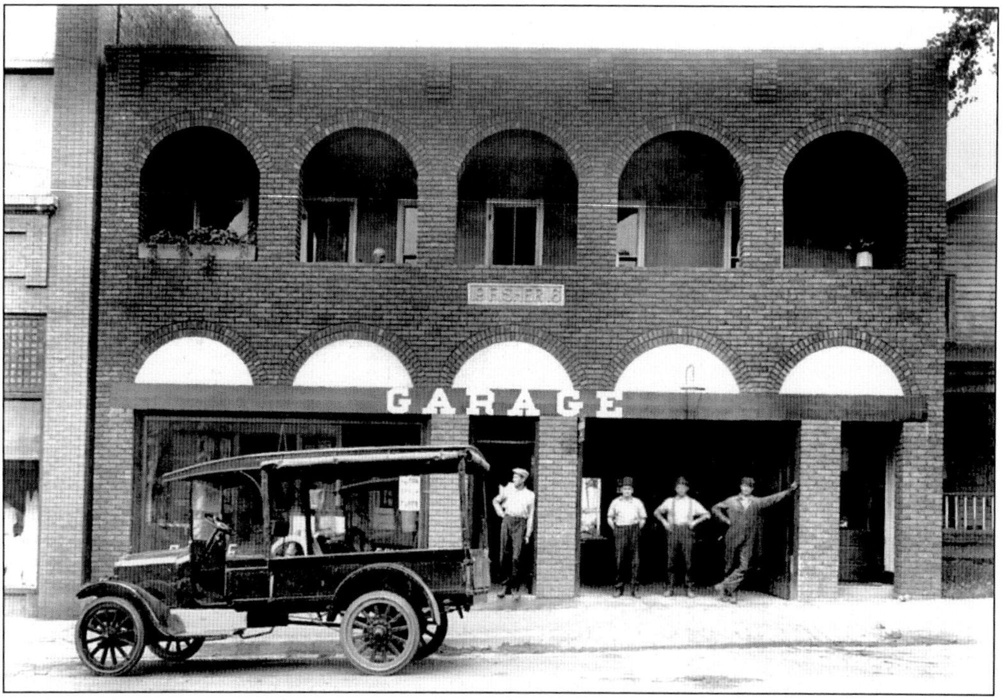

As the 20th century moved into its second decade, automobiles became more common. Hence, a number of automotive garages opened in Platteville. One such garage was located in the Fisher Building on Main Street, which was built in 1916. This photograph was taken around 1920.

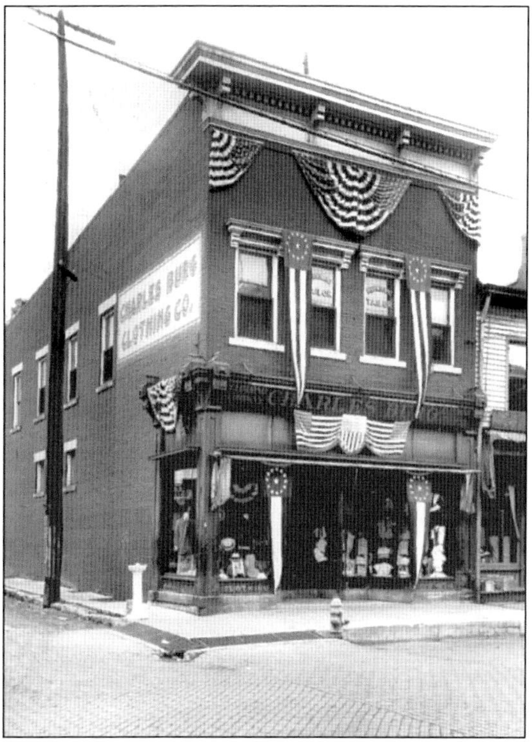

On July 4 and 5, 1923, Platteville's American Legion sponsored an event, "The historical Pageant of Grant County," held at the Big Badger Fairgrounds (Legion Field). The Platteville Journal noted that "the entire business district is festooned, giving a patriotic atmosphere." This image and the next show part of that festooning. Here is Charles Burg's Clothing Store, at the northeast corner of Main and Fourth Streets. In his advertisements, Charles emphasized hats, "HATS are a barometer of a store's modus operandi." Today this is the site of Badger Brothers Coffee and Internet Café. (Courtesy of Bob Metzger.)

This is a view of the Independent Order of Odd Fellows (IOOF) building on Main Street, built in 1912. Platteville's Lily of the Mound Lodge was one of the oldest IOOF lodges in the state, having formed in 1846.

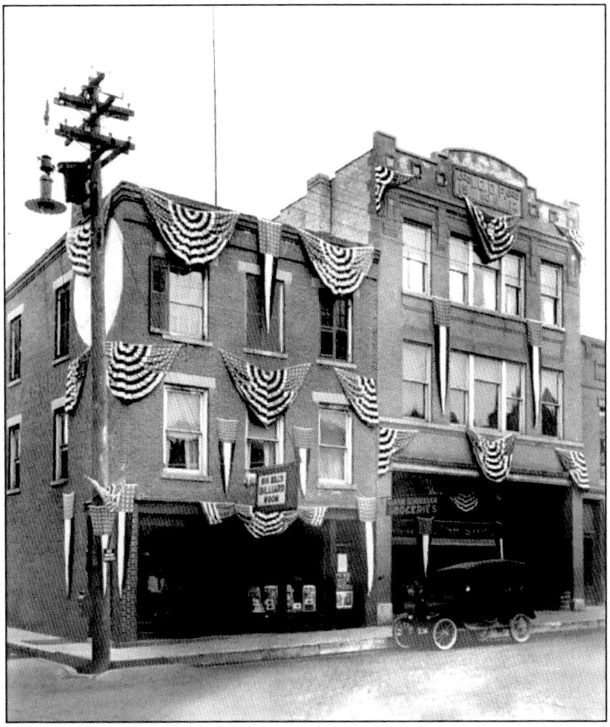

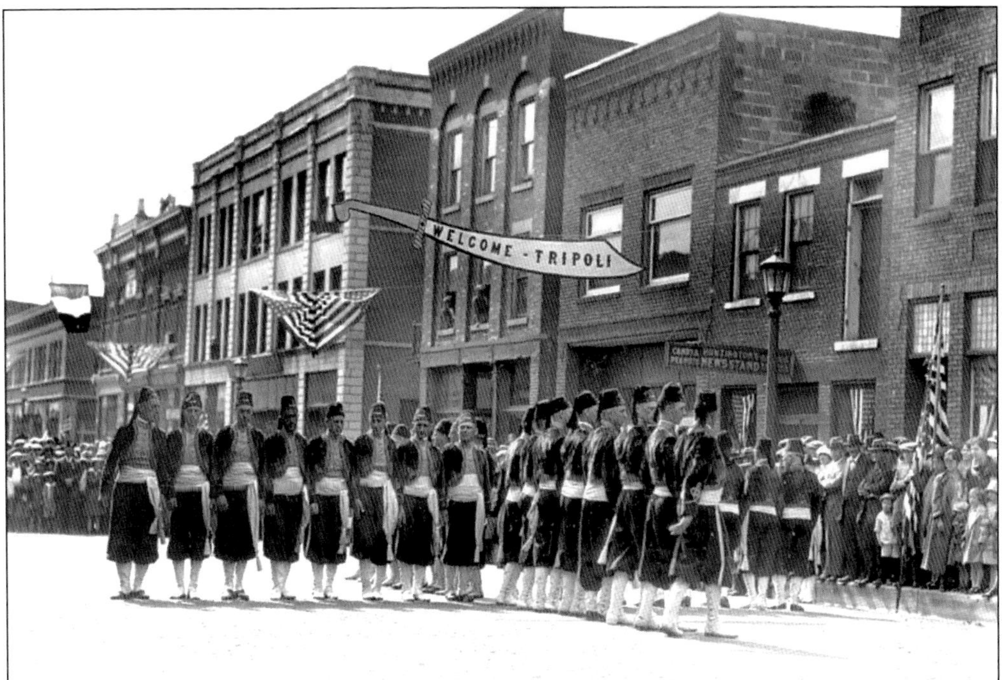

For their part, the Platteville's Masons dedicated their new Masonic Temple on June 27, 1925. One of the high points of the celebration came when the members of the Tripoli Temple of Milwaukee, shown here, performed their maneuvers on Main Street. The old Masonic Temple, dedicated in 1882, may be seen in the background, second building from the left.

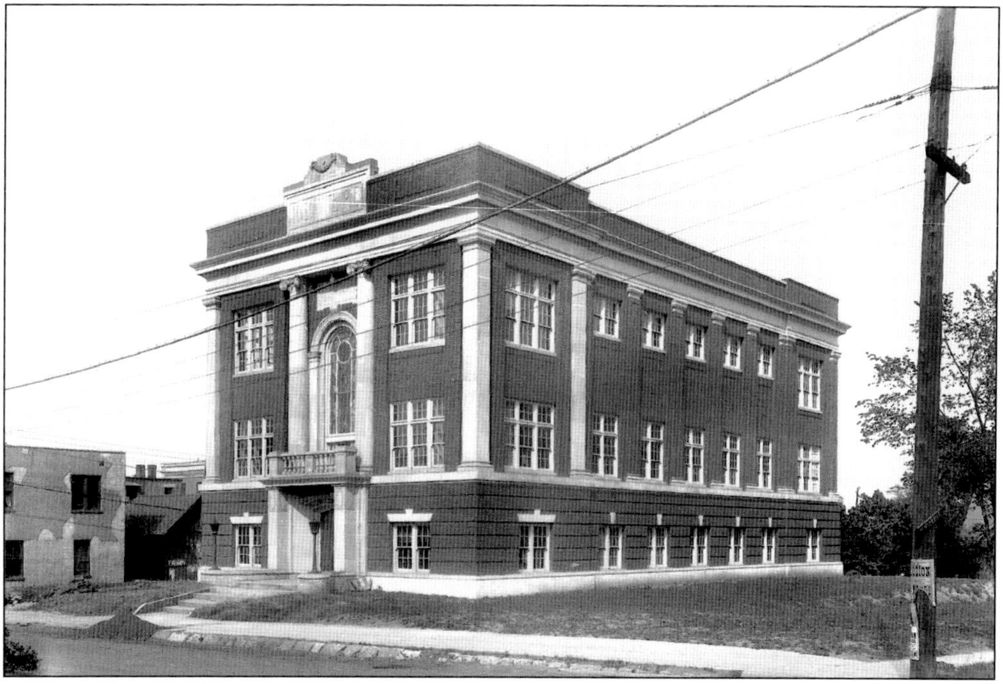

This is a photograph of the new Masonic Temple when it was dedicated. It was located on Pine Street, just east of the post office. It was razed in 1981.

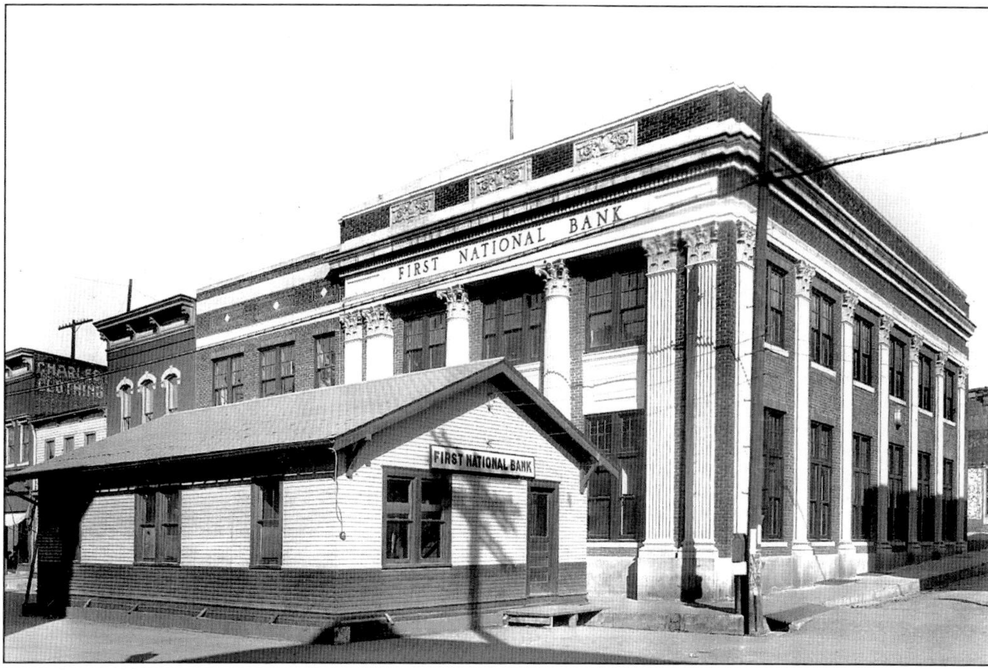

Another addition to Main Street in 1925 was the new First National Bank building, which replaced the bank's first building (see page 54). The small building in front of the new bank was the First National Bank's building from August 1924 until February 23, 1925, when the new bank was opened.

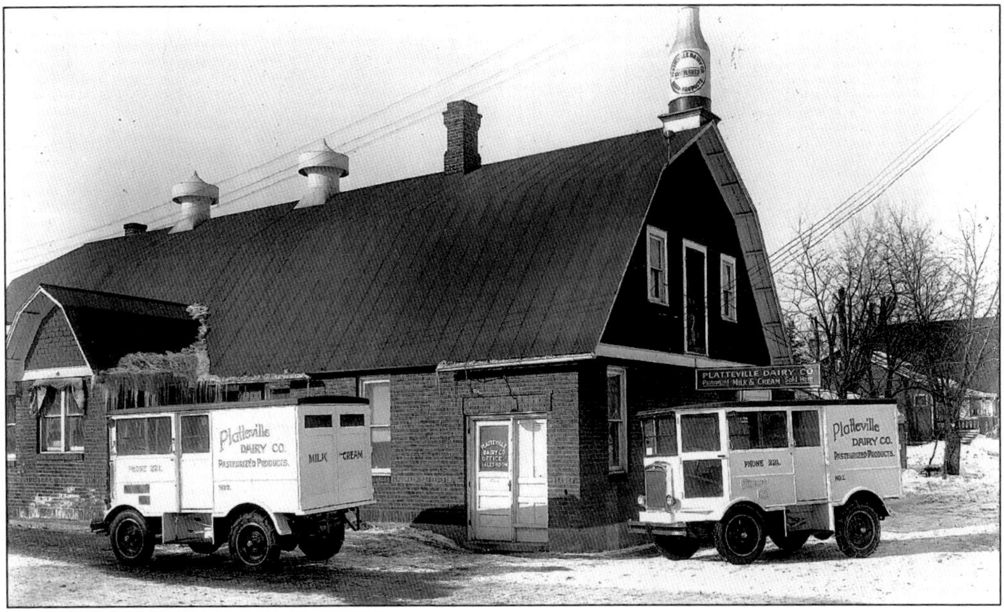

Two blocks northeast was the headquarters of the Platteville Dairy Company. This image, c. 1930, shows the dairy's new delivery trucks parked in front of their headquarters. This building had been the dairy's headquarters since it was built in 1919. It is located on Second Street between Mineral and Furnace Streets. Today it has a shorter roof.

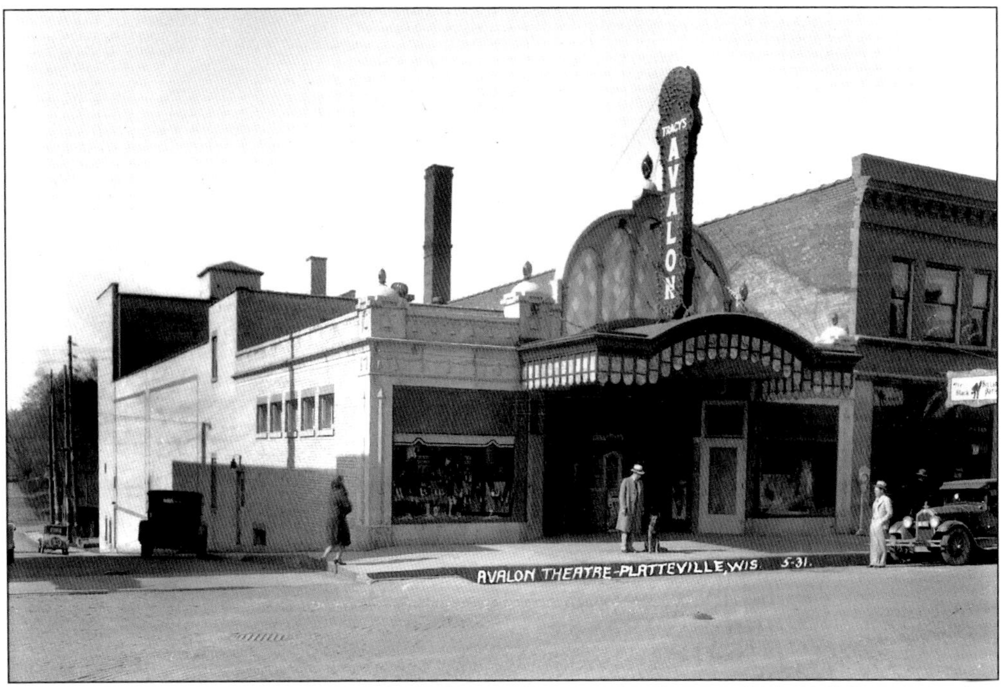

Two of Platteville's landmarks were built during this era. The first would be Bill Tracy's Avalon Theatre, which opened on December 11, 1930. Its first feature film was *Up the River* starring Humphrey Bogart. Tracy, who also owned the GEM Theatre in town, stated that he wanted the Avalon Theatre "to be a place where people love to come." (Courtesy of WHS.)

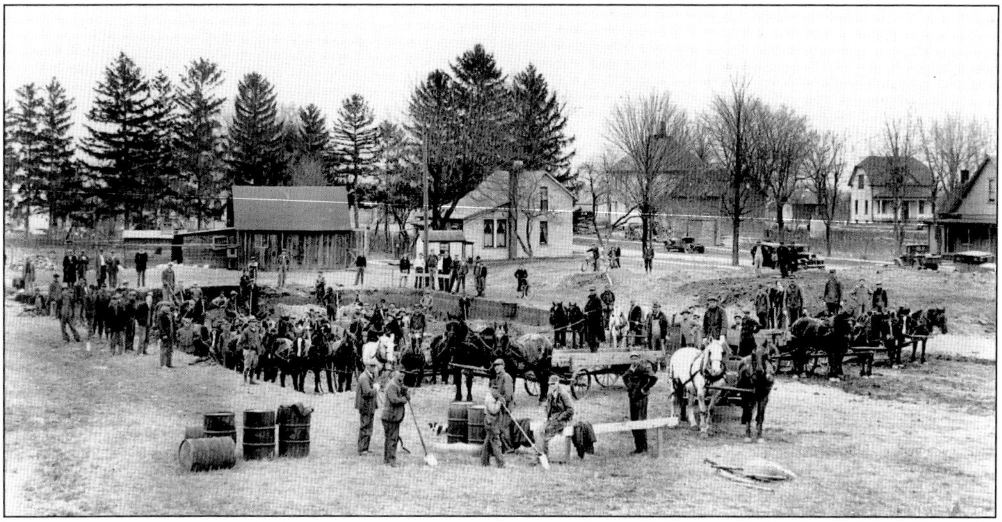

The second landmark was the public swimming pool, shown here in the spring of 1934. The pool, which cost $25,000, was dug by hand and the dirt hauled away by horses. "Jack" Tiedemann, a boy of 10 at the time, vividly recalls the day the pool opened on July 2, 1934. He and a group of children "sat around the edge of it, waiting for the adults to give them the ok to jump into the pool."

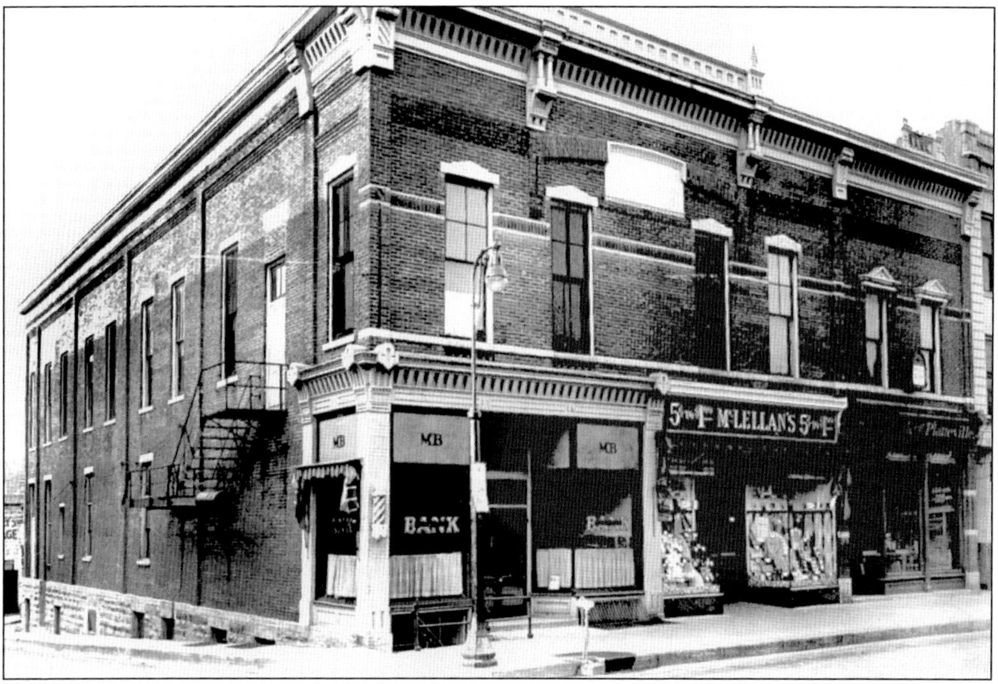

Over the years, most of Platteville's commercial buildings have served multiple purposes. Here is the old Masonic Temple, *c.* 1940, at the southwest corner of Main and Third Streets. Constructed in 1882, the Masons used its second floor until they relocated in 1925. Its first floor, however, had been the home of several businesses. The Mound City Bank, for example, which was established in 1915 with just $50,000, had occupied the corner of this building since 1919. (Courtesy of Dick Brockman.)

Four

MINERS AND PIONEERS
The Making of the University of Wisconsin-Platteville

"The local mining district, affords unusual opportunities for the practical education of students in mining methods."

–Homer B. Morrow, director, Wisconsin Mining School, 1926

At the beginning of the 20th century, Platteville had reached a crossroads in higher education. The increasing enrollments at the Normal School had caused it to relocate two blocks west into a larger building. At the same time, the resurgence of mining in Southwest Wisconsin created a need for an institution that would educate mining engineers. Platteville was the obvious place to locate such a school, because it was located in the heart of the zinc mining region. This led to the establishment of the Wisconsin Mining Trade School in 1908.

The Wisconsin Mining Trade School opened its doors in January 1908 in the old Normal School building. Over the next 50 years, it expanded its curriculum and changed its name twice, to Wisconsin Mining School in 1915 and Wisconsin Institute of Technology in 1939. In 1952, it was finally able to grant bachelor's degrees.

Change also came to the Normal School. In 1914, it established its Department of Agriculture. Its first farm was located south of the new Main Building. And in 1927, when the school changed its name to the Platteville State Teachers College, it could, for the first time, award bachelor's degrees. In 1951, its name was changed once more, this time to Wisconsin State College.

It was after 1927 that the school's nickname, the Pioneers, emerged. Originally the title of the Normal School's annual in 1910, the term Pioneer referred to the school being the pioneer, or first, state normal school and a pioneer in education. It was not long before it also meant the quintessential pioneer in buckskin.

Both schools, Normal and Mining, developed legendary rivalries. For instance, they competed in only nine football games and twelve basketball games against each other before the two administrations ended contact sports between them. Both schools also have their own traditions—the Pioneers with their old Normal School Bell and the Miners with their "M" on the Platte Mound.

In 1959, the schools merged, forming the Wisconsin State College and Institute of Technology. The name was changed again in 1964, when it became the Wisconsin State University-Platteville. Finally, in 1971, when the state of Wisconsin consolidated its institutions of higher education into one system, it became known as the University of Wisconsin-Platteville (UWP).

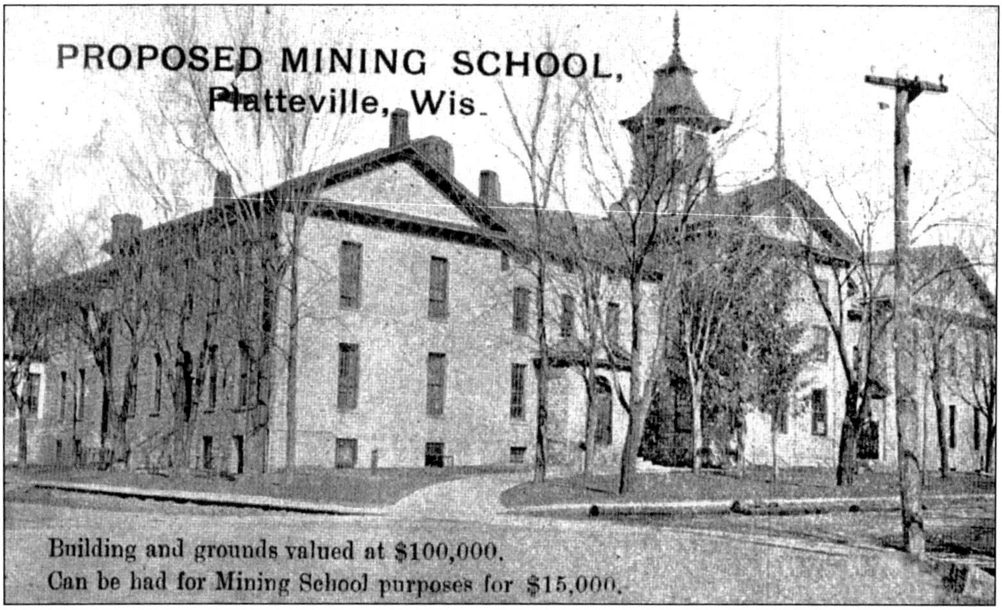

It took a concerted effort to establish a mining school in Platteville. This was an advertisement postcard used in a mailing campaign that was conducted in May 1907 to promote the use of the old Normal School building as a mining school. The state legislature passed the mining school act in July 1907 and after updating the old Normal School building it was reopened on January 27, 1908, as the newly established Wisconsin Mining Trade School (popularly known as the Mining School). During its first semester, the school had five faculty and eleven students. (Courtesy of RJM.)

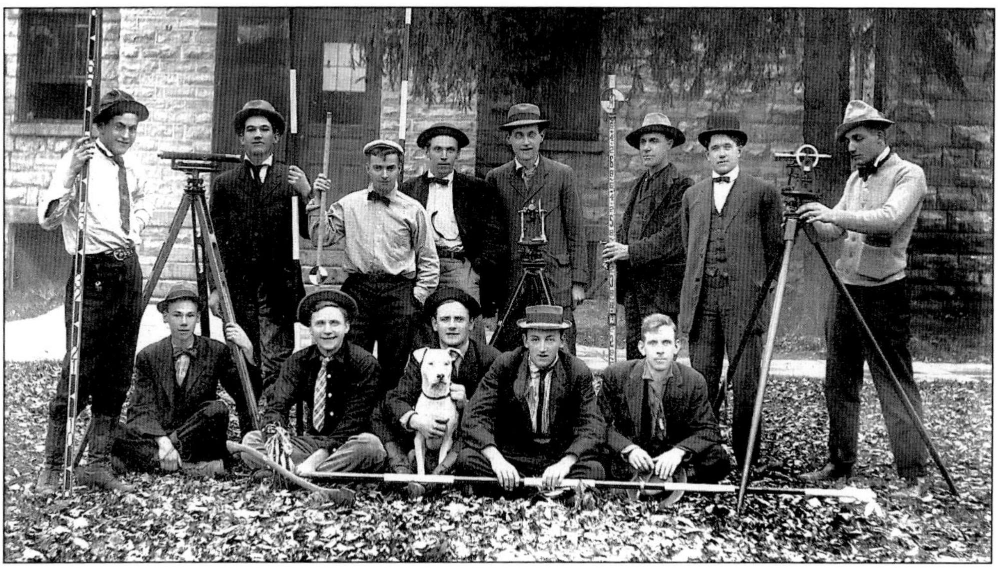

From its beginning, Plattevillians could count on seeing Mining students surveying the Mining School grounds and City Park. Shown here, in 1908, is the first Survey Corps of the Mining School. The 1908 catalog stated that "for land, railroad, and mine surveying there will be a full set of the most modern instruments, including transits, levels, compasses, sextants, clinometers, aneroids, rods, tapes and chains."

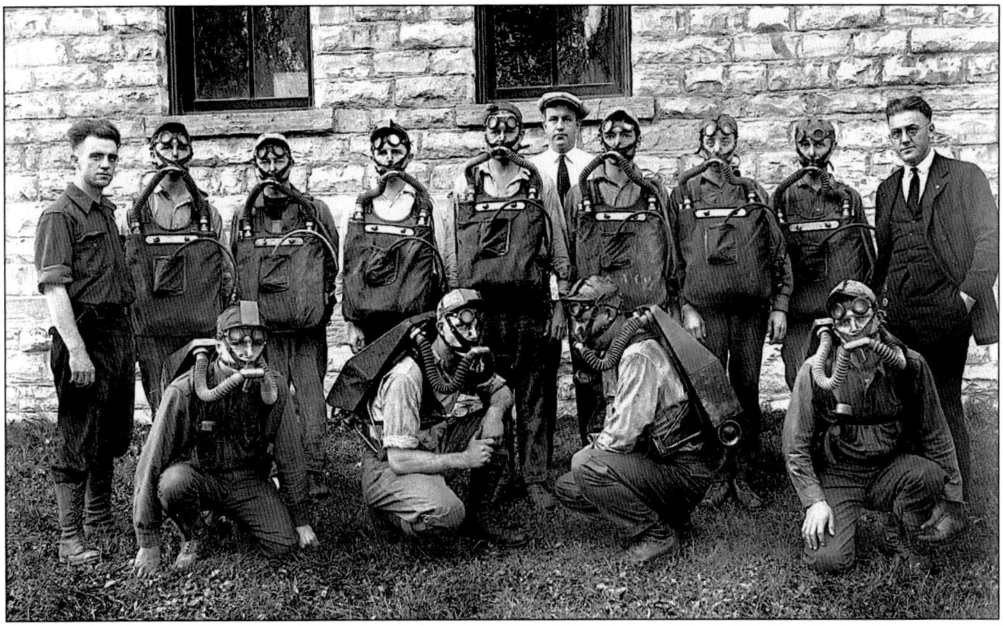

Mine rescue training began at the Mining School in the fall of 1914. The mine rescue squad of the 1922–23 school year is shown here. According to the 1915 *Miner* yearbook, "the training consisted of the operation, care, and the use of the self contained breathing apparatus of the Proto-Fleuss type." The students practiced in the Mining School's basement, part of which was "filled with smoke and ammonia gas."

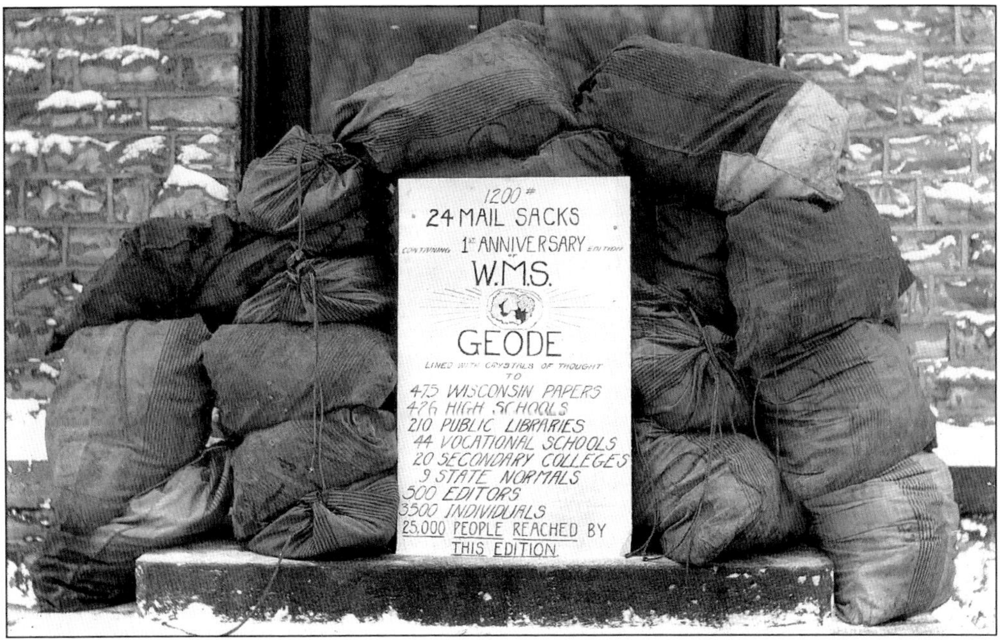

Like the Normal School, the Mining School also had a newspaper, the *W.M.S. Geode*. These mail sacks are filled with 5,274 copies of the February 21, 1926, issue. It was the first anniversary of the *Geode* and Henry Morrow, the director of the Mining School, used the occasion to promote the school to a larger audience than usual.

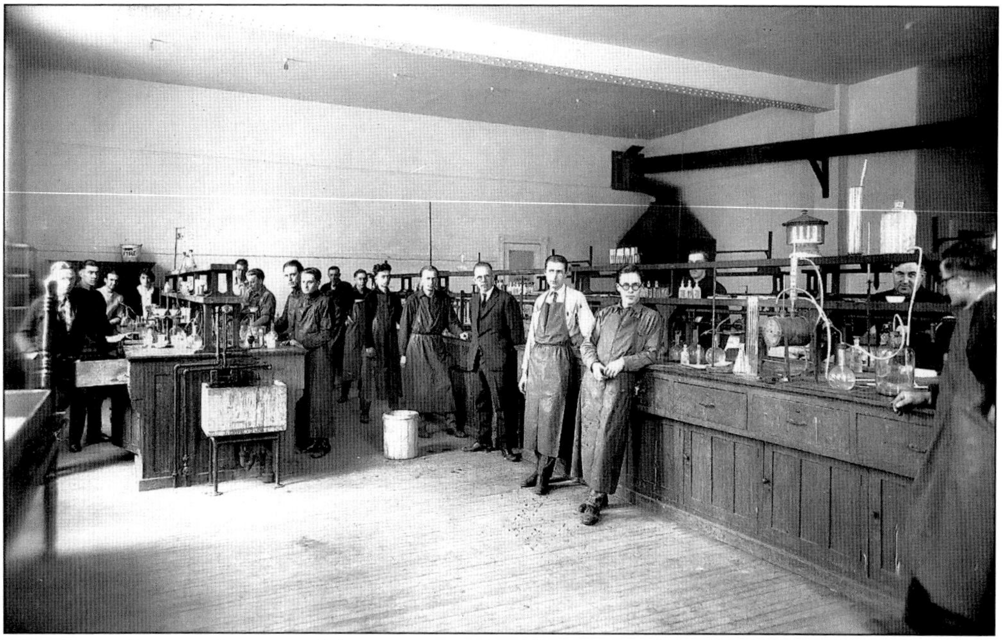

The above photograph is one of the images used in the anniversary issue. It shows the "Chemistry Laboratory" in 1926. The man standing in the center (without an apron) is the instructor of the class, George Dobson, affectionately known as "Dobbie." Outside of the classroom, Dobbie was the Mining School's legendary basketball and football coach—for over forty years.

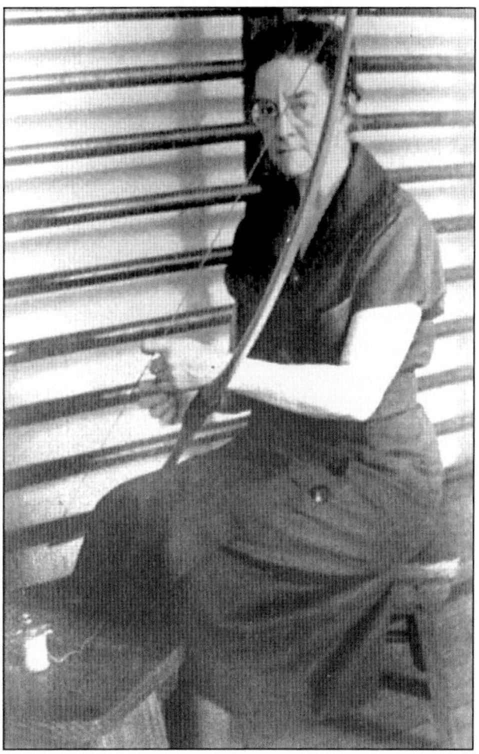

The person who could be considered Dobbie's counterpart was this lady, Agnes Otis Brigham. Brigham, shown here *c.* 1910, was affectionately called Briggie. She came to Platteville in 1903 and served as the Normal School's physical education director for 38 years. It was Briggie who organized and coached the Normal School's first basketball teams, both men and women. Brigham Hall was named in her honor in 1951.

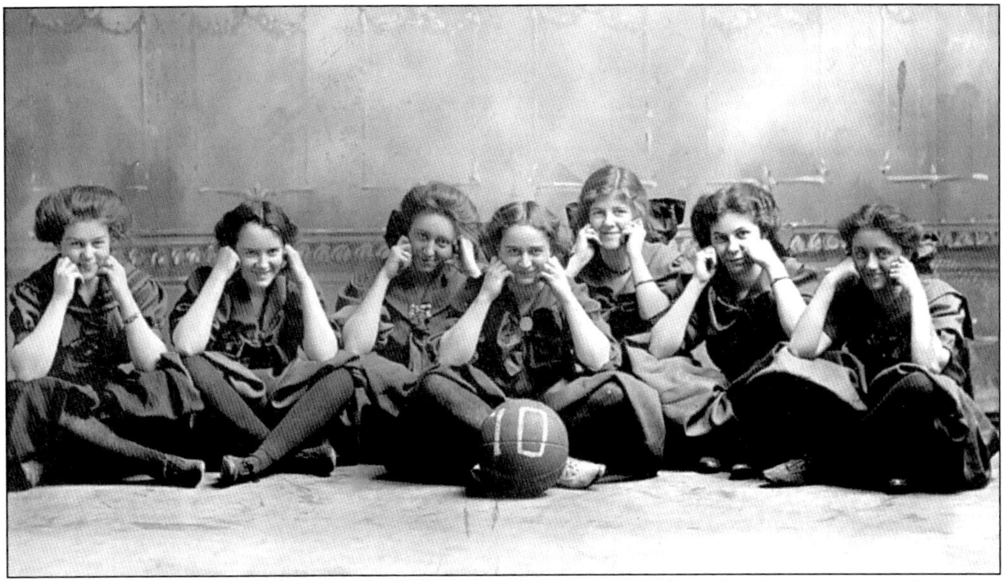

This is Briggie's 1910 "Girls' Basket Ball" team. The women played only two games that year, losing both to the Monroe High School girls. Seated from left to right are Rose Poland, Alice Doyle, Mary Mueller, Bessie Murphy (Captain), Gail Guilford, Genevieve Schuster, and Kathleen Beardsley.

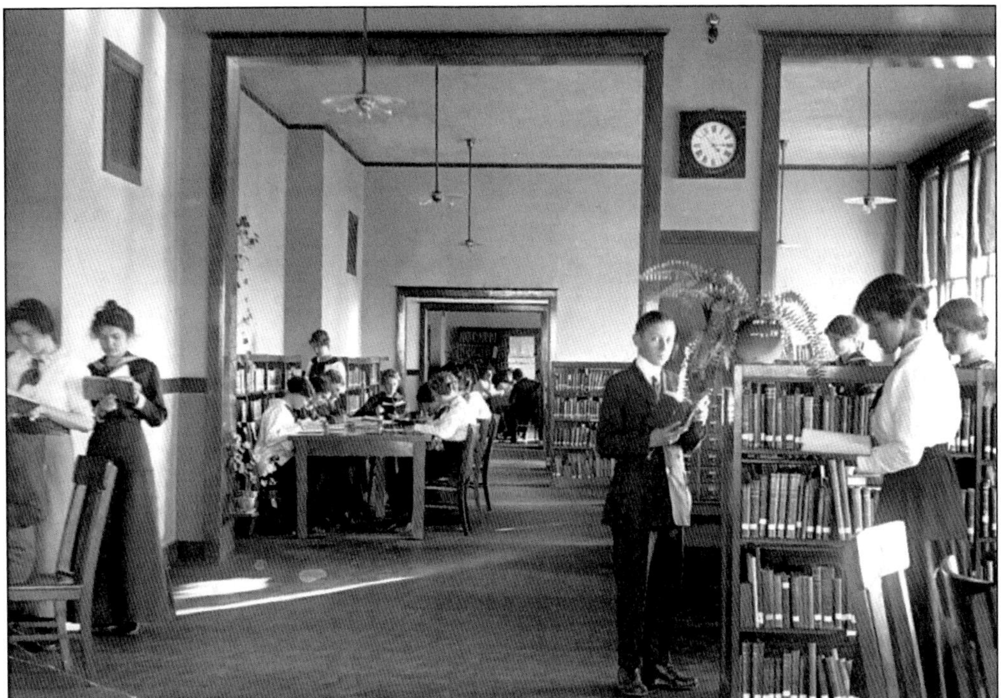

The Normal School's academic programs were supported by a library, shown here around 1914. According to the college catalog, the library's reading room contained over "seventy-five leading periodicals of the day." Myrtle Parmley (Class of 1915), standing at right with an open book, is the only identifiable person in this image.

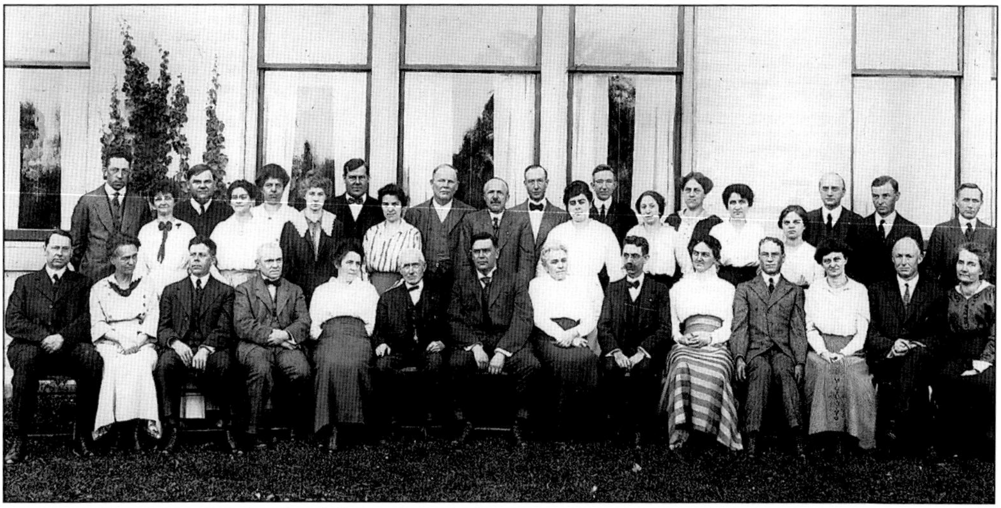

In 1916, the Normal School celebrated its 50th anniversary. Pictured above is the faculty at that time, from left to right: (seated) E. Riley, A. Durant, V. Russell, W. Williams, C. Schuster, D. McGreggor, President Asa Royce, B.A. Gardner, J. Wilgus, M. Mitchell, E. Reynolds, E. Fenton, I. Warner, and B. Burke; (standing) C. Burns, M. Hendrickson, F. Ullrich, A. Brigham, G. Gribble, C. Crouch, C. Roberts, unidentified, G. Haverson, F. Churchill, W. McConnel, G. Branigan, C. Riege, unidentified, W. Edsel, A. Sinclair, ? Roesler, M. Stormzand, G. Wilson, and J. Brockert.

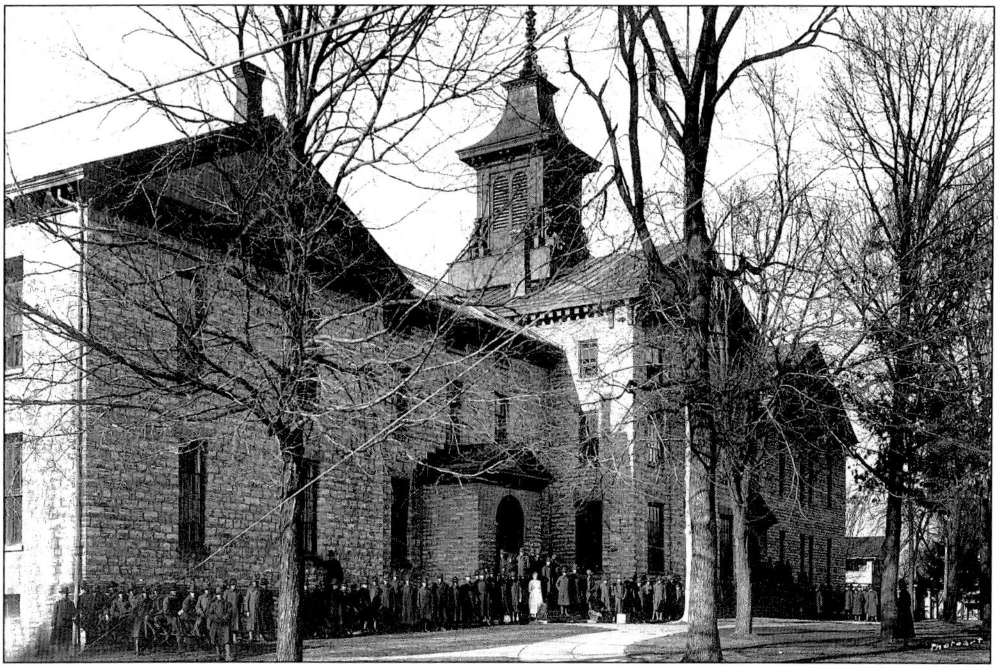

Two years later, in the fall of 1918, both the Normal School and Mining School participated in the United States War Department's Students' Army Training Corps (SATC), similar to the ROTC. The SATC students used both the Mining School's building and the Normal School's new Agricultural-Manual Arts building (see page 90) as their barracks. This photograph of the SATC students in front of the Mining School was taken around November 1918. The SATC was disbanded shortly after World War I ended.

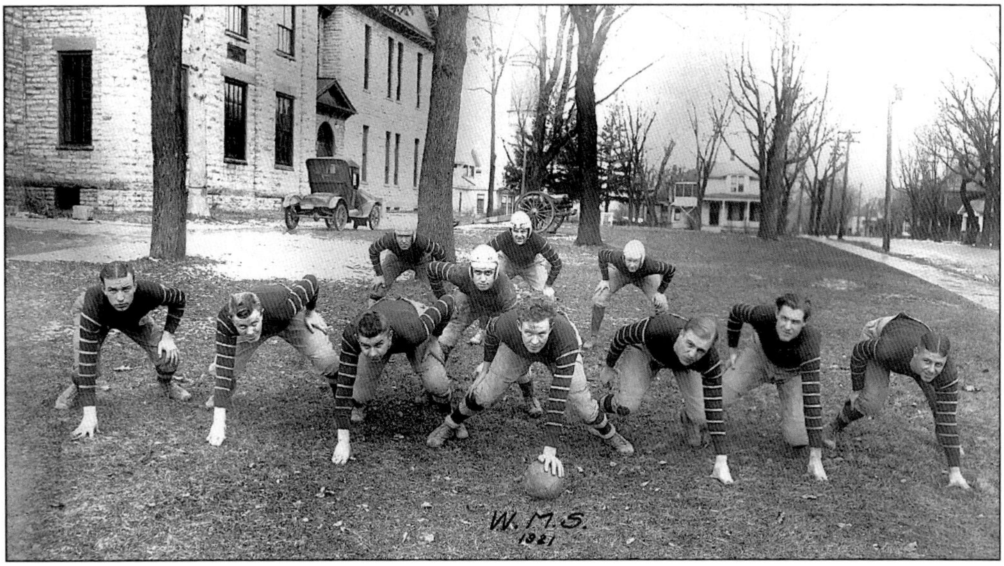

The two schools also shared an intense rivalry—in almost everything. The unthinkable happened to the 1921 Mining School football team, shown here. According to the Mining School's annual, "for the first time in the history of the school, the Normals scored on the Miners." They lost seven to zero. On at least one occasion, the Miners attempted to move the Normal School's Bell. The Normal School students countered by charging the World War I cannon (in the distance) with gun powder and firing it. The cannon was scrapped during World War II. In 1958, an old mining drill was placed on the same spot.

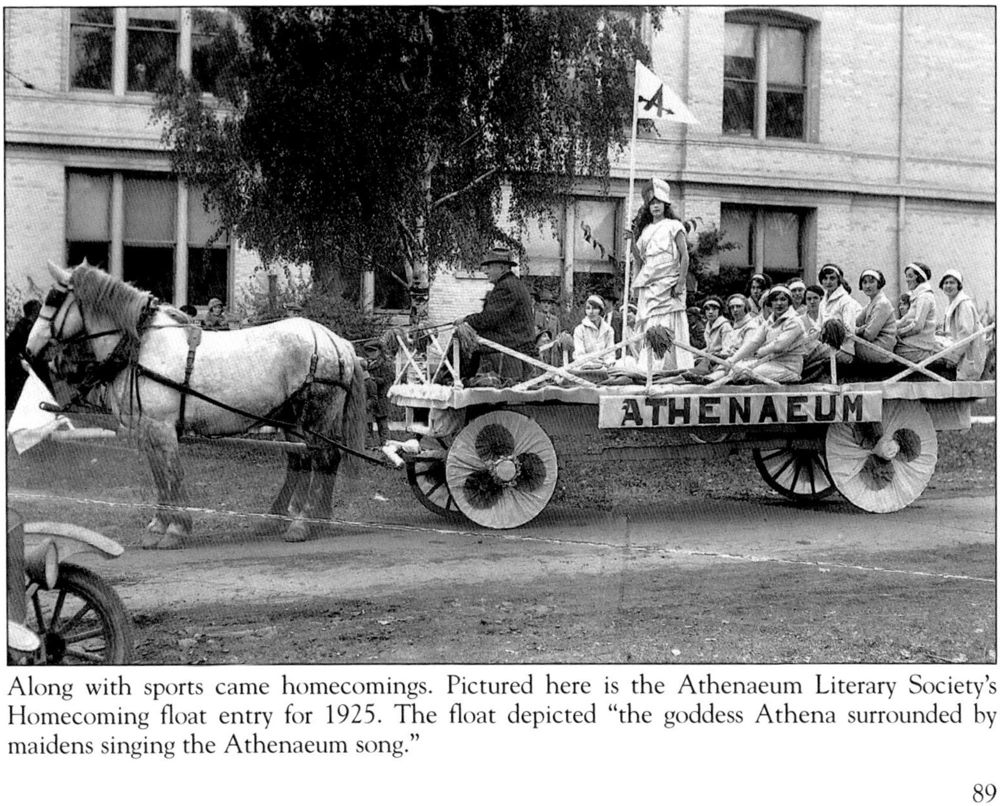

Along with sports came homecomings. Pictured here is the Athenaeum Literary Society's Homecoming float entry for 1925. The float depicted "the goddess Athena surrounded by maidens singing the Athenaeum song."

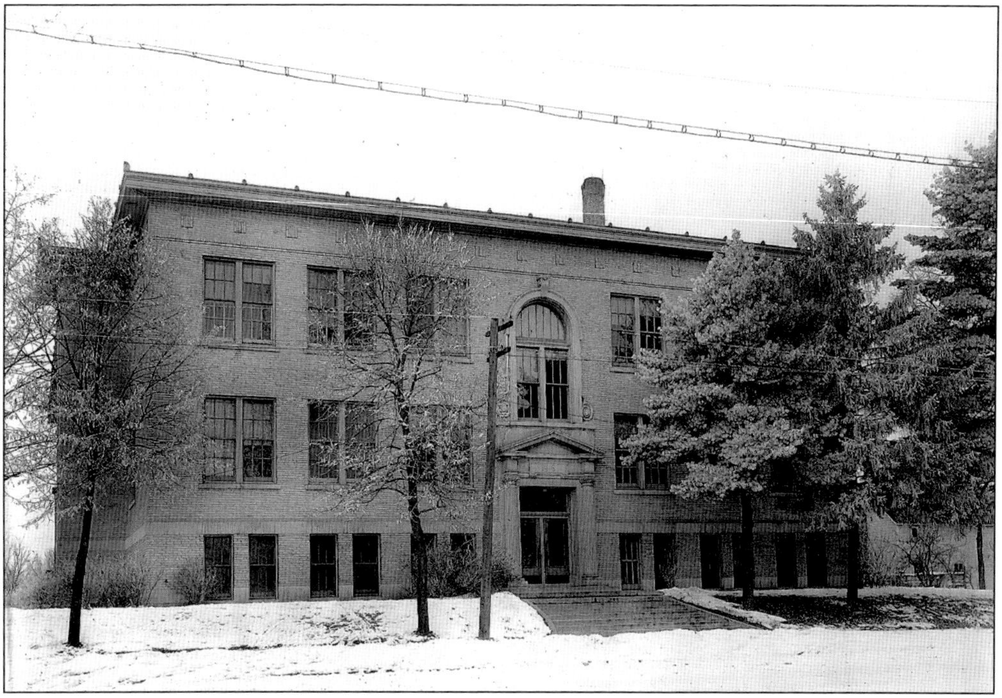

One of the Normal School's significant initiatives during this era was the establishment of a Department of Agriculture in 1914. In 1916, the Agricultural-Manual Arts building (shown above, *c.* 1920) was built to house the new department. In addition to classrooms, it had a forge room, farm carpentry shop, and a gymnasium. In 1966, the building was renamed Ullrich Hall, in honor of Fred T. Ullrich, the director of the Department of Agriculture from 1914 to 1941.

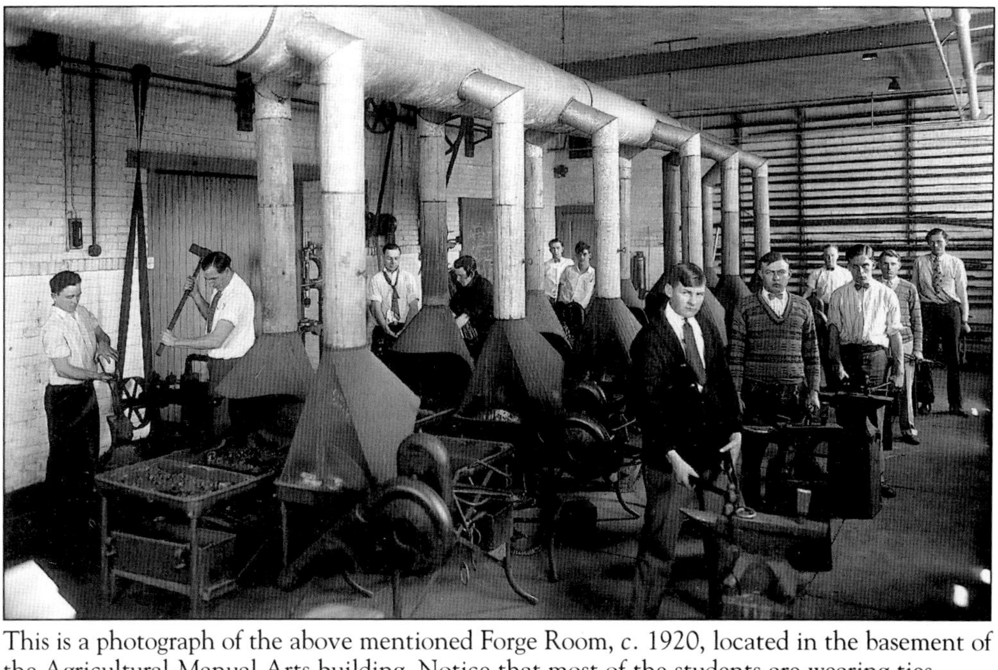

This is a photograph of the above mentioned Forge Room, *c.* 1920, located in the basement of the Agricultural-Manual Arts building. Notice that most of the students are wearing ties.

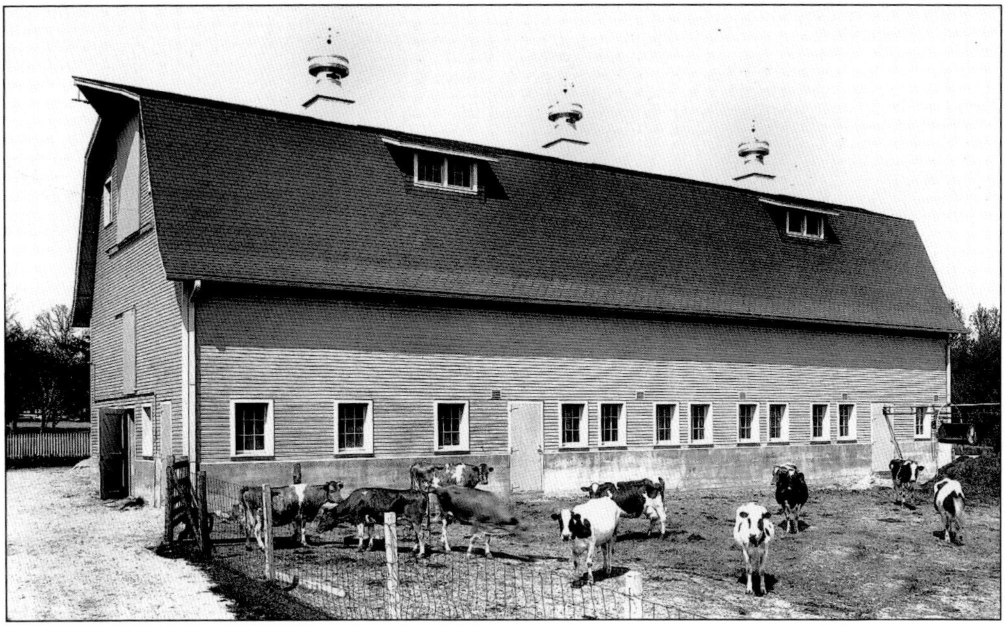

The Normal School's farm was located on the south side of campus. The central feature of the farm was the barn above, built in 1928, located approximately where the Pioneer Student Center is today. The barn had a large livestock judging room, 30 stanchions, and a classroom. This photograph was taken around 1928, before a silo was added. Since 1960, the Pioneer Farm has been located about five miles southeast of Platteville, in Elk Grove Township, Lafayette County.

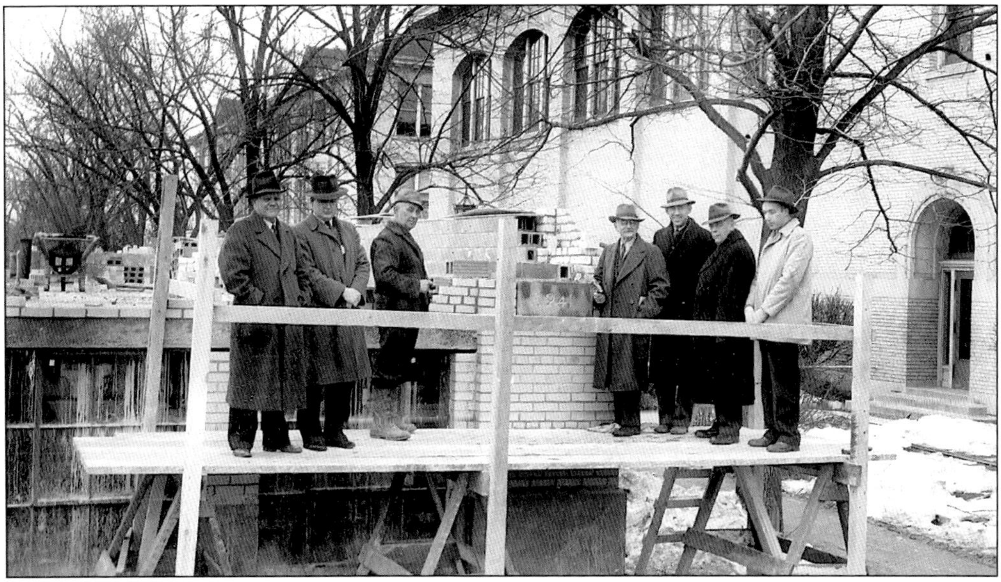

In the fall of 1941, ground was broken for a new Industrial Arts building located just west of the Agricultural-Manual Arts building. As reported in the *Exponent*, the purpose of this building "is to provide our industries with skilled labor, thus helping to fill the gap which at present is hampering our rearmament efforts." This is the cornerstone ceremony, which occurred on January 21, 1942. Robert I. Dugdale, Platteville's representative on the Board of Normal Regents, is holding the trowel.

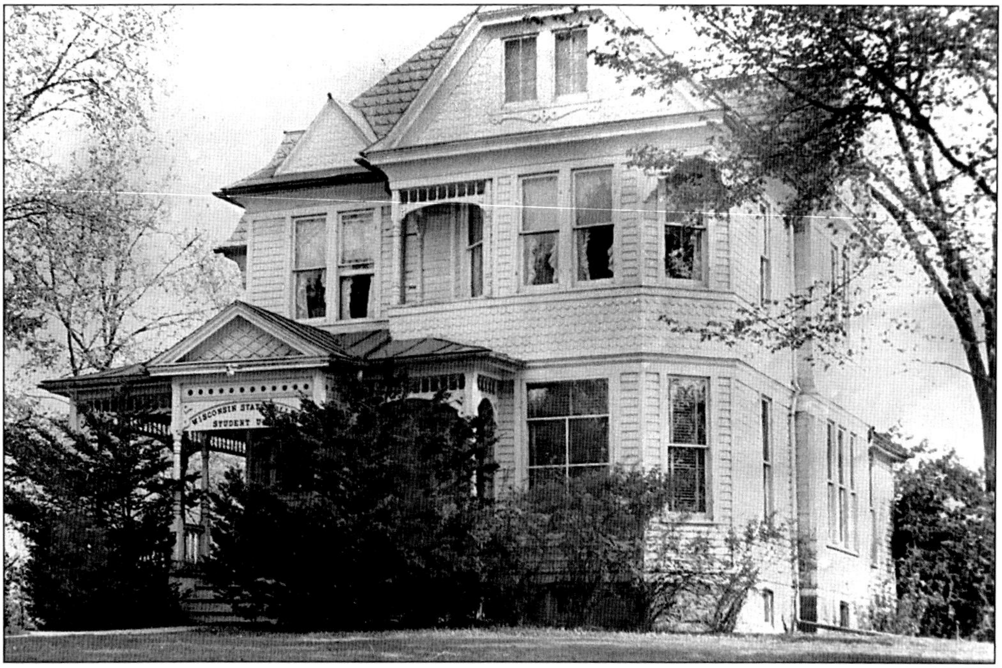

In June 1936, the Normal School, now called the State Teachers College, opened its first Student Union, shown here *c*. 1955. Affectionately known as the May House, only women could use it until 1953, when men were allowed. As a contemporary college catalog stated, it was a place where "the young women of the college may go to rest, study, read or visit during their free hours." Originally located where the Ullsvik Center is today, it was moved in 1957 to 500 Lancaster Street.

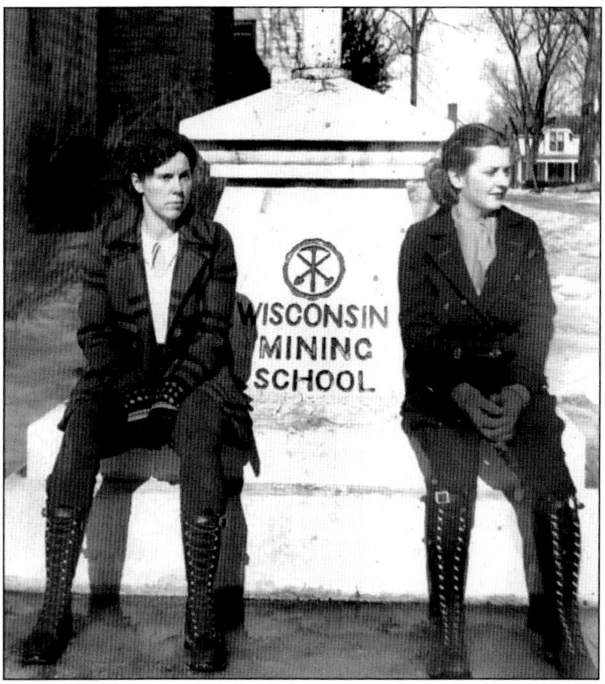

Women, moreover, were making an impact at the Mining School during the 1930s. Shown here in February 1937 are the first women admitted to the school. Seated on the flag pole base erected in 1926, are, left to right, Fay Bible and Nancy Morrow. When asked why they desired to attend the Mining School, Nancy stated, "we believe in the future of science, and hope to have a place in the scientific world." They both graduated in 1938.

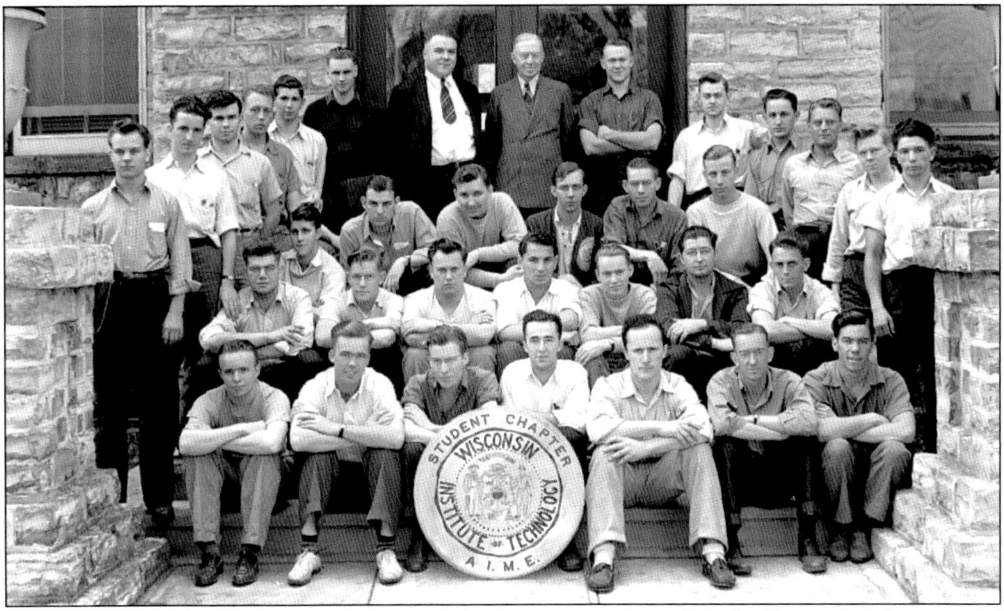

One year later, in 1939, the Mining School's name was changed to the Wisconsin Institute of Technology, to reflect the school's broader engineering program. On the heels of that change, a charter student chapter of one of the more prominent engineering organizations, the American Institute of Mining, Metallurgical and Petroleum Engineers (AIME), was established on campus. Pictured here is that charter student chapter of AIME in May 1941.

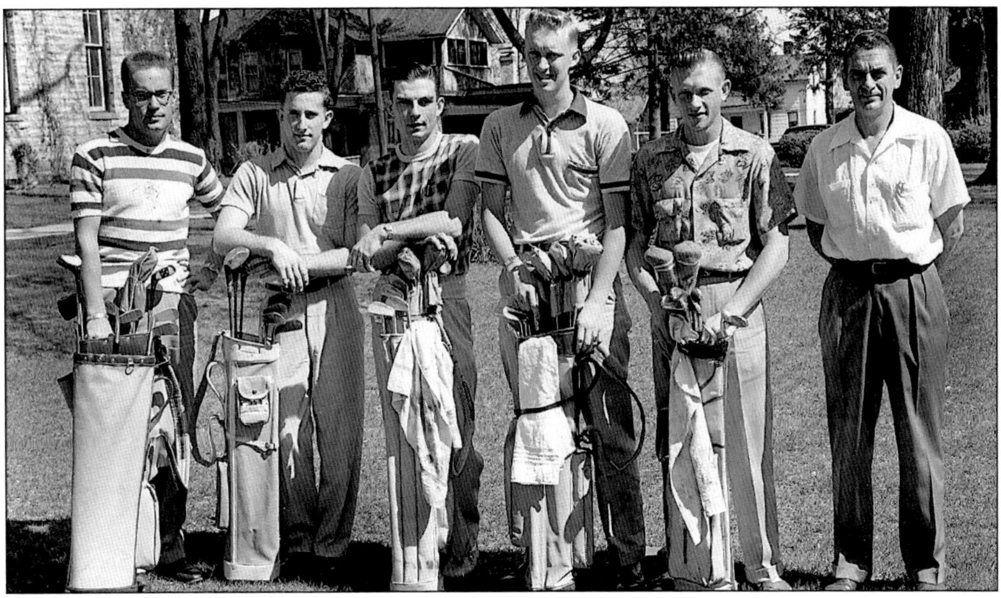

Both schools were ably led. Shown here is Dale C. Dixon, a faculty member of the Wisconsin Institute of Technology. Dixon, himself a 1936 graduate of the Mining School, returned to the Mining School in 1939. He taught chemistry and eventually became the dean of the College of Engineering. He also became deeply involved with the athletic program, coaching basketball, football, golf, baseball, and track. In this May 1953 photo he is shown with his golf team, from left to right, B. Carthew, J. Keene, H. Seeley, B. Nabblefeld, J. Sutliff, and Dixon.

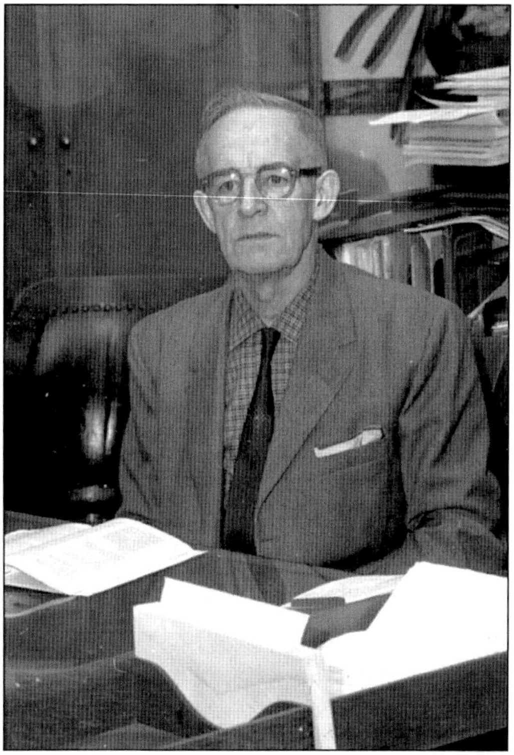

Another Mining School faculty member was Milton Melcher, shown here around 1960. Melcher began his career at the Mining School in 1923 as a geology instructor, served as the president of the Institute of Technology from 1941 to 1959, and closed out his career as a dean. It was under his guidance that the institute was finally given the right to grant bachelor of science degrees in 1952 and he played a primary role in the merger of the Institute and the State College in 1959.

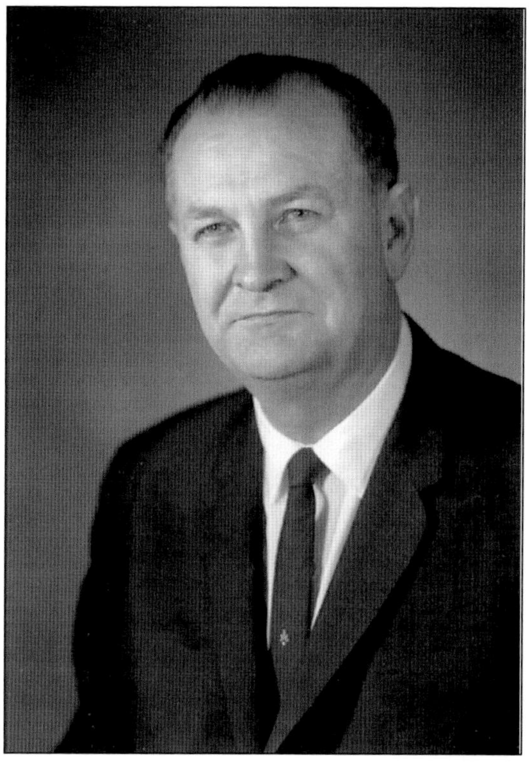

The other person instrumental in the 1959 merger of the two schools was the State College's President Bjarne Ullsvik, shown here around 1965. Ullsvik served as president (later chancellor) from 1958 to 1975. It was under his tenure that the college really became a liberal arts university, increasing its enrollment from 1,284 in 1958 to 5,024 by 1968.

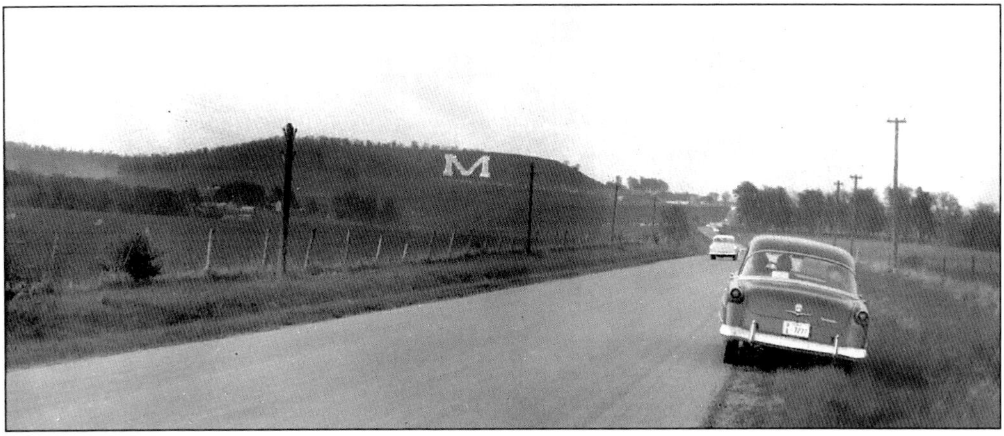

Both the Institute of Technology and the Teachers College had their symbols. For the Institute it was the "M," for Mining School. The Mining students constructed the "M" with limestone in 1937 on the west face of the Platte Mound. It is usually whitewashed once a year and lighted twice a year, during fall homecoming and during the Miners' Ball in the spring. This photograph, taken around 1958, shows a time-honored tradition of vehicles lining up to see the "M" lighted.

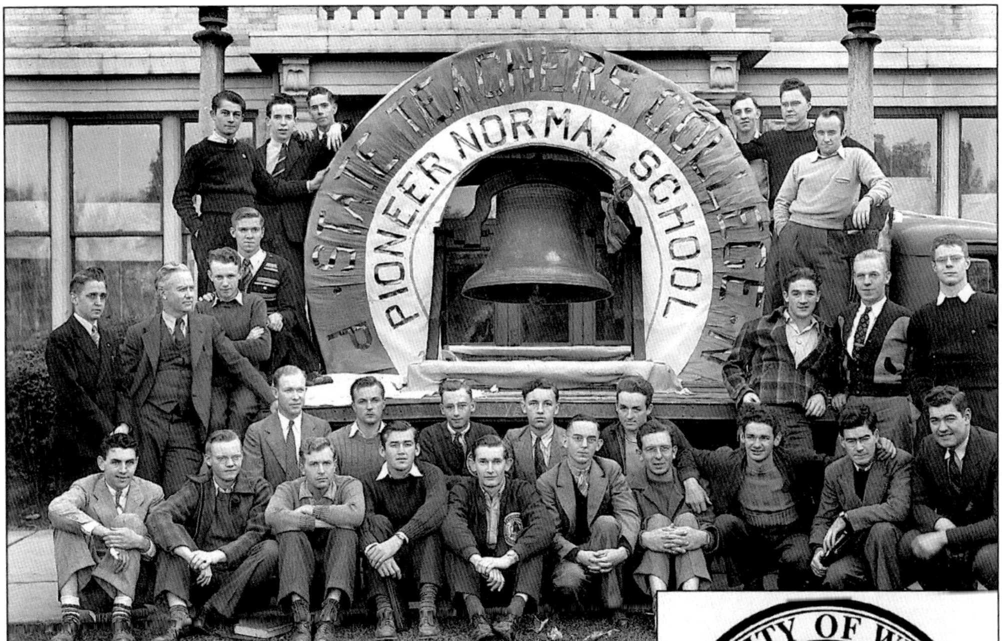

The Teachers College's symbol was their old Normal Bell, shown here on the Philadelphian Society's first place float for the school's Jubilee Homecoming in October 1940. The bell, cast in Troy, New York in 1870, first hung in the old Normal School's belfry. After being stored away in the Main Building for 45 years, it was hung on the side of Doudna's Little Theater in 1953. In 2002 it was moved again, this time it was hung outside of the new Pioneer Student Center. The Normal Bell and "M" were later incorporated into the UWP's official seal, shown at right.

UNIVERSITY OF WISCONSIN 1866 PLATTEVILLE

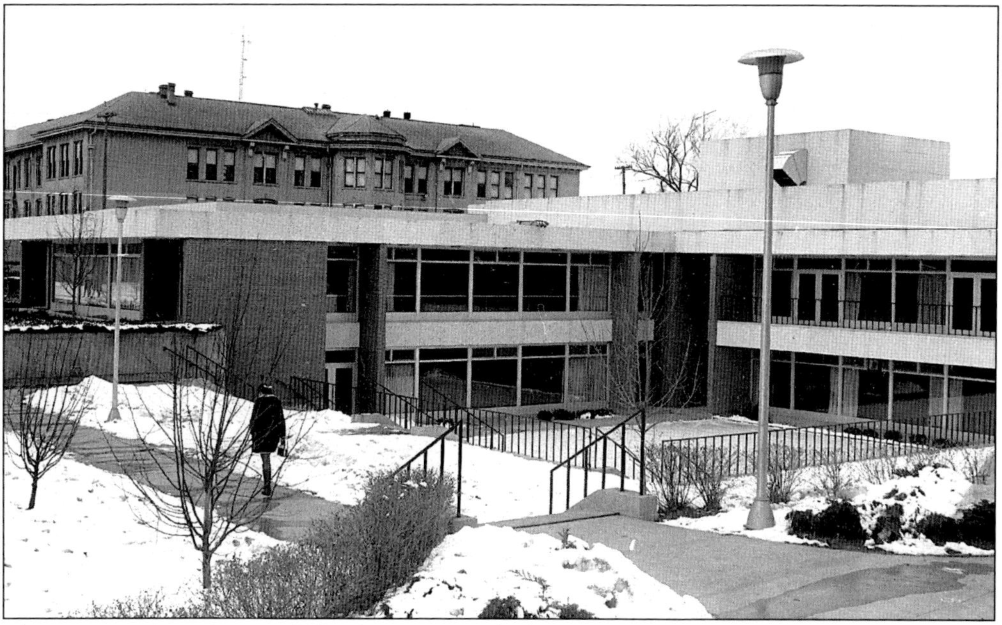

The new Student Center (Ullsvik Center today), shown here around 1965, was a tangible symbol of the transition from college to university. Dedicated on April 30, 1959, the Student Center replaced the old May House and was initially a joint venture between the Institute of Technology and the State College. In the foreground is a sunken ice skating rink that was often used by students—today it is the site of the Nohr Gallery.

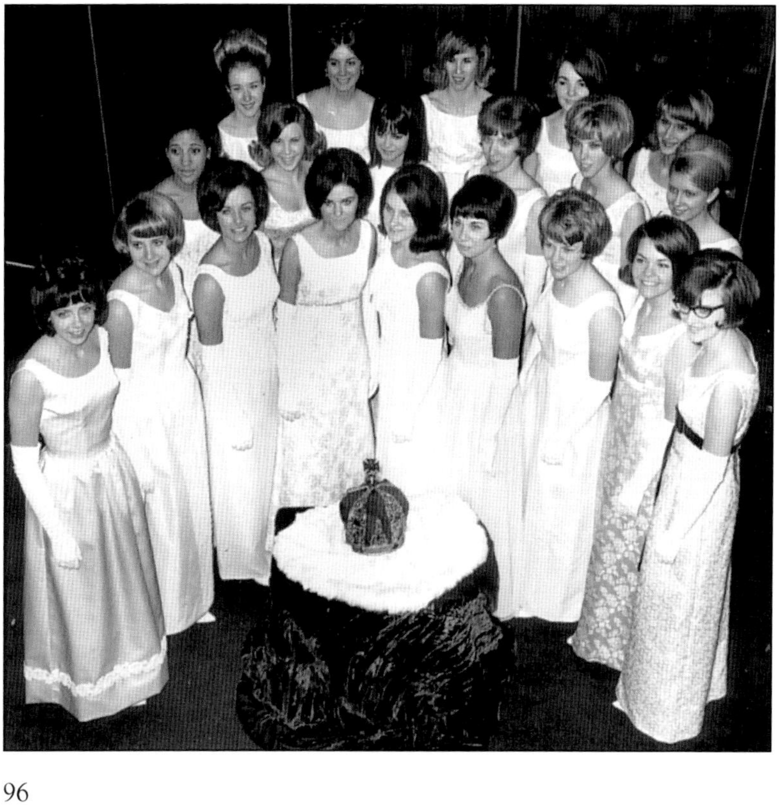

The Student Center provided needed space for new social activities, such as the Madrigal Dinner and Crystal Caprice. The Crystal Caprice was a winter follies activity that was usually held in February. Shown here are the 1967 contestants for the Queen of the Crystal Caprice.

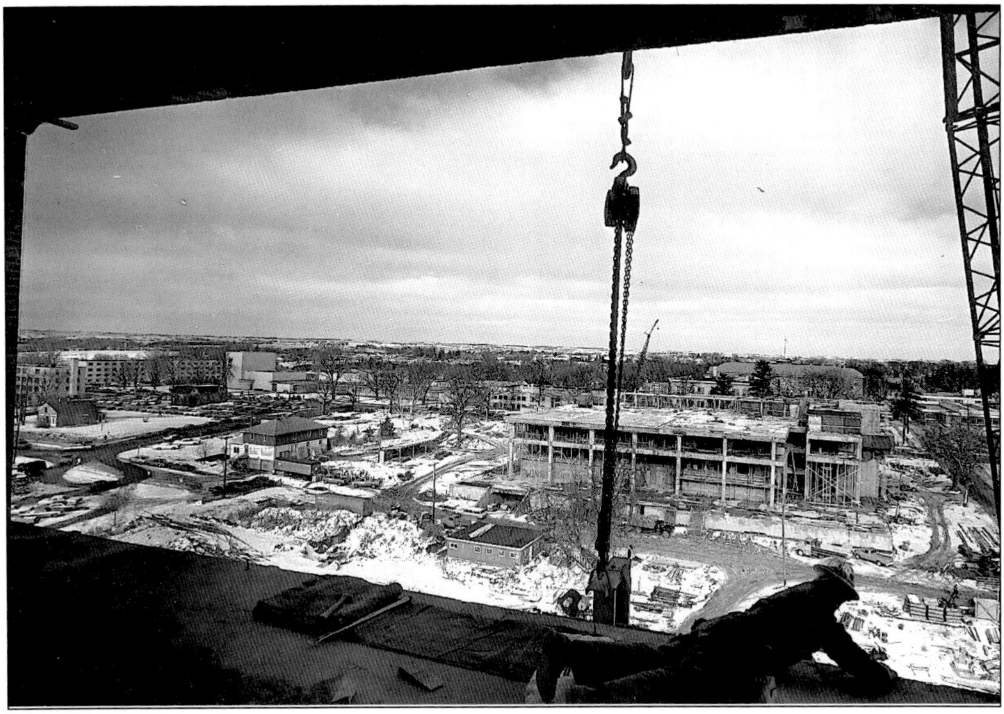

During Dr. Ullsvik's tenure more than 20 major construction projects were completed. This photograph, taken from the Pioneer Tower, shows both the Tower and the Elton S. Karrmann Library under construction during the winter of 1968–69.

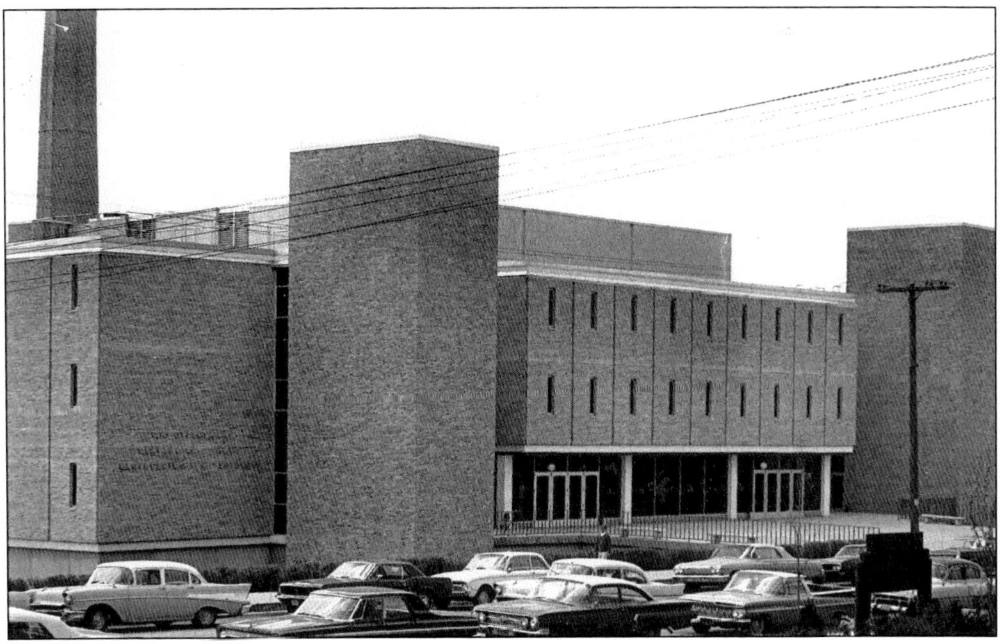

The C.W. Ottensman Centennial Hall of Engineering-Science, shown here around 1966, was also one of those construction projects. Opened on the school's Centennial Day, September 11, 1966, it became the new home of the School of Engineering, the successor of the old Mining School.

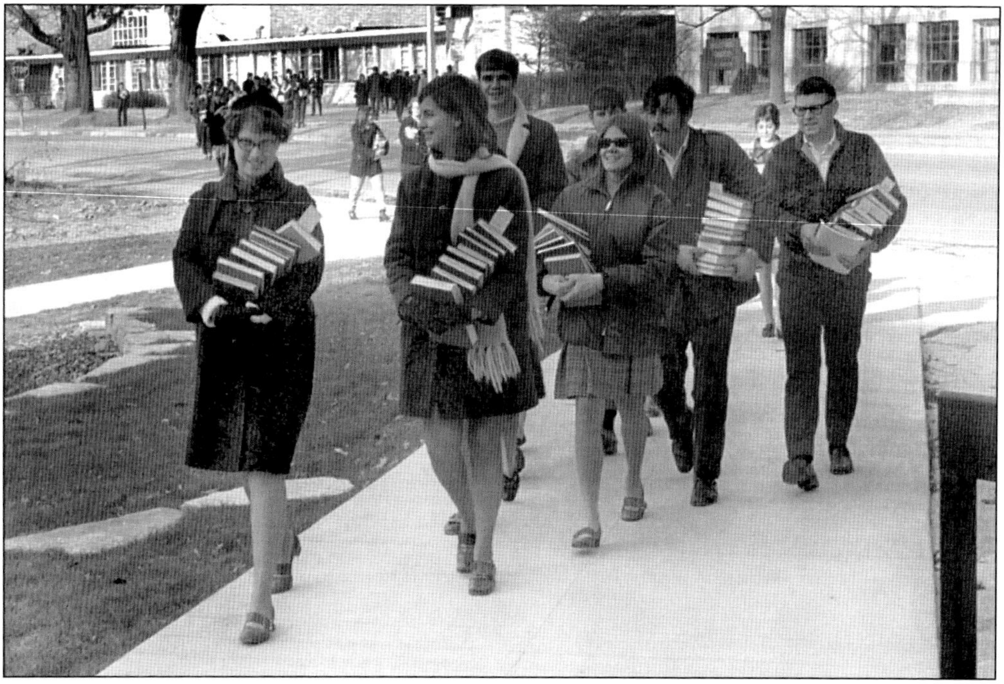

The one constant that has always been a part of the university is its commitment to education. Shown here are just some of the 1,500 students who transferred 89,000 library books from the old Karrmann Library to the new Karrmann Library on December 3, 1969.

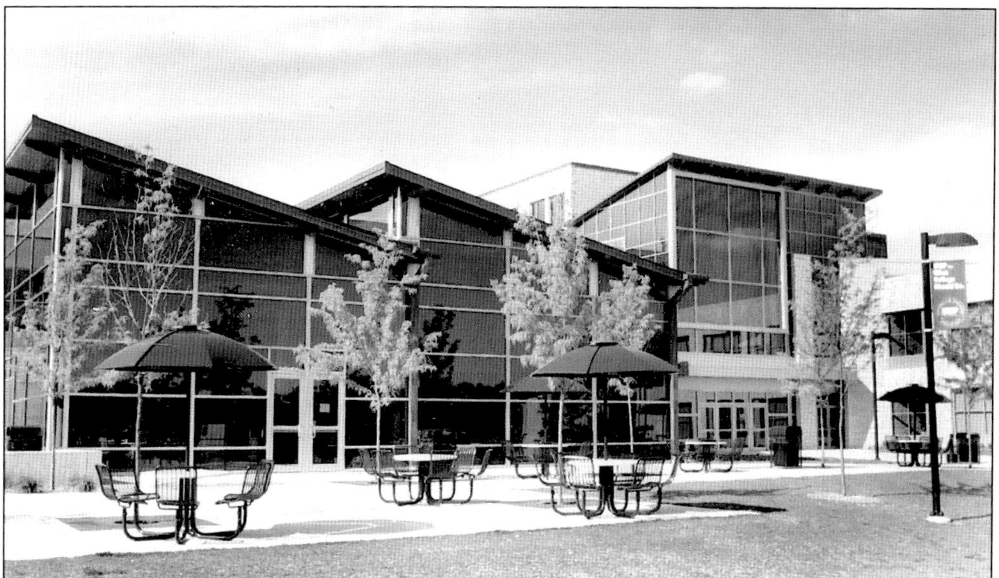

Today, the pioneering spirit of the University of Wisconsin-Platteville continues. In April 2002, the new 92,000-square-foot Pioneer Student Center (shown above) was dedicated. It functions as the crossroads of the university, bringing students, faculty, staff, and alumni together. And in 2004, UWP's Tri-State Initiative was approved. The goal of the initiative is to increase the student body by 2,000 students over the next decade.

Five

THE MOUND CITY AT HOME

"Platteville is as plesent a little a Town as I have seen. Here is plenty of stores or Shops. We can buy any thing we want, and here is plenty of good Schools both in the town and Country. We have a large Academy at Platteville, and here is six Churches. The stage Coach runs through our Town every day."

–Thomas Shepherd writing to relatives, March 31, 1854

Throughout its history, people of strong character have shaped and molded Platteville. It took the hard work of the early pioneers, such as Mary Mitchell Goodell, Samuel Moore, and August Kettler, to build the town. Their hardships created opportunities for the following generations. A good example of this would be Vera Hemphill. The daughter of John, a carpenter by trade, and Bell Hemphill, Vera was the first in her family to attend college. She graduated from the Normal School in 1918 and became a teacher. Another example is Laura Rountree Smith. She graduated from the Normal School and became a writer of children's books. Legend has it that she got her inspiration for her "Bunny Cotton Tail" series from watching rabbits in Duncan McGregor's garden, which was down the hill from her home, Major Rountree's house.

Along the way, Platteville became known as the Mound City. This is not surprising—the Platte Mound has always been an integral part of Platteville's social fabric. It was from the Mound in 1827 that Major Rountree first saw the future site of Platteville, for generations Plattevillians have held social events at it, and the Mining School students even used it as a backdrop for the world's largest "M."

Most of all, however, Platteville has been a town of small shops, enterprising individuals, and loving families. For the youngsters who thirsted for adventure, one of the popular refrains was "Let's go out to the Powder Mills," which were located west of town on the Little Platte River. Favorite picnic areas were Tuffa Falls and the Platte Mound. At the end of summer, everyone looked forward to the Big Badger Fair. Platteville also witnessed Scott Cairy lead Company I, 4th Wisconsin Volunteer Infantry into World War I, and, 20 years later, sent another generation off to fight World War II. It was the people of Platteville who became its merchants, built the city, and filled their homes with love and laughter. They made the Mound City what it is today.

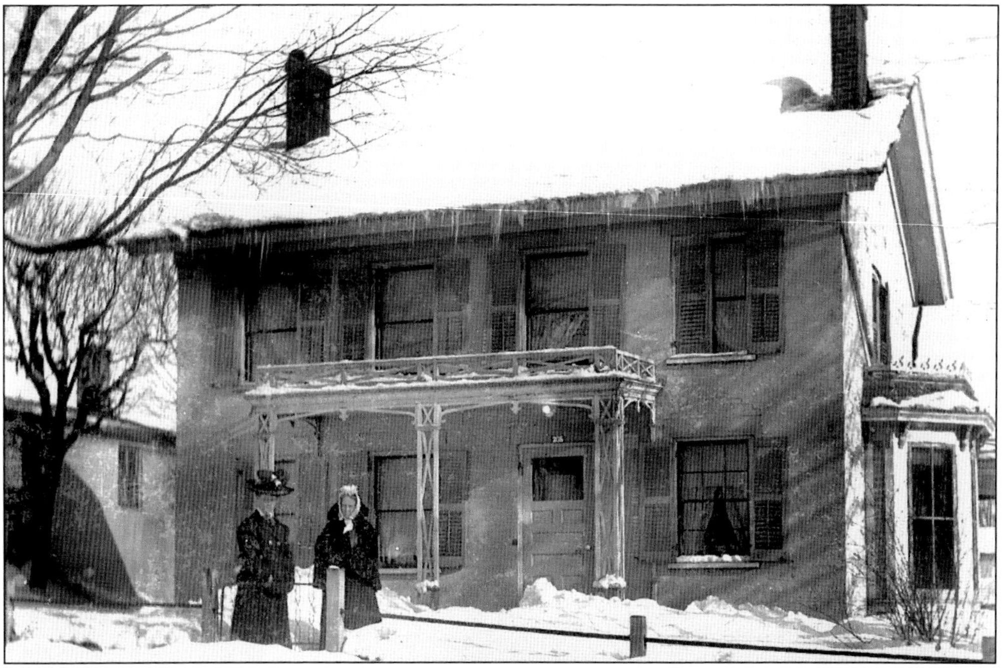

The story of Platteville is really the story of its people. One of Platteville's earlier residents was Mary Mitchell Goodell, shown here (on the right) in 1910 with her daughter, Nettie Goodell Jones. Mary came to Platteville as a child with her parents in 1839. In 1854, she married Lemuel Goodell, a druggist in town; the couple had three daughters.

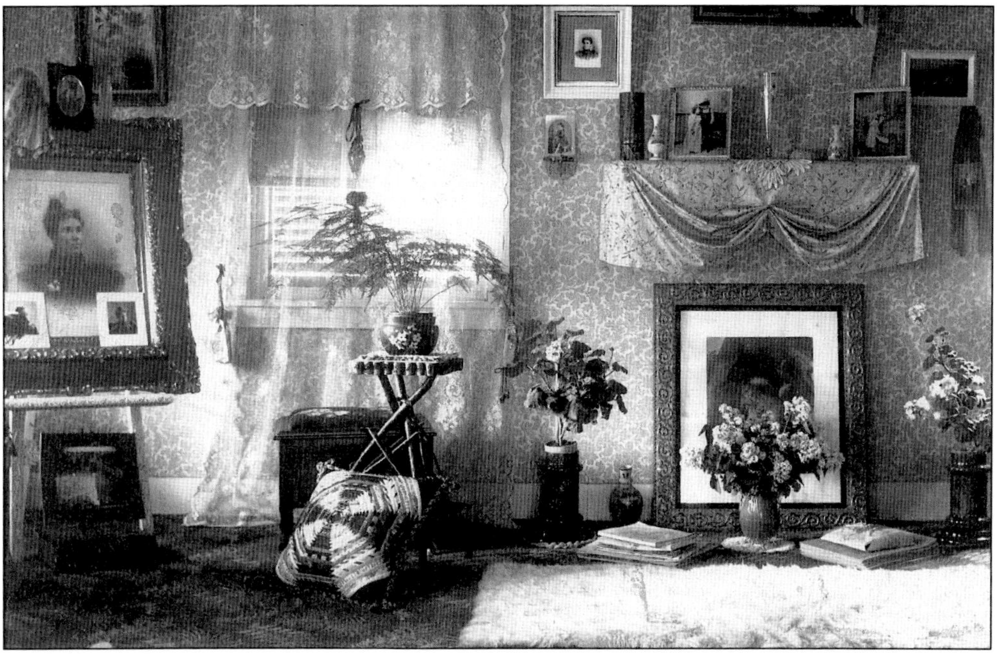

By 1855, the Goodells purchased the house shown in this and the previous image (135 North Water Street). Peter McIntire, a blacksmith, constructed this Greek Revival in the late 1840s. This photograph shows what one of the house's parlors looked like around 1900.

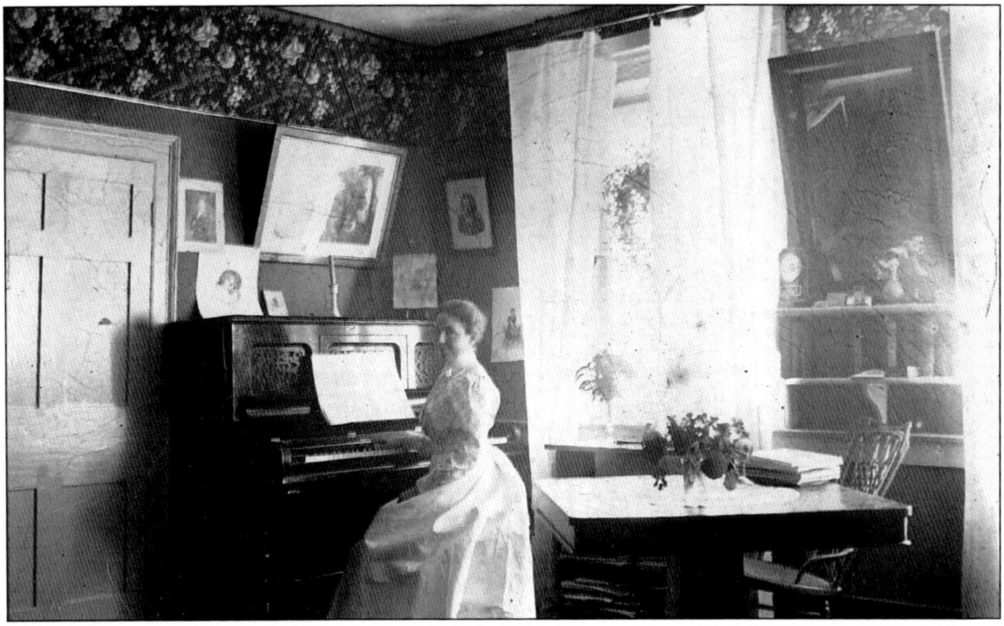

Here is Laura Rountree at her piano inside her sitting room in the Mitchell-Rountree Stone Cottage, *c.* 1910. The daughter of Samuel and Sophia Rountree and granddaughter of Major John Rountree, Laura never married. She lived in the cottage for most of her life, becoming a good painter, musician, and calligrapher. In 1959, she deeded the cottage to the Grant County Historical Society. She died in 1966 at the age of 95. (Courtesy of GCHS.)

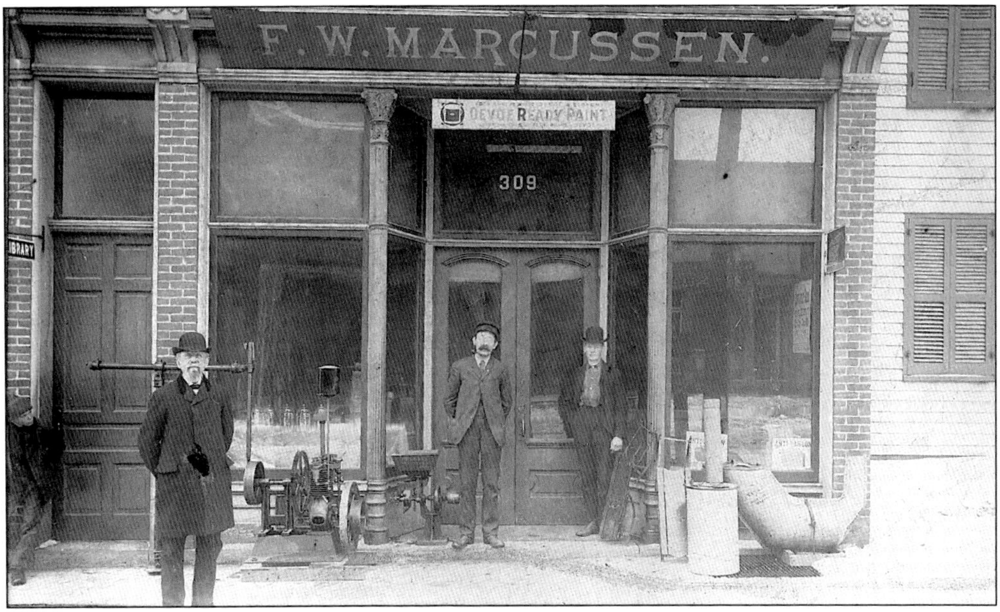

In the 19th century, Platteville had a fairly substantial influx of immigrants from Germany. Among them was Frederick W. Marcussen, the man with the dark mustache. Born in Holstein in 1861, he arrived in Platteville in 1880 and made his living as a hardware dealer. Here he is in front of his store, located at 133 East Main Street, *c.* 1905. Notice the "Library" sign on the far left. The public library was located there from 1904 to 1907 (see page 118).

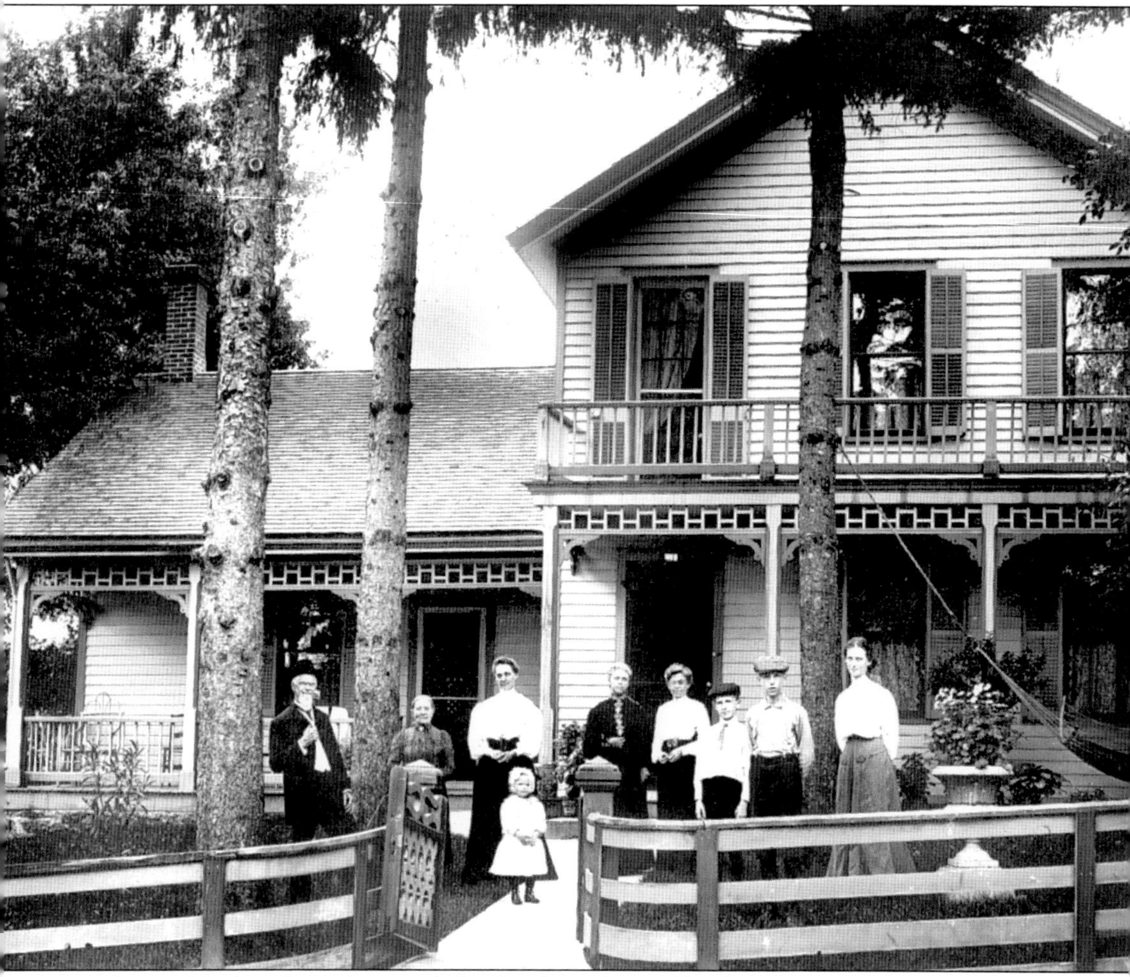

August Kettler, shown here with his family in front of his house, was another individual from Germany. August had this house, located at the southwest corner of Furnace and Water Streets, built in 1868. The photograph, c. 1905, shows, from left to right, August and his wife Julia; their two daughters, Louise Schambow and Carrie Burg; Lou Clabe; Carrie's two boys, Leo and Frank Jr.; and Clara Schambow, Louise's daughter. The little girl in front is Carrie's daughter, Julia Burg. August, who was born in Hanover in 1837, came to Platteville with his parents in 1856. He made his living as a general merchant at Main and Second Streets. Incidentally, he lost two of his store buildings to fire, after which he rebuilt with brick.

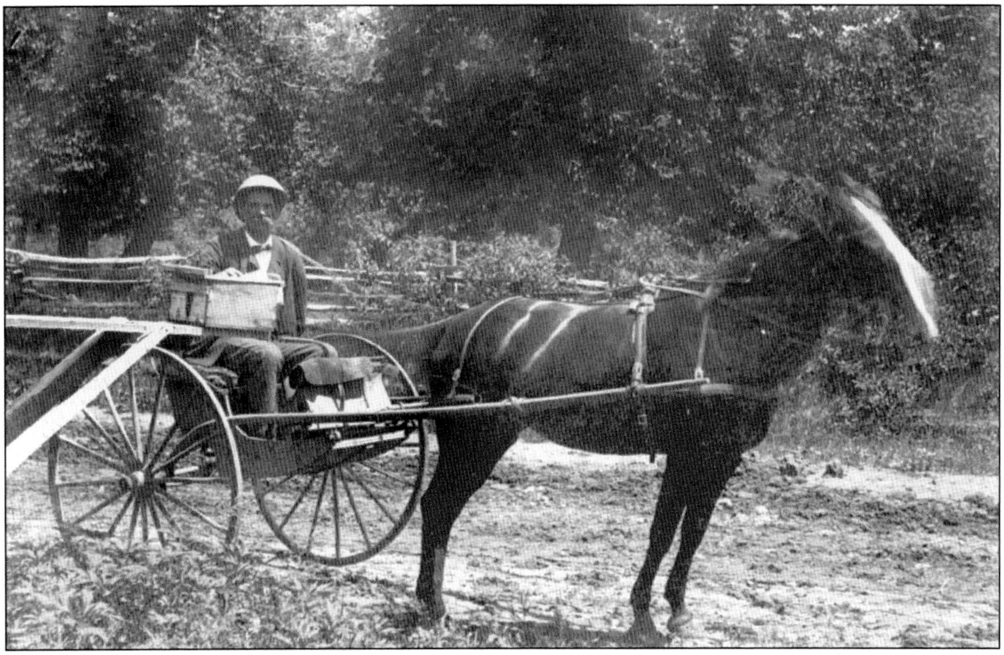

Christian Graeser, a veteran of the Franco-Prussian War of 1870–71, arrived in Platteville in 1881. In 1889, he lost his left arm in an accident at the Powder Mill, but by 1899 he became the first rural free mail carrier of the Platteville Post Office. Christian is shown here on his mail route, c. 1900. He delivered mail until his death in 1918. (Courtesy of Dick Brockman.)

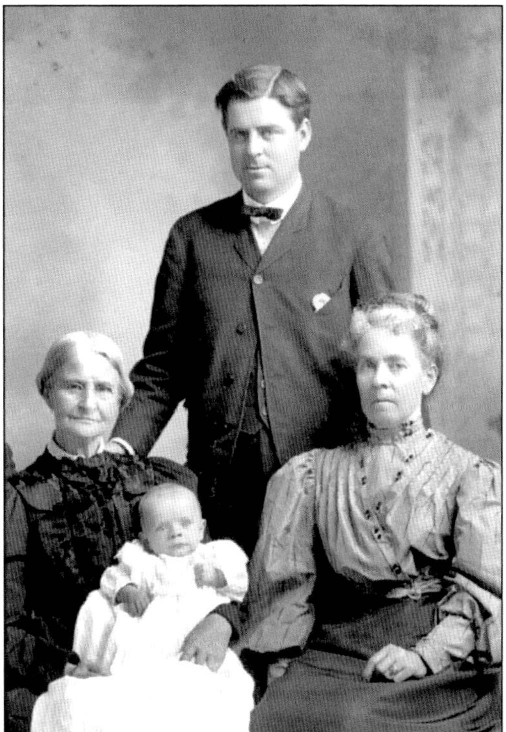

For his part, Arthur W. Kopp, whose paternal grandfather was from Germany, combined both German and Cornish heritage. Pictured here (c. 1905) are, from left to right, Jane Thomas, Kopp's maternal grandmother; William Roy Kopp, Kopp's son, born in 1905; Arthur Kopp (standing); and Elizabeth Jane Kopp, his mother, who was born in Cornwall. Kopp, a well-known lawyer and congressman from Platteville, was also a big supporter of the Mining School.

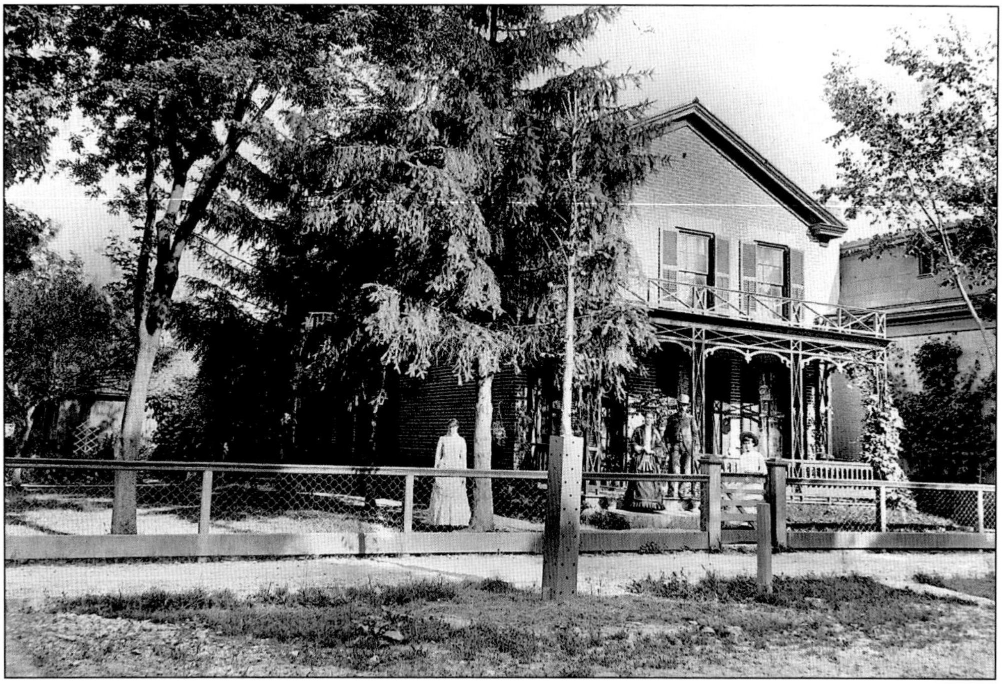

Architecturally, Platteville's 19th and early 20th century houses reflect the prominent styles of the era. This Greek Revival at 85 North Elm Street was built around 1847. In this image, c. 1887, are Dempster Gardner, a Normal School mathematics instructor, and his family. From left to right are Bertha, daughter; Etta, wife; Dempster; and Mabel, daughter.

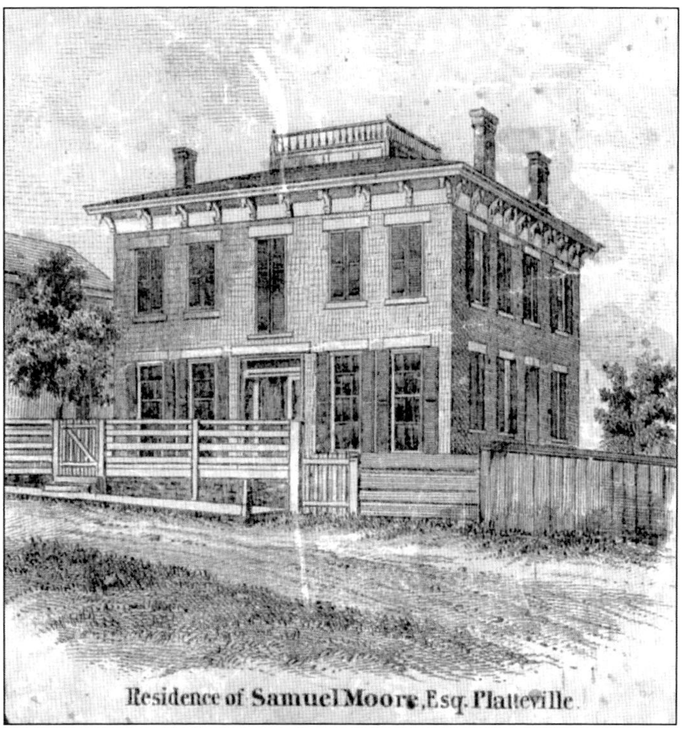

In 1868, the first detailed map of Grant County was published. It included maps of all townships, villages, and engravings along its border of prominent businesses and dwellings. This image of Samuel Moore's house was one of those engravings. Moore, who arrived in Platteville from Indiana in 1834, became a prominent merchant and was instrumental in securing railroad service for Platteville. He had this Italianate house built in 1863. Located at 45 South Oak Street, it was later enlarged and turned into a hotel. (Courtesy of Dick Brockman.)

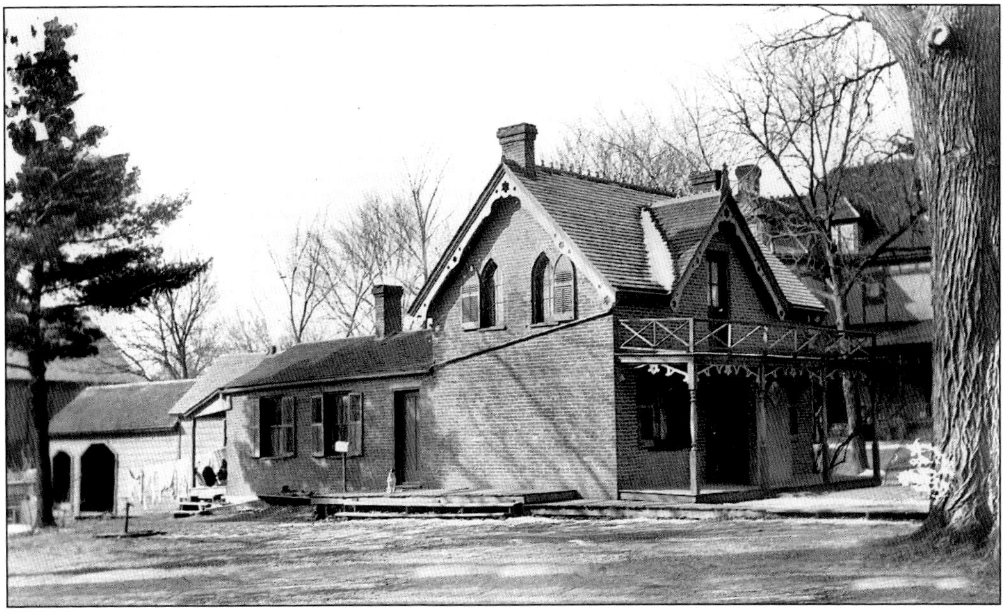

William F. Grindell, a successful furniture dealer, and his family lived in this Gothic Revival house after the Civil War. It was constructed in 1858 and was located just south of where Elm Street meets Pine Street. It is an empty lot today.

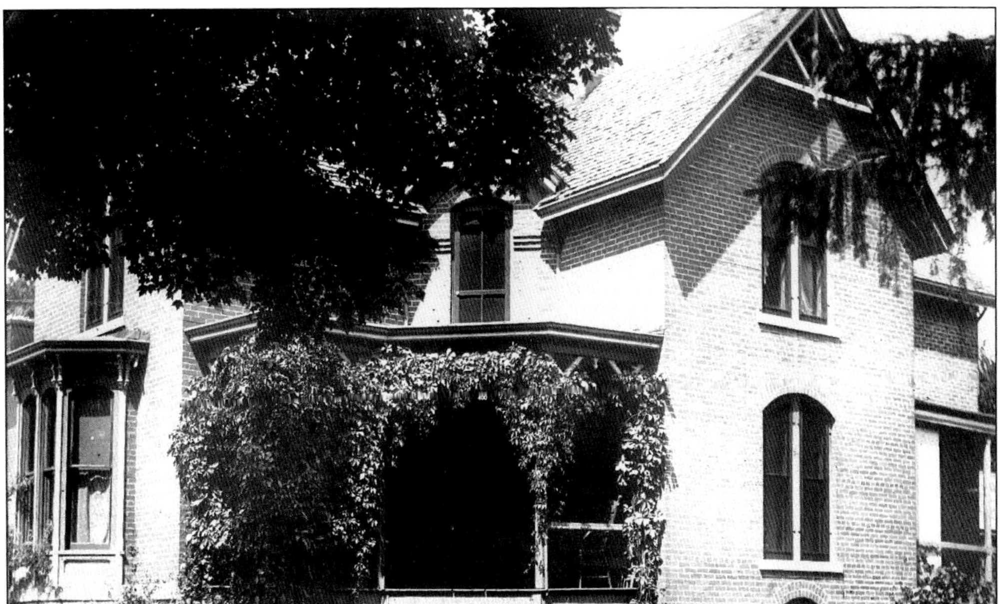

John Grindell, William's brother and partner in the furniture business, constructed this beautiful Italianate-style house in 1885. It was located at the northwest corner of Main and Chestnut Streets. (Courtesy of GCHS.)

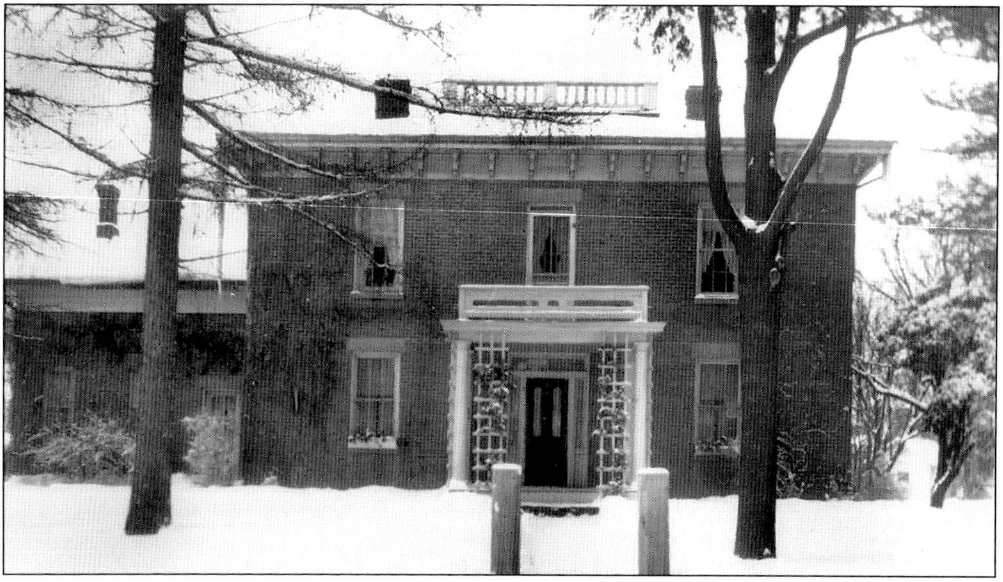

For his part, Leonard Coates, a lead furnace entrepreneur, constructed this stately Italianate in 1870. In the 19th century, its front porch extended across the whole front of its main section. Located at 250 Southwest Road, one of it owners in the 20th century was Roy Kopp. Notice that when this photograph was taken, in the late 1920s, it had a widow's walk.

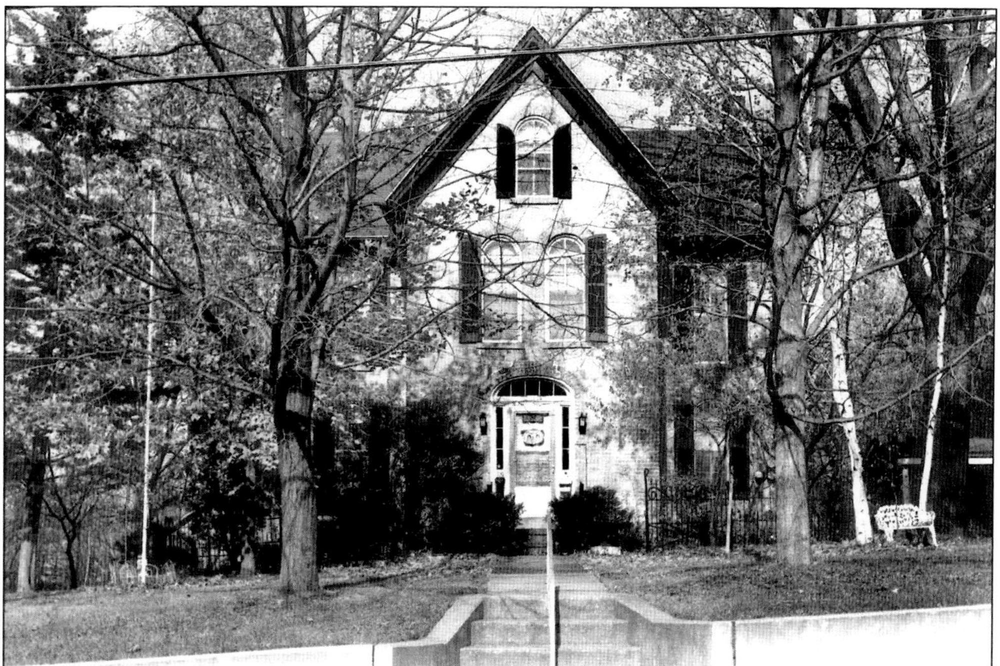

That same year, 1870, William Homer Beebe built this Italianate house at 390 West Adams Street. A Civil War veteran and a lawyer by profession, Beebe's claim to fame, however, was the telephone line that he installed between Platteville and Lancaster in 1879. When General Ulysses S. Grant visited Platteville on November 22, 1879, he used Beebe's telephone and talked to a journalist from the *Grant County Herald* "sixteen miles apart" in Lancaster.

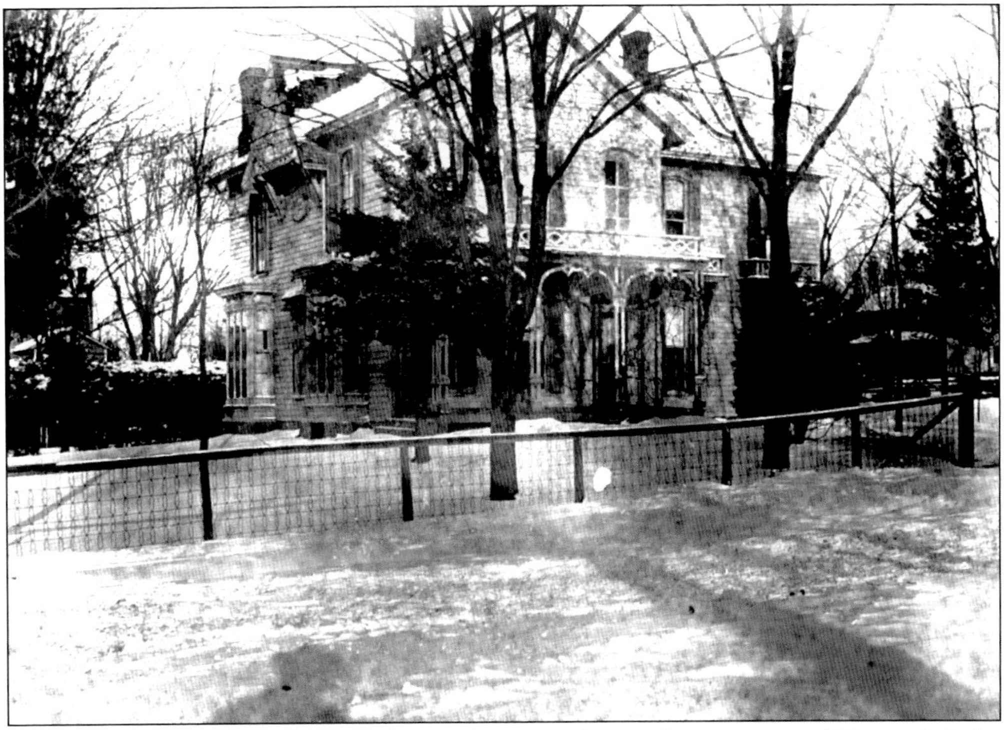

Henry Gribble constructed this Italianate house at the northeast corner of Elm and Cedar Streets in 1873. Gribble operated a general store at Main and Third Streets in the latter half of the 19th century. This photograph was taken about 1900. (Courtesy of GCHS.)

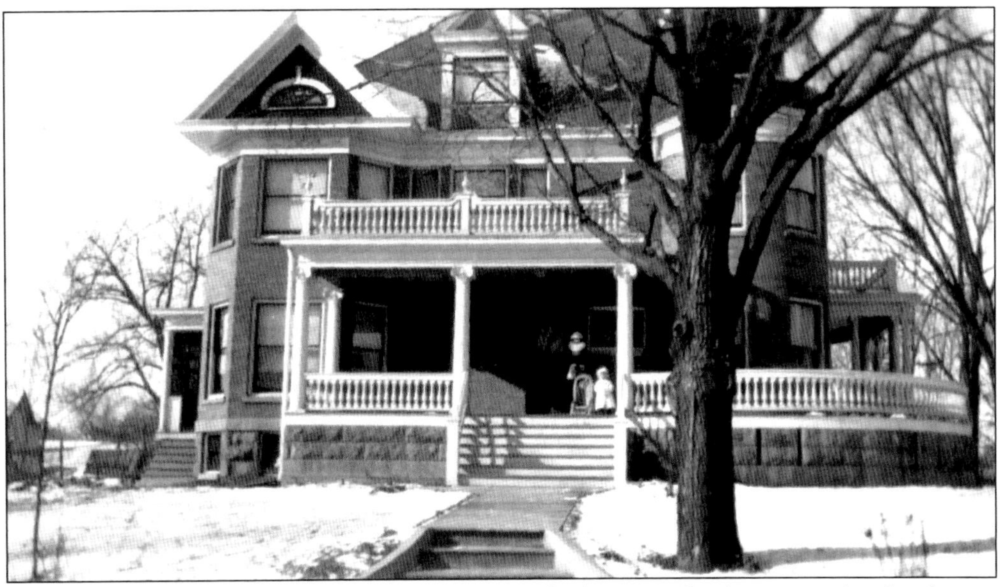

In 1909, Frank Burg, a prominent clothier in town, had Henry Kleinhammer, a local architect, design and construct one of Platteville's most architecturally significant houses. The house, located at the southwest corner of Main and Elm Streets, is shown here in 1919. In wood alone, it had $4,200 of "Lumber & mill work" in it.

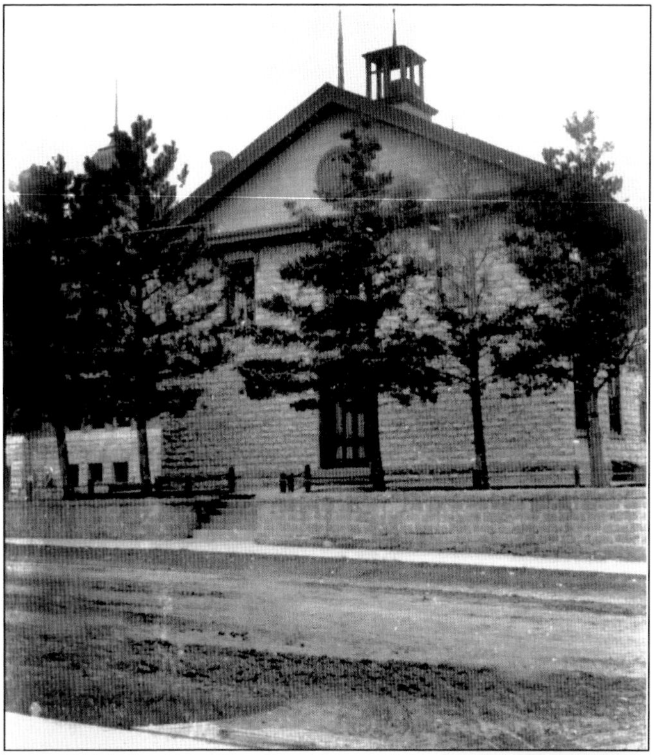

The foundations of Platteville's school system were also laid in the 19th century. The first schoolhouses were log cabins, but this changed when the Rock School, located at the intersection of Broadway and Main Street, was constructed between 1858 and 1863. This image was taken around 1905. Today the Rock School building houses the Mining Museum.

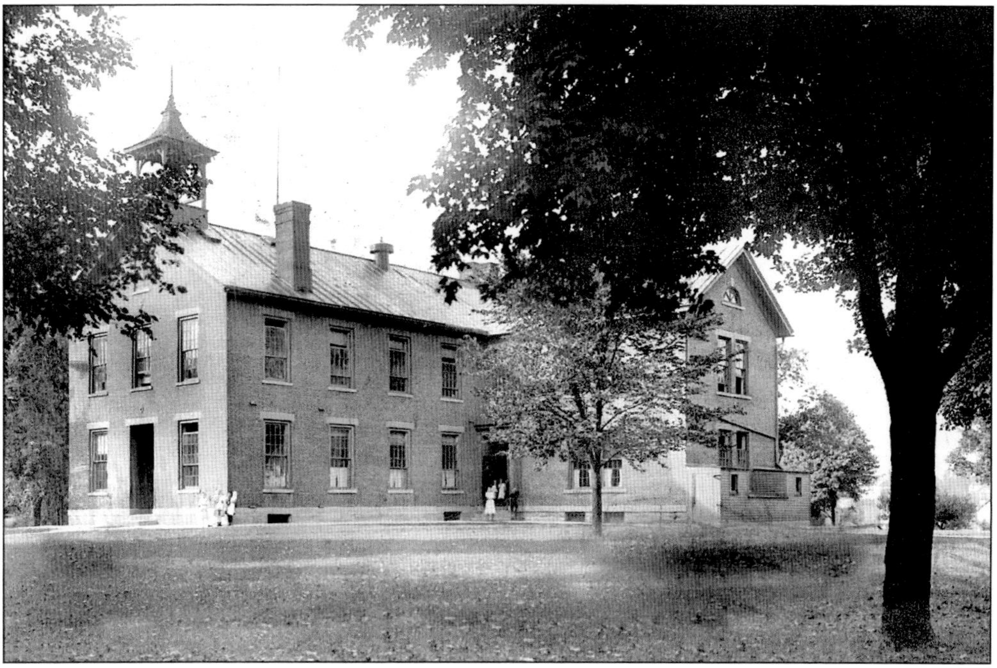

Around the same time, *c.* 1860, Platteville's second permanent schoolhouse, the Brick School, was constructed. Located on Adams Street just east of Chestnut Street, the Brick School, shown here *c.* 1905, was completed in 1863. In 1953, it burned down and the O(liver).E. Gray School was built on the same ground.

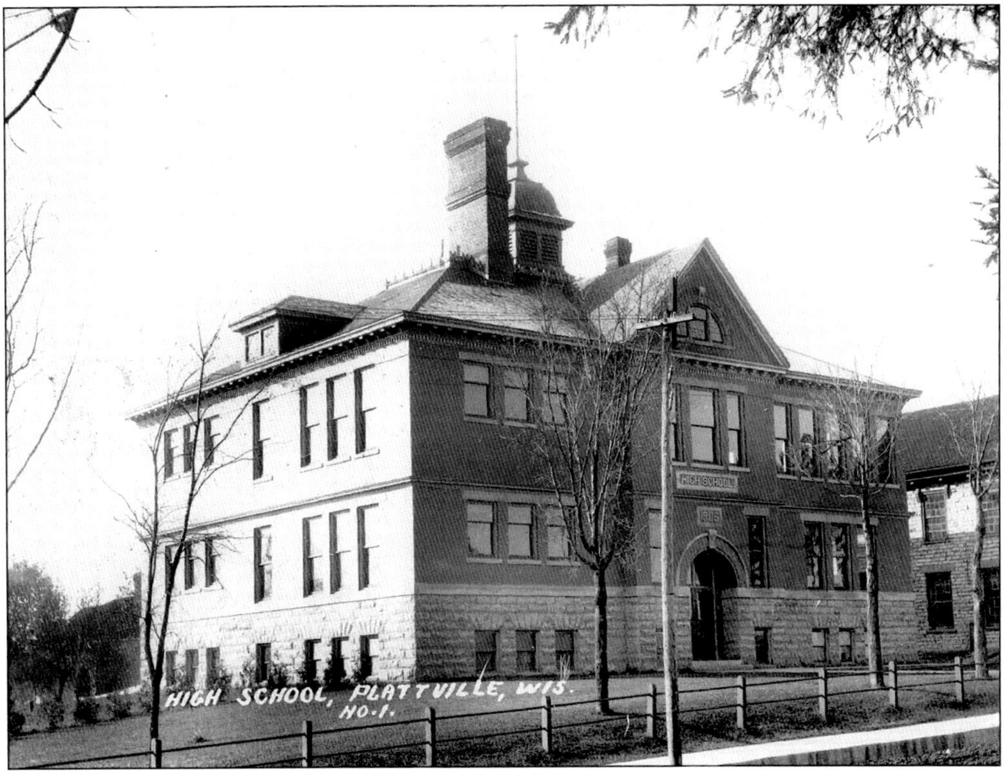

After the turn of the 20th century, Platteville built its first high school building. Constructed next to the Rock School, it was called the Hanmer Robbins High School and was opened in 1906, about the time this image was taken. Today this building houses the Rollo Jamison Museum.

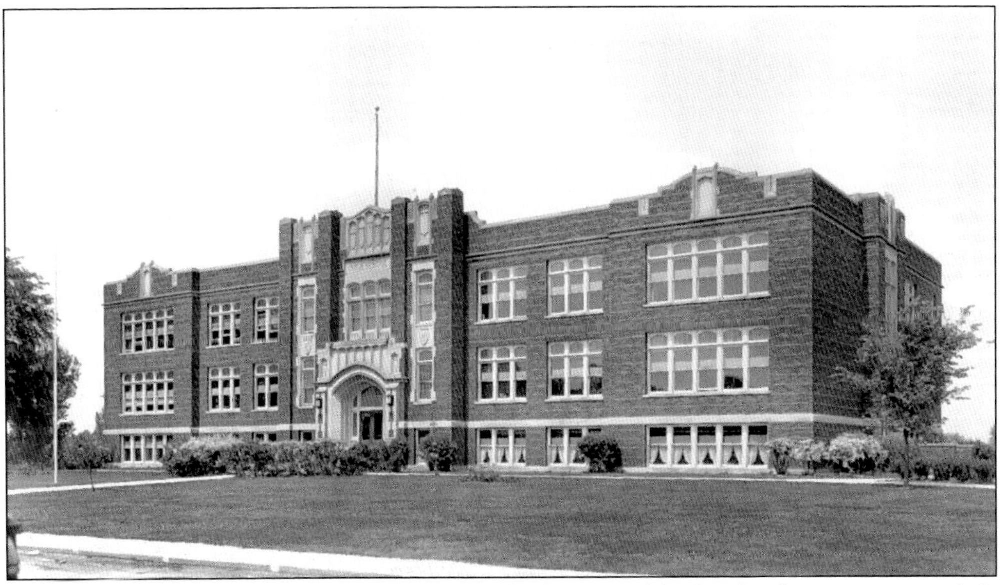

A little over a decade later, from 1917 to 1919, the second high school was constructed. It was located at 710 East Madison Street. This photograph was taken c. 1919. This high school became a middle school in 1968 and was razed in 1998.

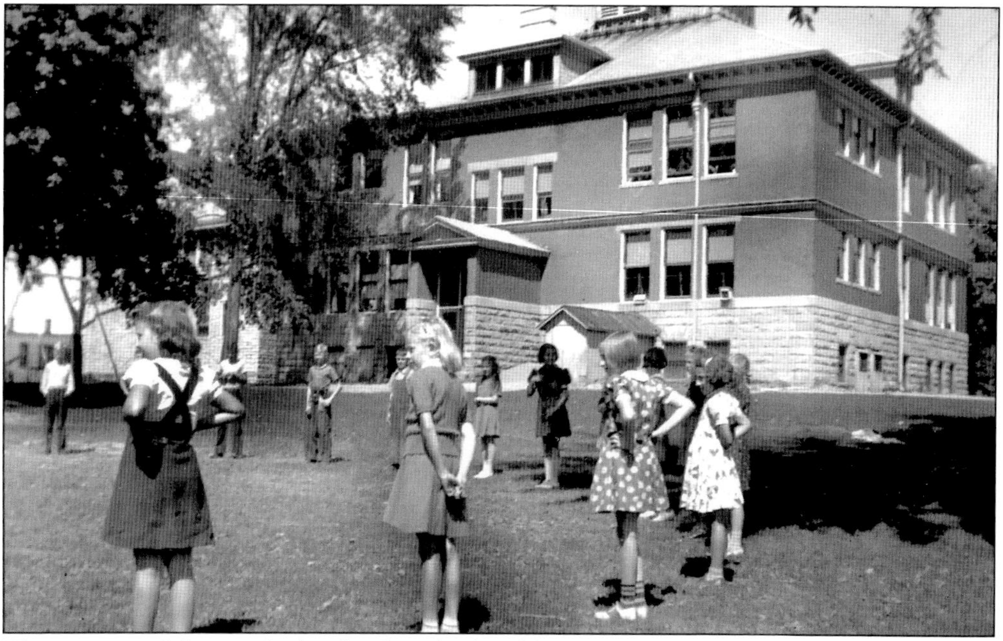

The opening of the new high school made the old Hanmer Robbins School a middle school. Here, a group of students perform an exercise on the south lawn of the Robbins School. This photograph was probably taken in the fall of 1937.

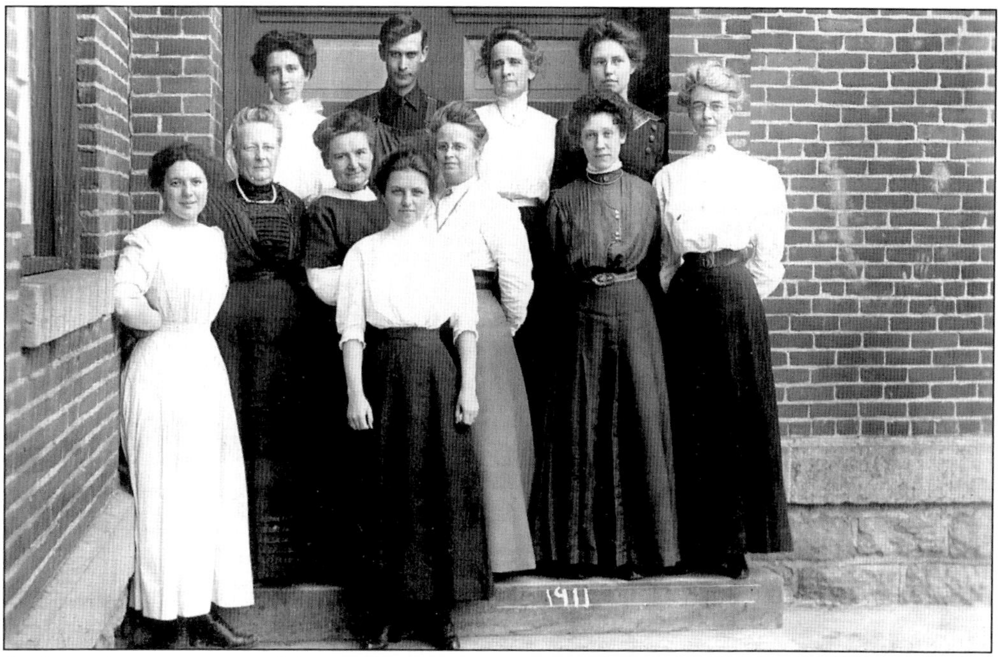

In the early years, many of the teachers were women and not a few of them had attended the Normal School. Here is a group of the Brick School teachers in 1911. From left to right are: (front row) Ruth Seaton and Sadie Schmidt; (middle row) Julia Main, Mattie Meyer, Mary Mackay, unidentified, and Elgie Ward; (top row) Ada Rundell, Walter Golden (janitor), Celia Gardner, and Myrtle Patterson.

Class sizes were small in the early 1900s. This is the Class of 1900. Shown seated, from left to right, are Georgia Wellers, her sister Emma Wellers, and Laura Vail. Edna Stephens is standing.

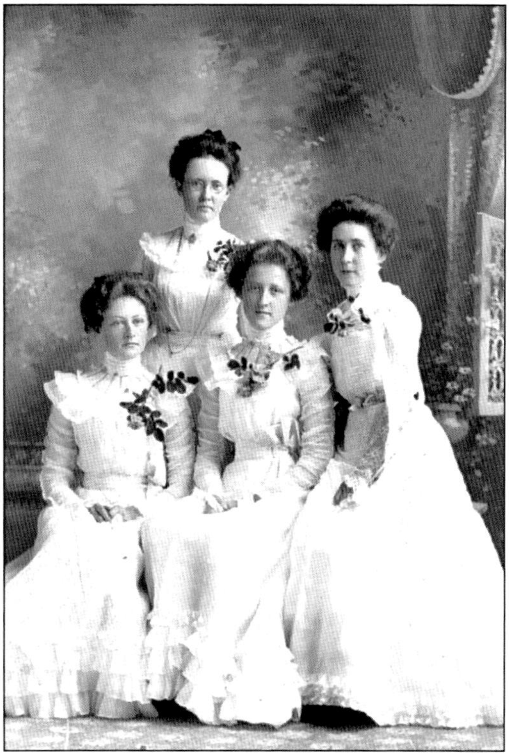

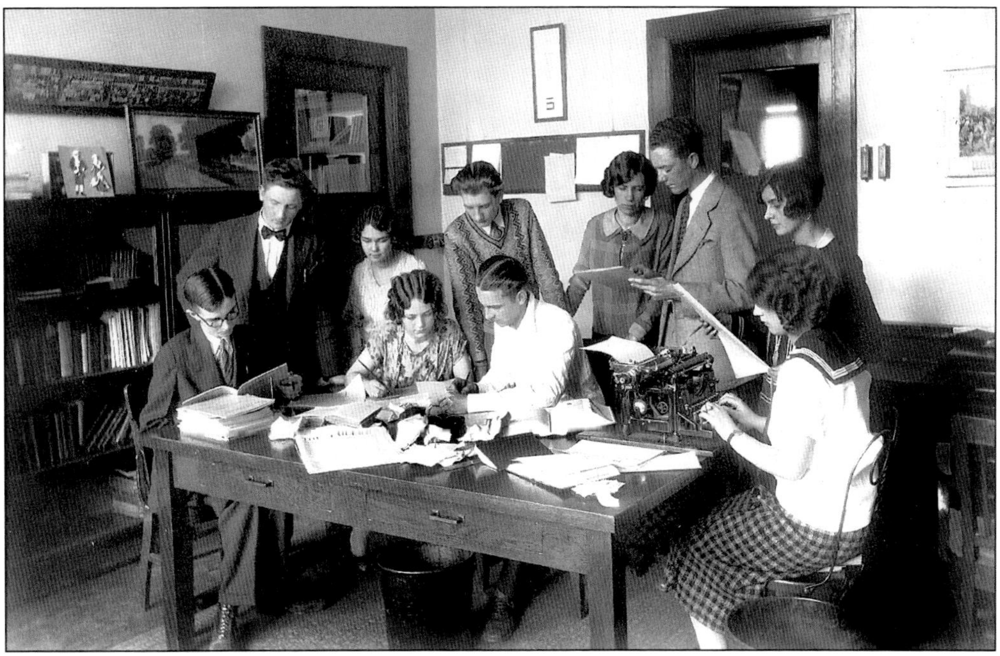

Over time, however, the increasing size of the student body justified the publication of a school newspaper, *The Tailings*. This is *The Tailings* staff in 1927. They are, from left to right: (seated) Richard Goodell, Dorothy Nehls, Harrison Roddick, and Mary Roser; (standing) Arthur Smail, Frances Young, Billy Thomas, Miss Chapman (teacher), John Gable, and Frances Webb.

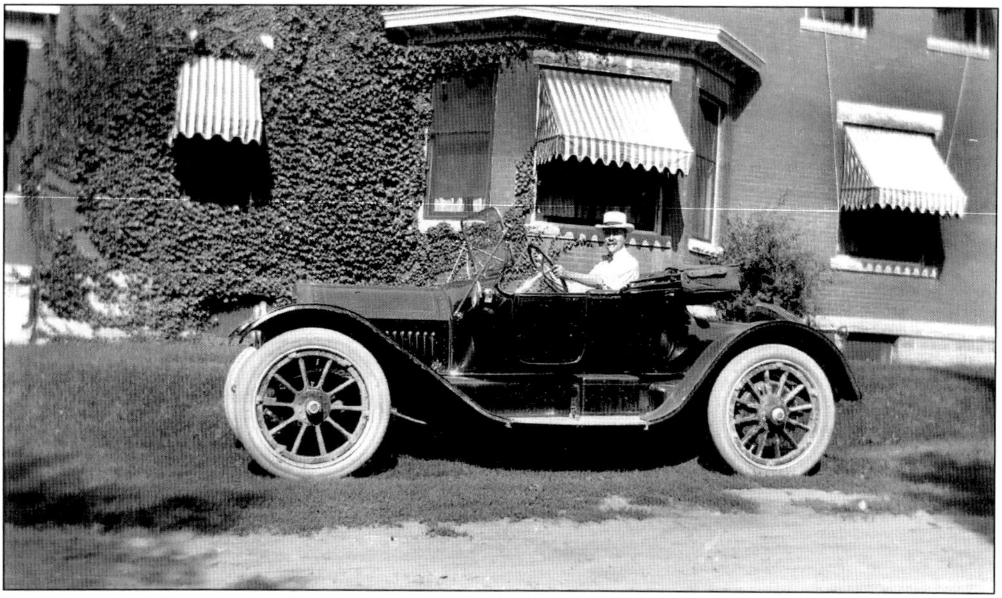

By the turn of the century the economic and educational opportunities that Platteville offered were attracting people from around the area. Dr. Wilson Cunningham was one of them. Here he is on the side of his house, which was built in 1906–07 on the north side of City Park. Cunningham became a renowned physician with his invention of the ox-bone splint, a splint made of actual bone that was affixed to a fractured bone. (Courtesy of GCHS.)

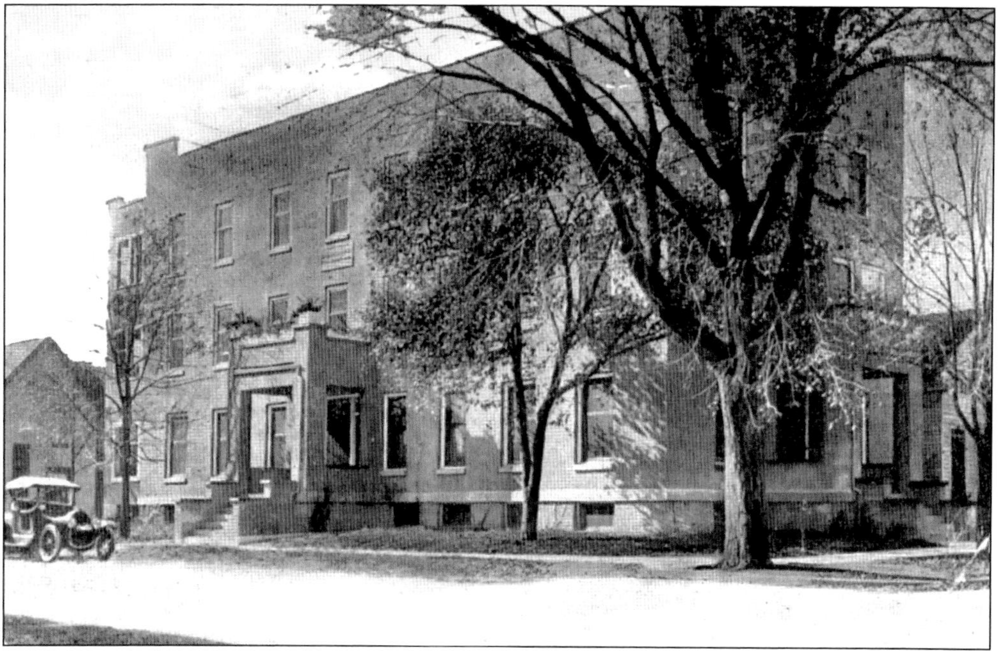

In 1914, Dr. Cunningham financed the construction of Platteville's first hospital building, the Cunningham Hospital. Located at the southwest corner of Main and Chestnut Streets, the three-story concrete structure came equipped with 30 hospital rooms. It remained a hospital until 1950.

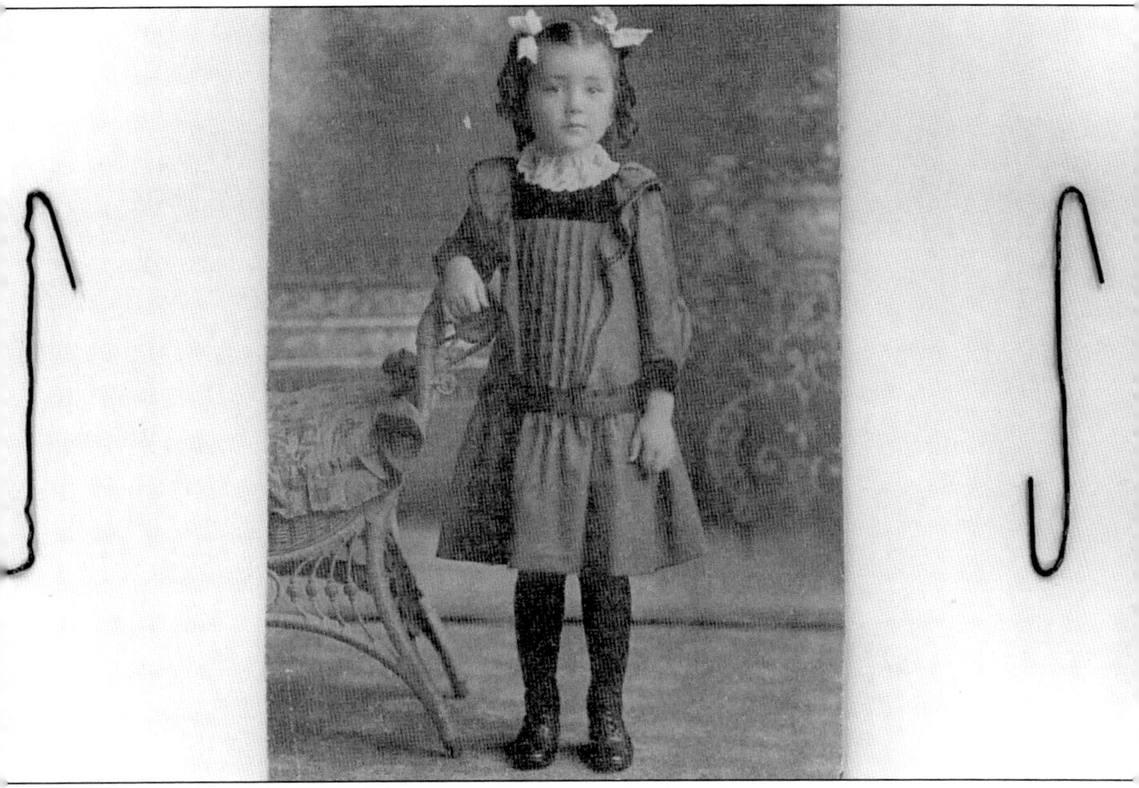

One of Dr. Cunningham's most dramatic cases occurred early in his career. Sometime around 1904 he received word that Hazel Brugger (above), who was suffering from diphtheria, needed immediate medical attention. By the time the doctor arrived at the little girl's house on the outskirts of Platteville, she had ceased breathing. In shock, her father told him, "Doctor, it is no use. My little girl just died." Cunningham, however, performed a tracheotomy, and as he later recalled, "I had difficulty in keeping the incision open, so I called out for two hairpins [shown above]. I bent these so as to make hooks on the ends, and inserted the hooks into the trachea. I fastened strings to the other ends and tied them around the little girl's neck, and in this way kept the incision open. It was a crude affair but it was all I had in the emergency, and it worked." Hazel recovered and lived a full life. Dr. Cunningham always called her his "hairpin" patient. (Courtesy of GCHS.)

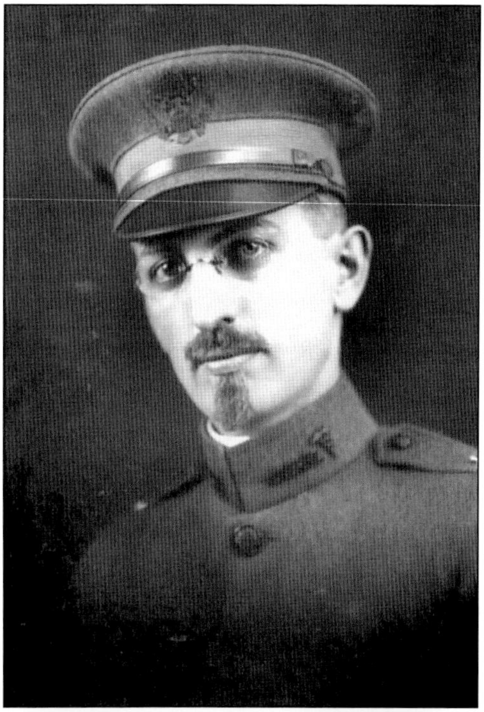

One of Dr. Cunningham's long-time colleagues at the Cunningham Hospital was Dr. Clarence M. Schuldt, shown here c. 1918. Born in Illinois, Dr. Schuldt came to Platteville with his parents when he was a little boy. After attending the Normal School, he earned his medical degree from Northwestern University Medical School in Illinois in 1914. He served as a lieutenant in the Medical Corps during World War I and returned to Platteville at the conclusion of that war to practice medicine. Affectionately called "C. M.," he died in 1949.

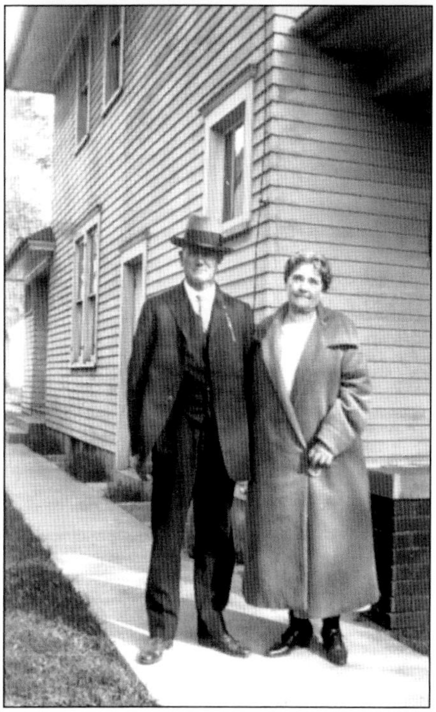

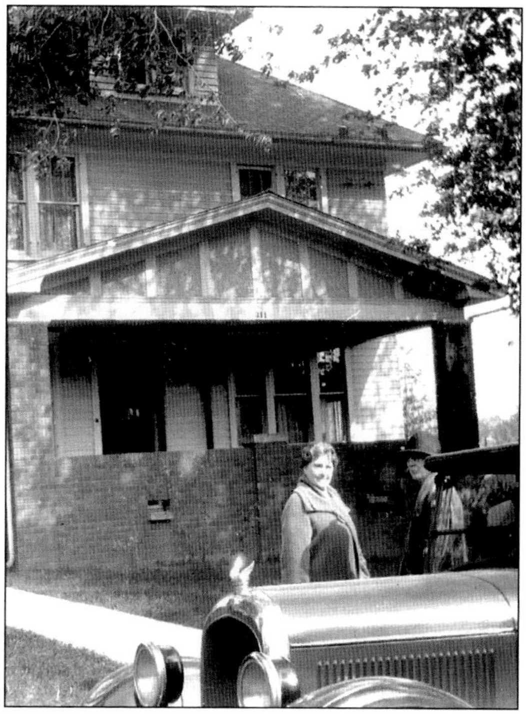

For their part, John and Bell Hemphill (at left), came to Platteville from Belmont in 1908. John, the city assessor, built the family's house (shown at right) in 1921. The image shows Bell on the left, with the couple's daughter, Vera, in front of the house at 145 South Chestnut Street, c. 1930.

Their daughter, Vera Hemphill, shown here about 1915, took full advantage of the educational opportunities. She graduated from Platteville High School in 1917, and enrolled in the Normal School's Rural School Course. This course, designed for high school graduates, allowed her to complete her course work in one year and begin teaching grade school by the fall of 1918.

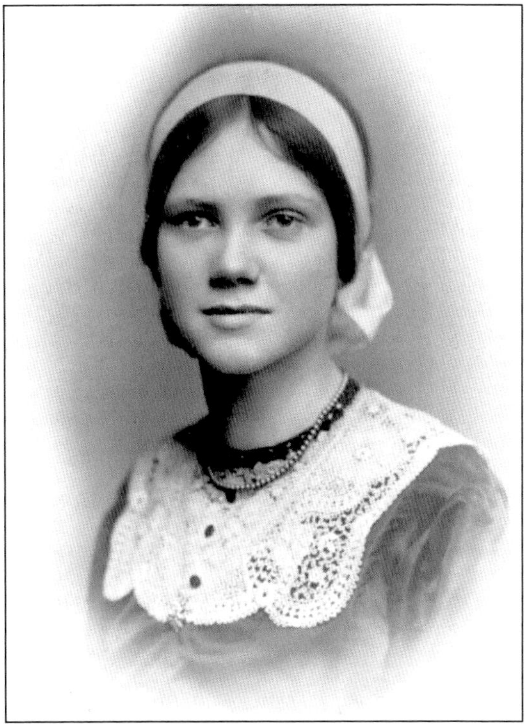

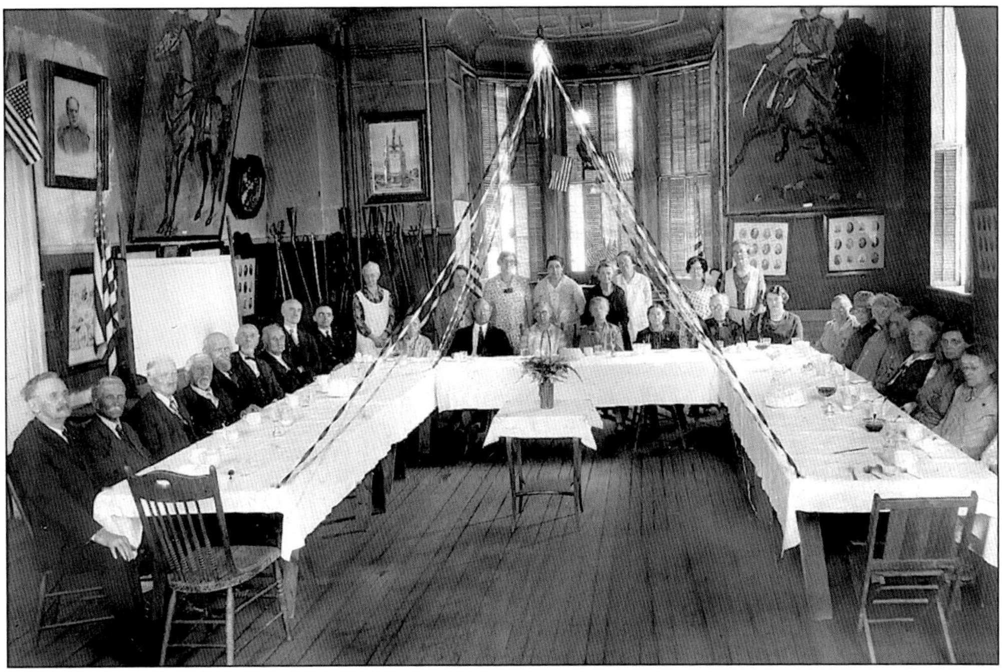

Platteville also had its share of societies and clubs. This image, taken April 6, 1929, shows the members of the Grand Army of the Republic's Sherman Post No. 66 attending a banquet. The banquet was sponsored by the Woman's Relief Corp and held in the post's hall, which was the bay window room of the Mining School. By that time, the post's minutes of their meetings often began with, "The Comrades were again called together to attend the Funeral of their late Comrade. . . ."

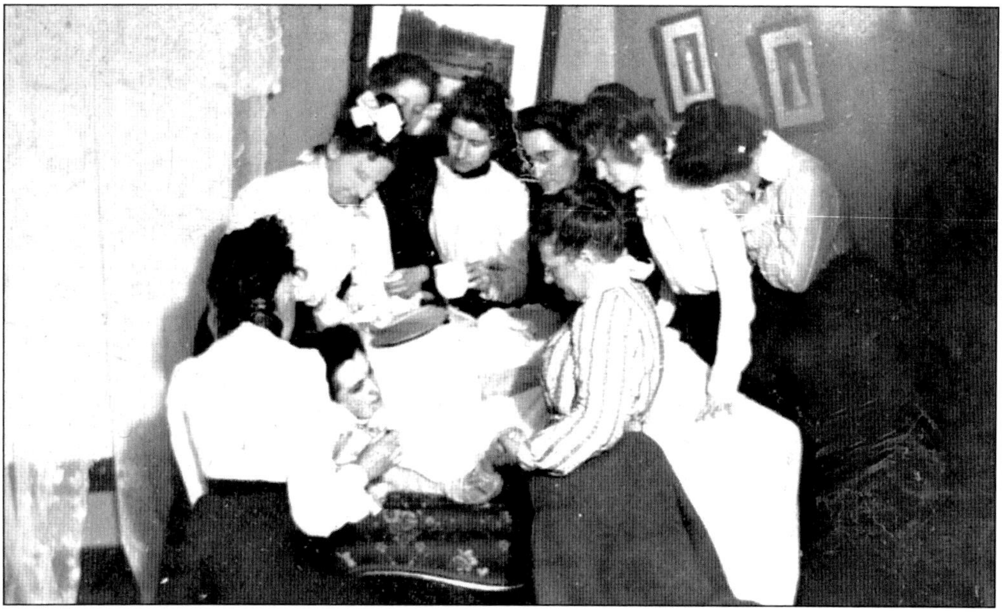

This era also witnessed the emerging role of women in the community. Many women formed their own clubs. Here is the Twentieth Century Reading Club, April 30, 1901. Jennie Jones, the lady who is acting "sick," is comforted by, shown left to right, Celia Gardner, Mattie Meyer, ? Bass, Cythia Thomas, Belle Burke, Gertrude Friedrich, Gretta Davis, and Julia Main.

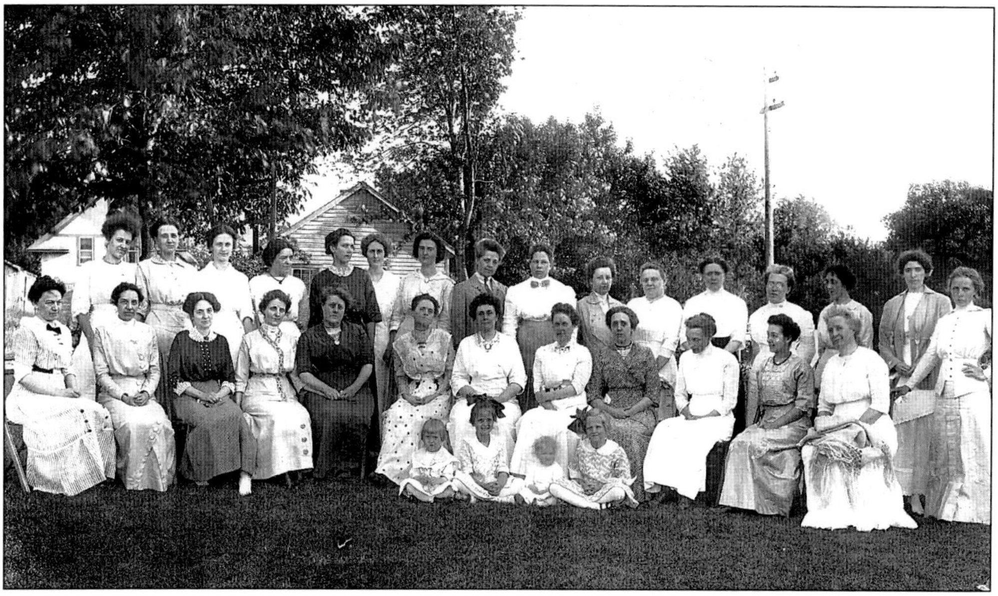

Here are the members of the Platteville's Tourist Club in the summer of 1913. Shown from left to right are: (standing), Euretta Davis, Clara Dana, Clara Merrifield, Julia Kuster, Marcia Grindell, Emily Fawcett, Frances Cleary, ? Russell, ? Martin, ? Aschaw, ? Butterworth, Minta Jones, Emily Kopp, ? Woodward, Nora Smith and ? Millwan.; (seated) ? Sutherland, Bertha Williams, ? Dudley, Clara Webster, Mina Grindell, Margaret Beardsley, Gertrude Sickle, Anna Pretts, Alice Dugdale, Carrie Nicklas, ? Kindschi, and ? Metcalf; (on the grass) Marjory, Elizabeth, Alice, and Leonora Dana.

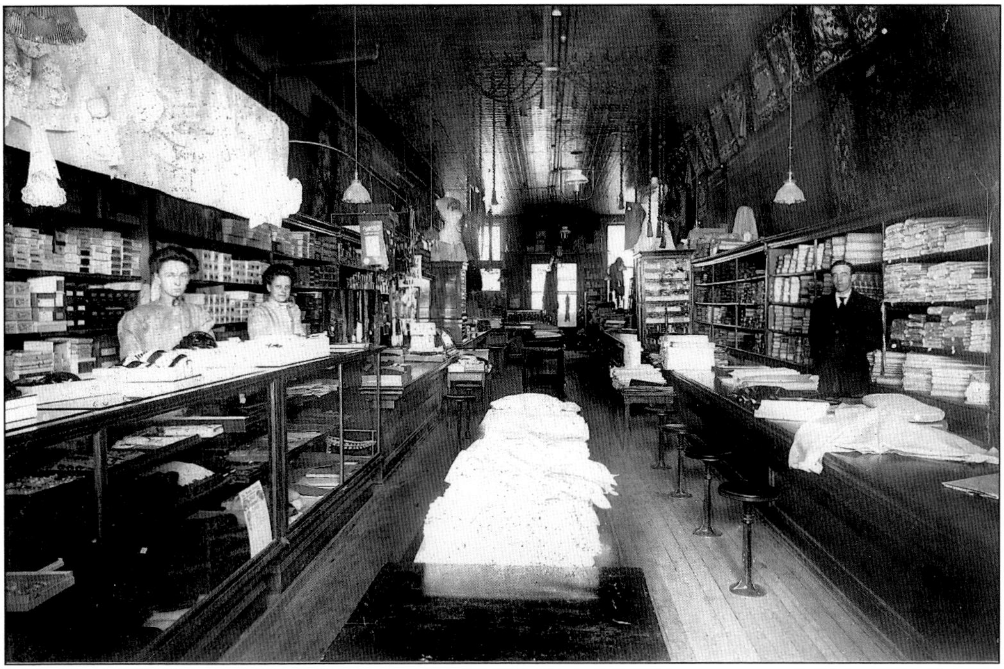

Women, moreover, began to break out of their traditional roles and move into a few professions, such as store clerks. This is a view of Henry Schambow's clothing store, *c.* 1912. Notice that two of the clerks are women. Schambow, who specialized in women's clothing, advertised "'Tapering Waist' R&G Corsets . . . They Unite Exquisite Lines with Easeful Flexibility."

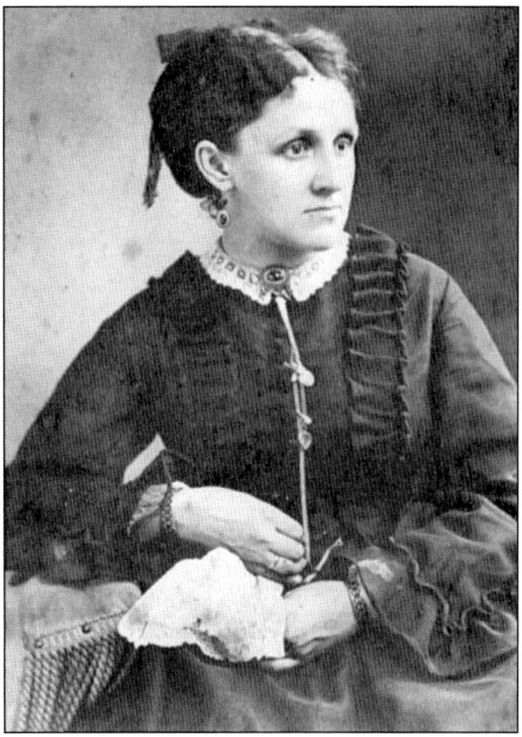

Other women, such as Laura Rountree Smith (shown here, *c.* 1900), Major Rountree's granddaughter, became entrepreneurs. A graduate of the Normal School in 1897, Laura became a successful author of children's books. Her first book, *The Tale of Bunny Cotton–Tail*, was published in 1905. She once stated, "My stories are so real to me that I write rapidly when the action is hurried."

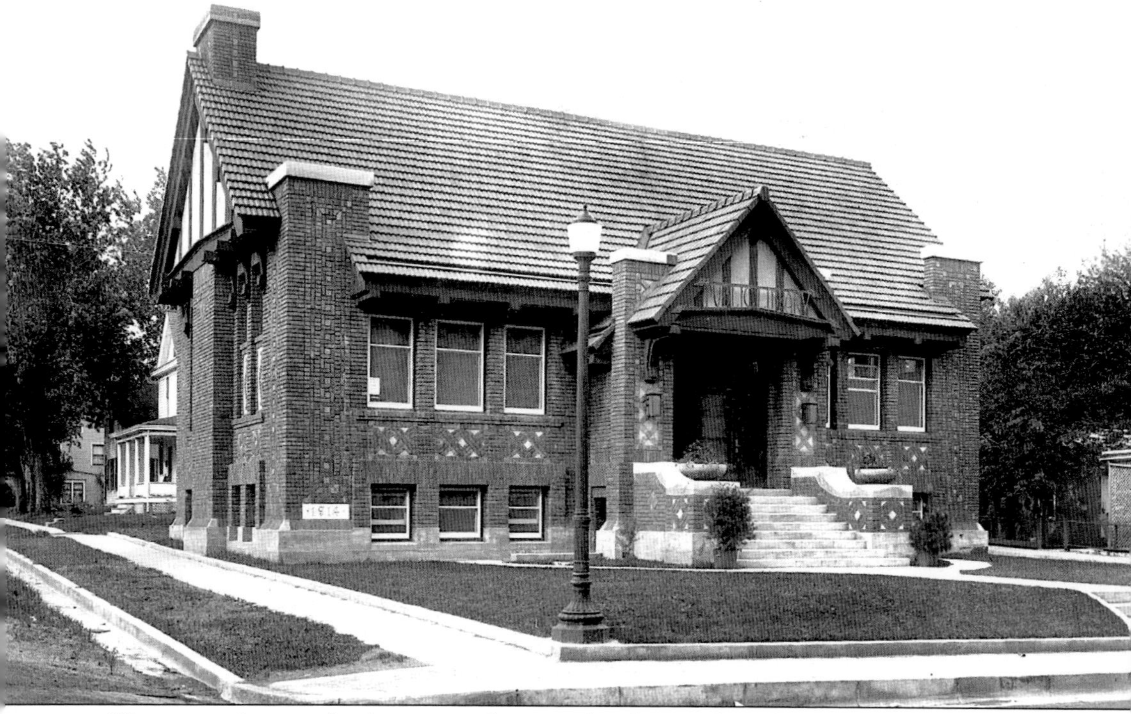

Women in these and other groups became the driving force behind the establishment of a public library in Platteville. Platteville had a subscription library in the 19th century, but by the turn of the century, the concept of a public supported library had taken hold. Hence, on August 6, 1904, a group called the Woman's Alliance, with $200 of books, opened Platteville's Free Public Library in a room next to Frederick Marcussen's hardware (see page 101). In 1907, the library was moved to a room in the old Normal School building. Finally, in 1915 the public library found a home of its own after the women had secured a donation of $12,500 from Andrew Carnegie. The new public library building, shown above *c.* 1916 and located at the northeast corner of Chestnut and Market Streets, was officially opened on December 17, 1915.

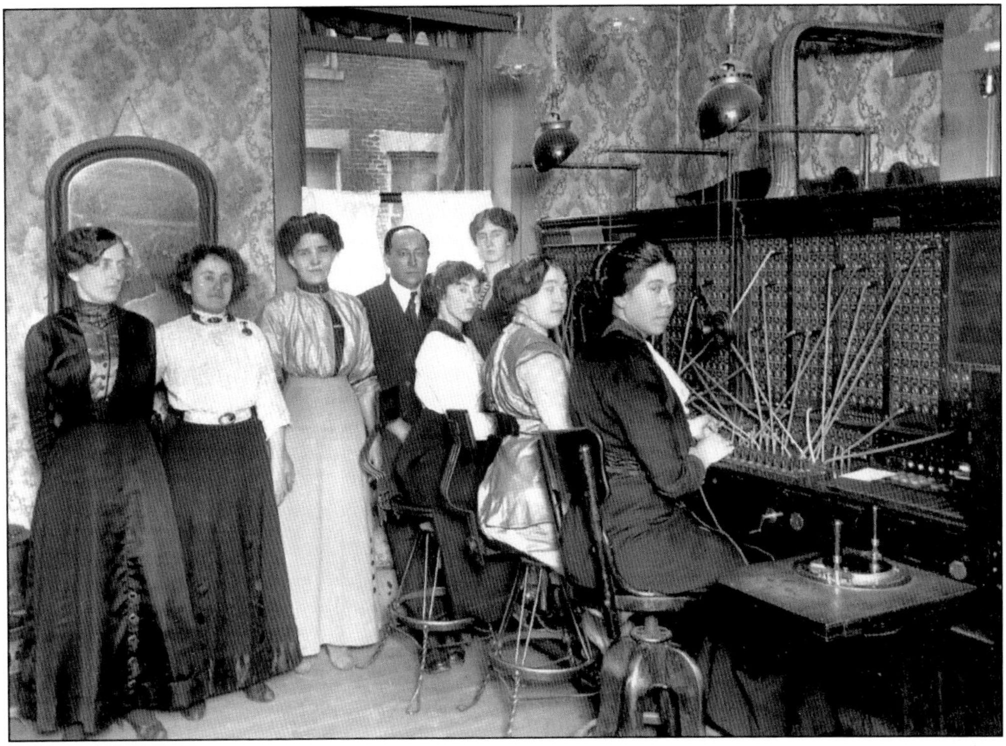

And a few women became telephone operators. Here is the switchboard crew of the Platteville, Rewey & Ellenboro Telephone Company, c. 1915. The switchboard was located on the second floor of the building at the northeast corner of Main and Bonson Streets.

In 1900, the Eastman Kodak Company revolutionized photography by introducing its Brownie Camera. At a cost of just one dollar, many Americans became amateur photographers. This and the next several images were taken by some of those new photographers. Here, for example, is a snapshot of Hotel Columbia, c. 1909. Located at the southeast corner of Main and Oak Streets, this hotel was a favorite of travelers. As a bit of free advertising, the utility pole in the foreground has "Hotel Columbia" painted on it. Today, this is the site of Hearthside Apartments.

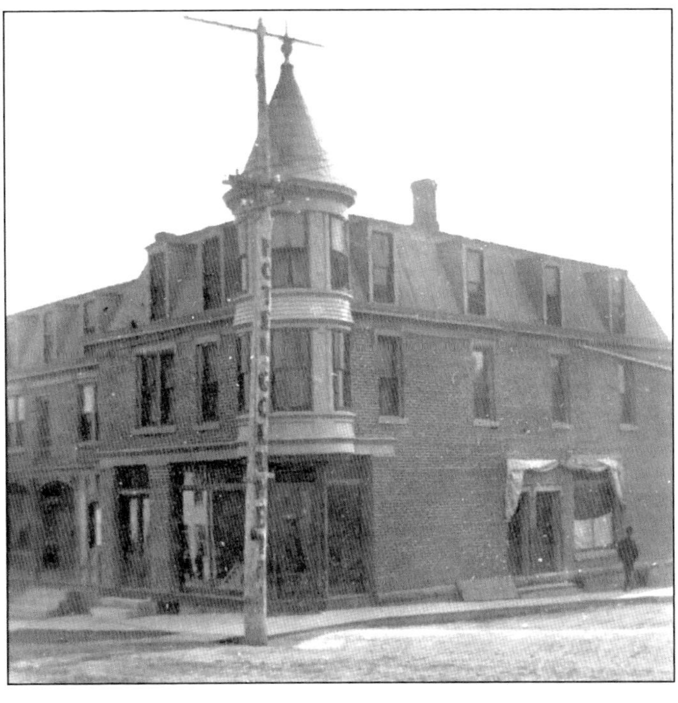

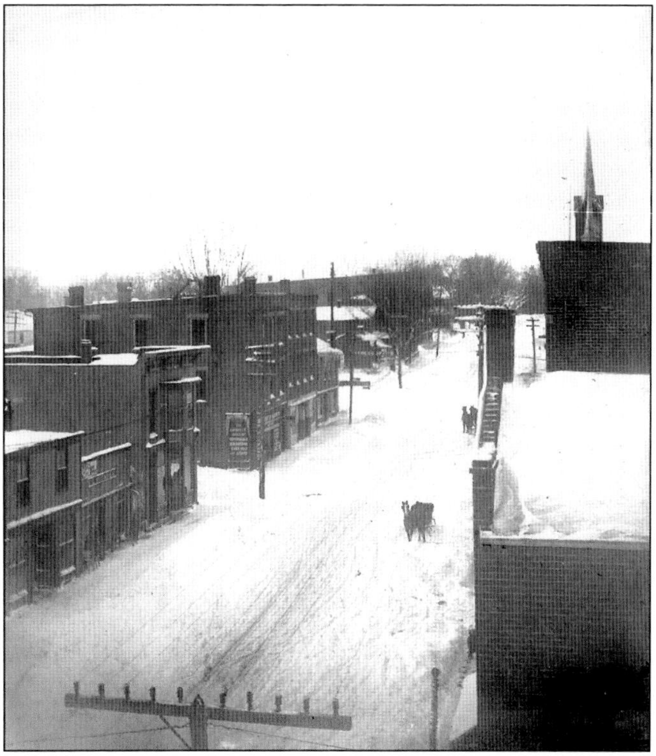

Sometime around 1910, Platteville was hit with a big snow storm. Shortly after the storm passed, an intrepid photographer went out on the roof of the building at the northeast corner of Main and Fourth Streets and took this image, looking west on Main Street. (Courtesy of John Tiedemann.)

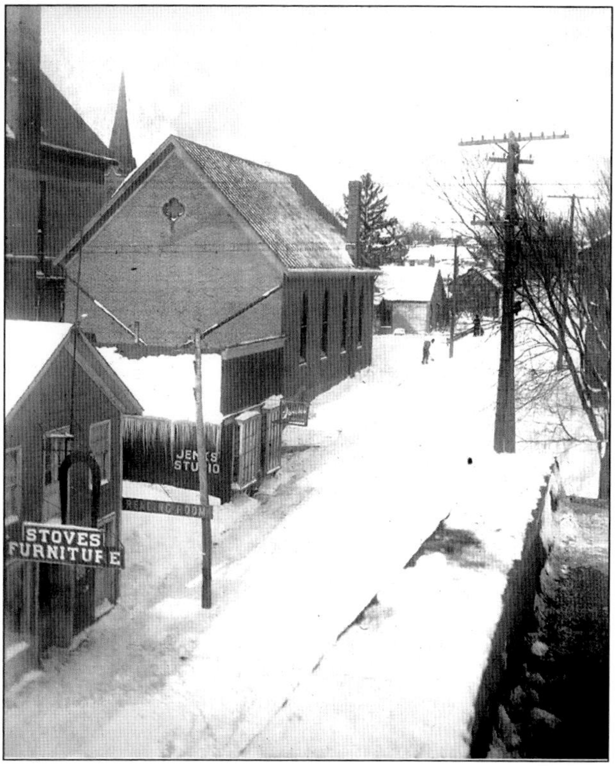

Turning 90 degrees to the north from the previous snapshot, the same photographer snapped this image of Fourth Street. The building in the middle is the "Jenks [photographic] Studio." The English Lutheran Church is north of that and the old City Hall is on the upper left. (Courtesy of John Tiedemann.)

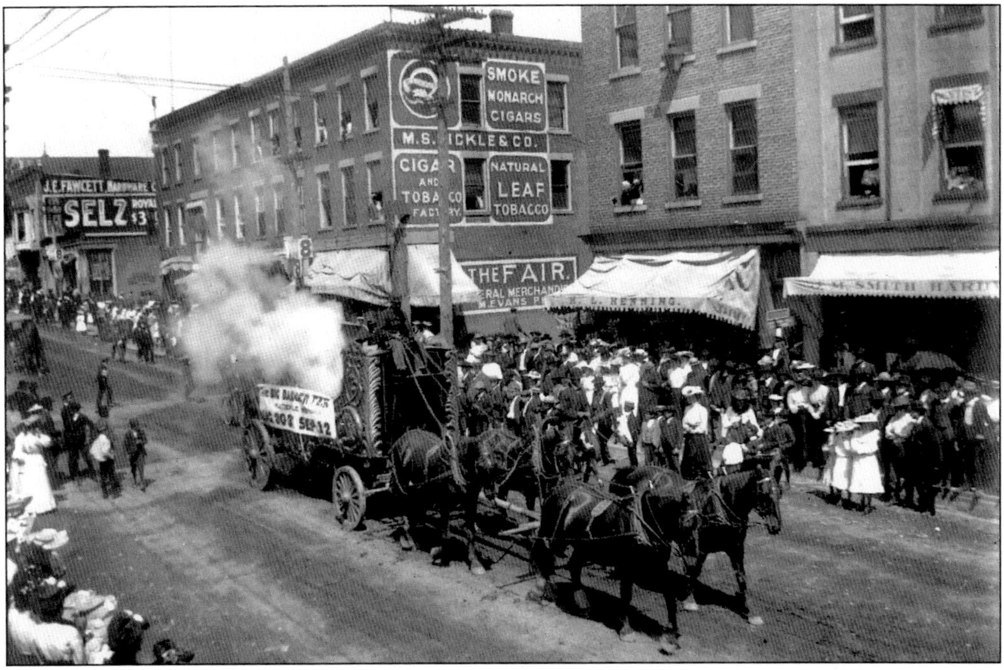

Like other towns, Plattevillians were entertained in an assortment of ways. In 1901, for example, the first Big Badger Fair was held. The fair was a combination county fair, circus, and sporting event. It was held out at the fair grounds, today's Legion Field. Shown here is part of an opening parade down Main Street in 1904. This image was probably taken on August 30.

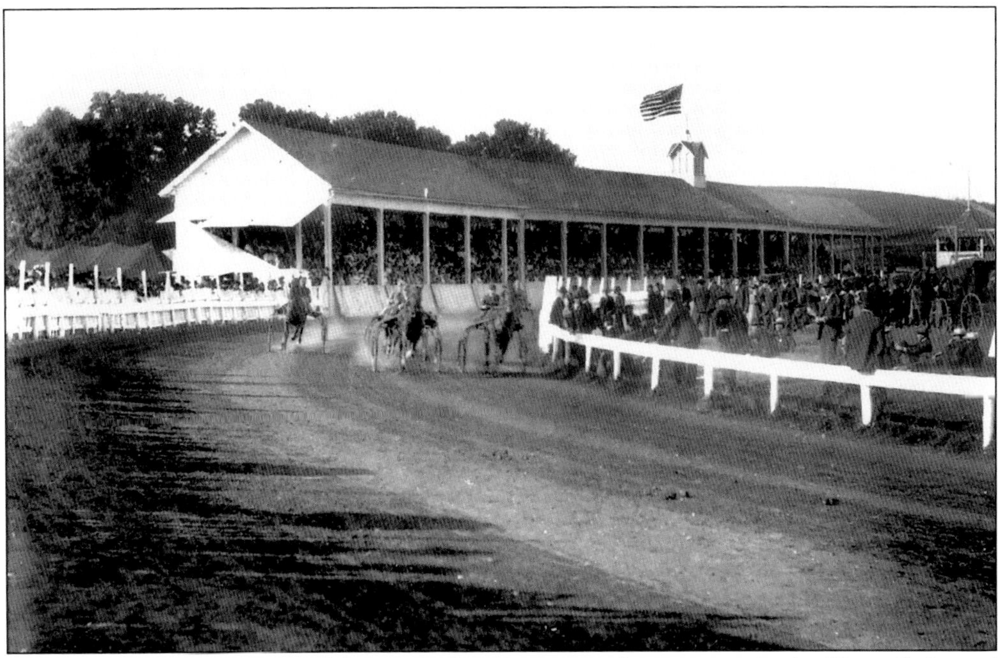

One of the main attractions of the Big Badger Fair was its horse races. As the *Platteville Journal* noted in 1908, "The races are filled. . . . Nearly 100 horses have entered and red hot excitement will prevail." This photograph was taken around 1904.

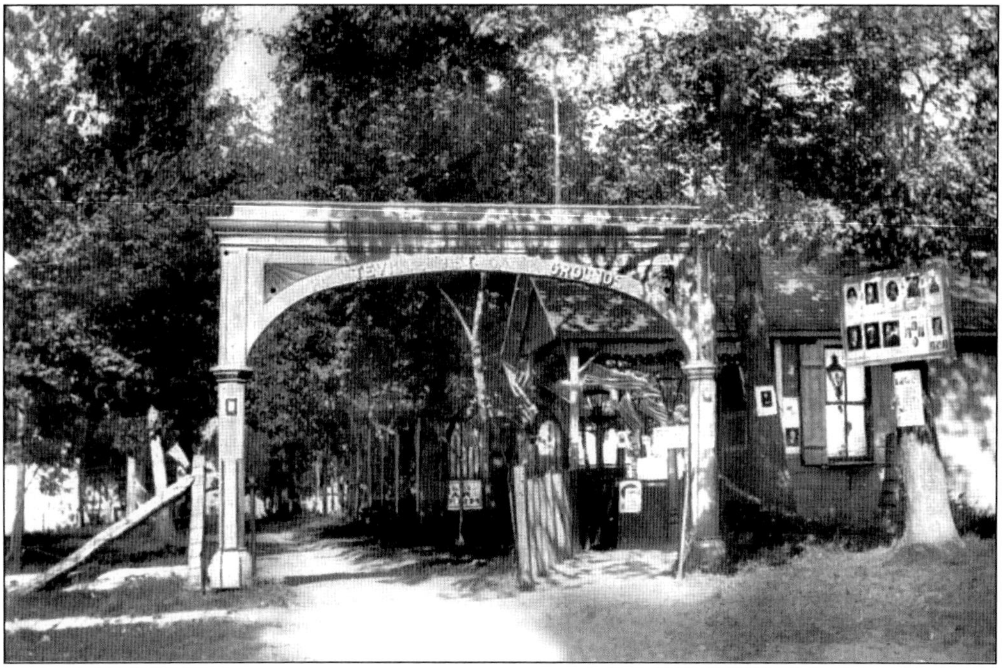

Platteville's first Chautauqua was held in 1908. This image, *c.* 1910, shows that event's entrance gate at the campgrounds, today's Smith Park. The Chautauqua, a combination lecture series and concert event, was sponsored by the Methodist Church.

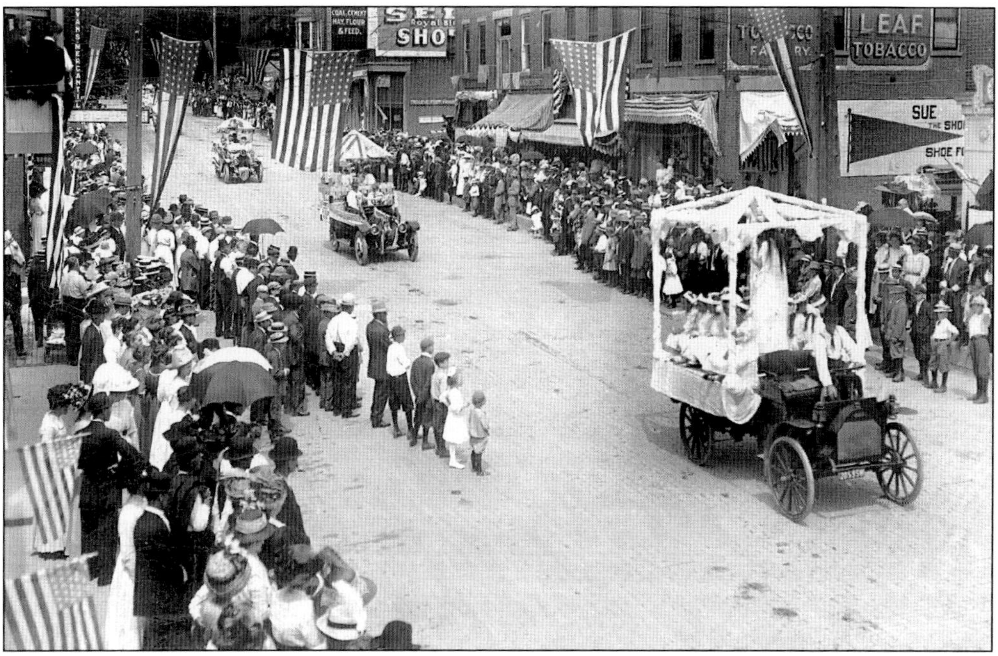

There was, of course, the perennial favorite event. Here is Platteville's July 4, 1912, parade, which featured an "Auto Street Parade." As one person commented, "The celebration on the fourth was dandy. . . . There were fifty automobiles besides the soldiers and childrens carriages in the parade."

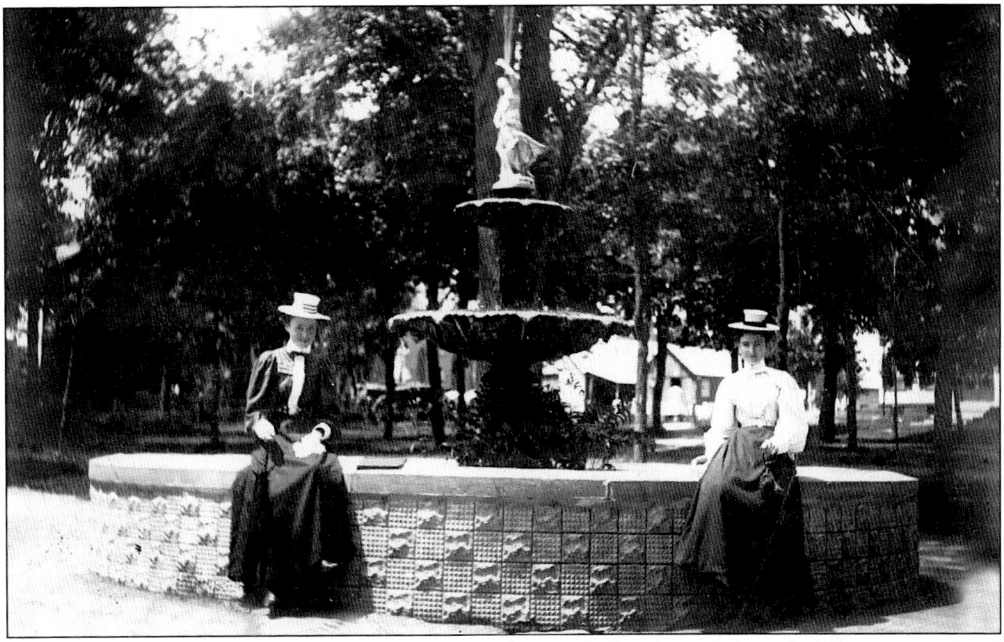

Plattevillians also enjoyed spending time together with family and friends. Here, a couple of young ladies, Alice March and Nellie McCauley, enjoy their time in City Park, c. 1900. Set aside in the original plat of 1835, City Park has long been a place where Plattevillians gather. The park has gone through several name changes. First called the Public Square, it became the Park by the 1870s and finally City Park by the early 1900s.

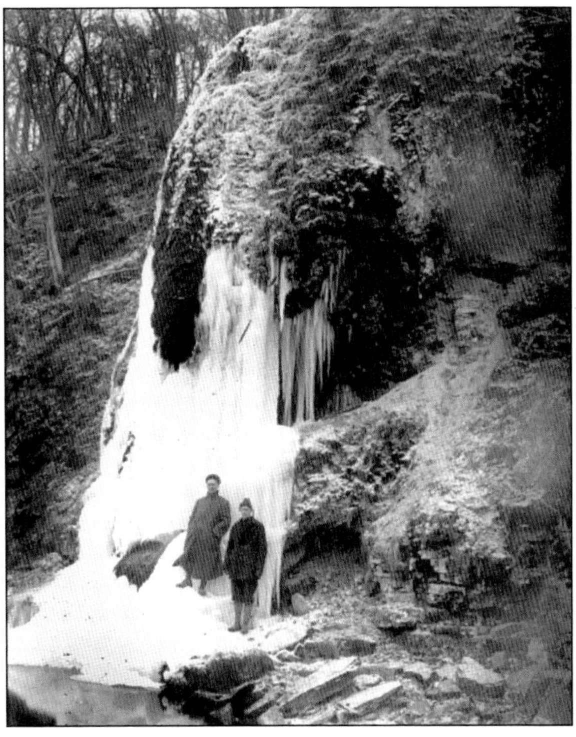

And Plattevillians enjoyed a good picnic. They had two favorite spots. One of them was Tuffa Falls, which is located a little south of town. This image was taken around 1912. (Courtesy of John Tiedemann.)

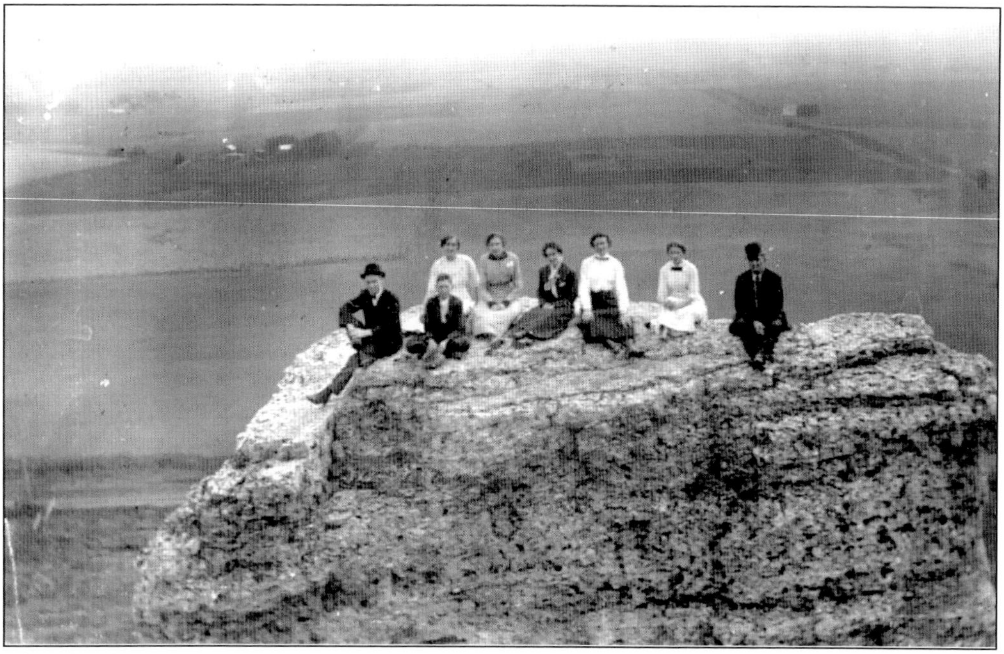

The other favorite picnic spot was the Platte Mound. Here is a family gathering "on top of Platteville Mound." This photograph was also taken around 1912. (Courtesy of John Tiedemann.)

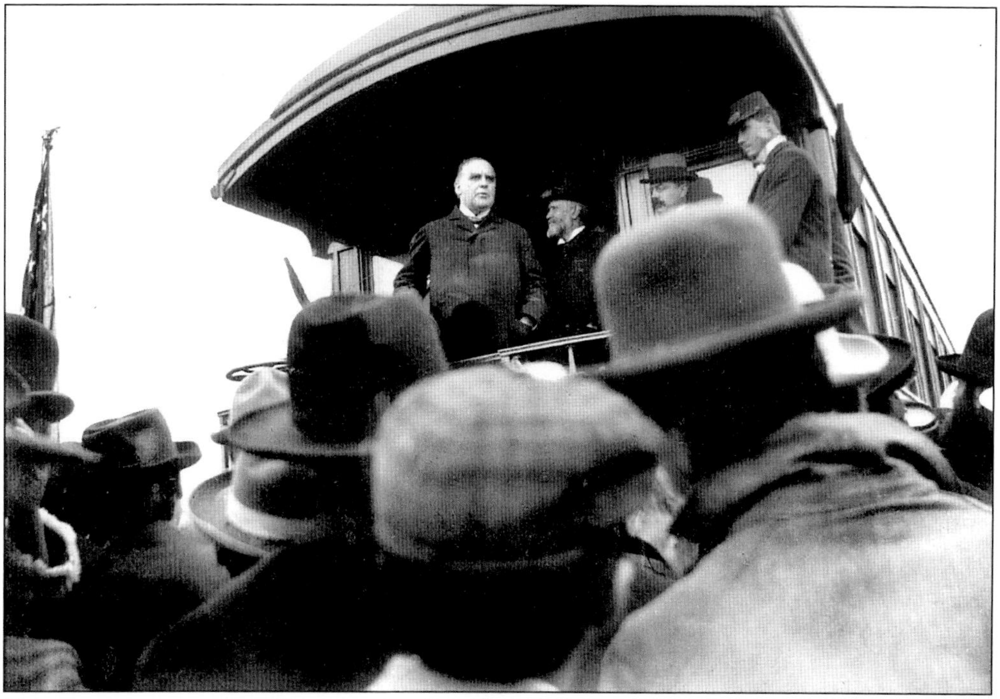

Some events were unique. Knowing that President William McKinley's train would make a brief stop at Ipswich (Lafayette County) on October 16, 1899, a small group of Plattevillians arranged for the Chicago & Northwestern Railroad to provide round trip rides to Ipswich for 22¢ per person. This snapshot of that event was taken by William Dudley, a Normal School instructor.

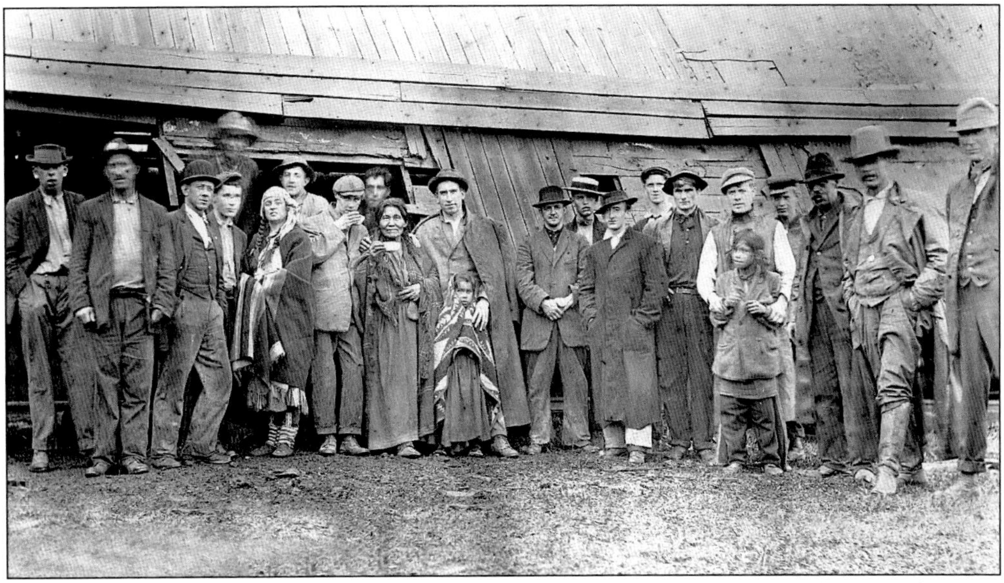

Some events, though, turned tragic. After it gave two performances in Platteville, tragedy struck the 101 Ranch Real Wild West traveling show in the early hours of August 10, 1912, when its train derailed at the Leslie station (formerly Belmont, the site of the First Territorial Capitol building). Nine of its horses were killed in the accident. Here, the 101 Ranch performers stand in front of a derailed boxcar, lying on its side. A hole cut into the roof to free the animals can be seen behind the performers on the left.

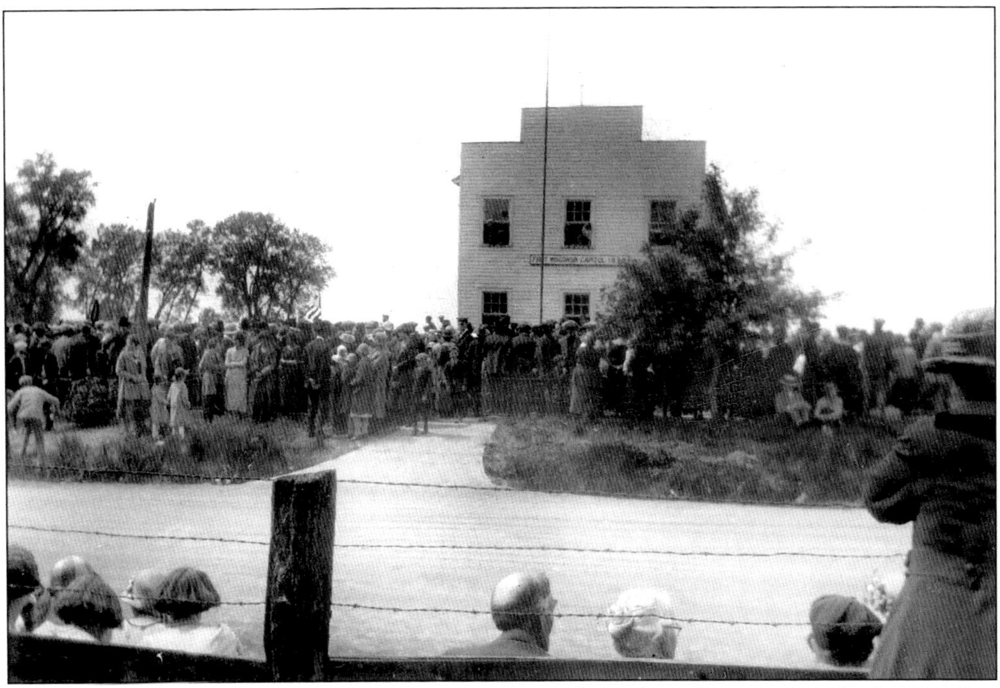

Twelve years later, on June 1, 1924, this image was taken of another event at Leslie. On that day, the recently restored First Territorial Capitol building, originally used by the Territorial legislature in 1836, was turned over to the State Park system.

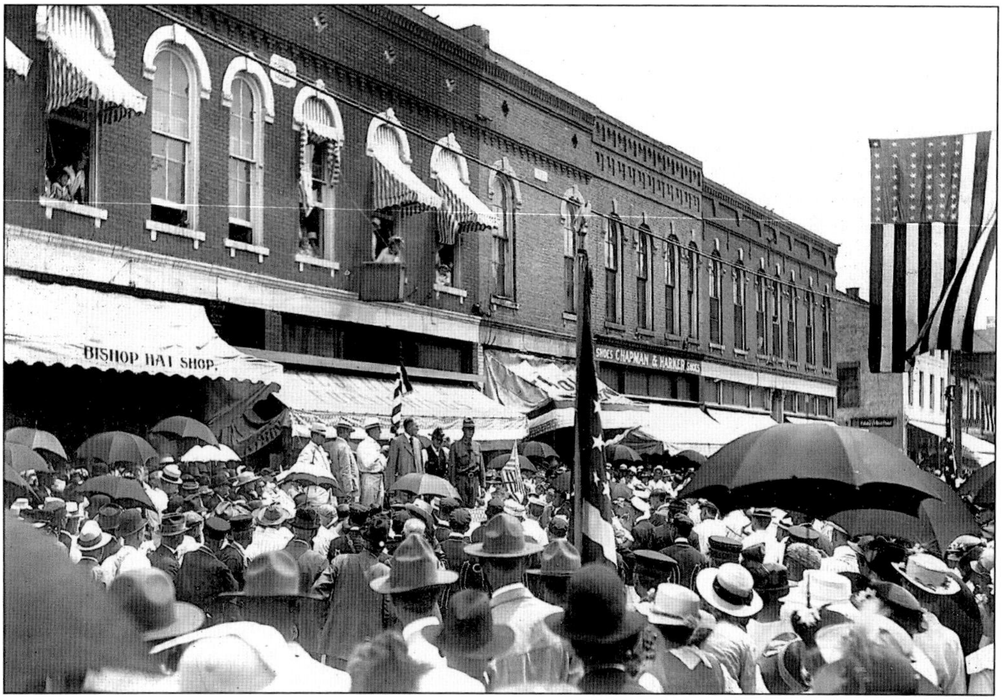

Platteville also carried its load during wartime. This photograph, taken on Main Street in early May 1917, shows the presentation of the United States flag to Platteville's Company I. Attorney Richard Goodell is the bareheaded man underneath the flag, and the company's captain, H.D. Wiedman, is on the right of the stage. The flag went to France during World War I and was buried with the company's first casualty, John Orweke.

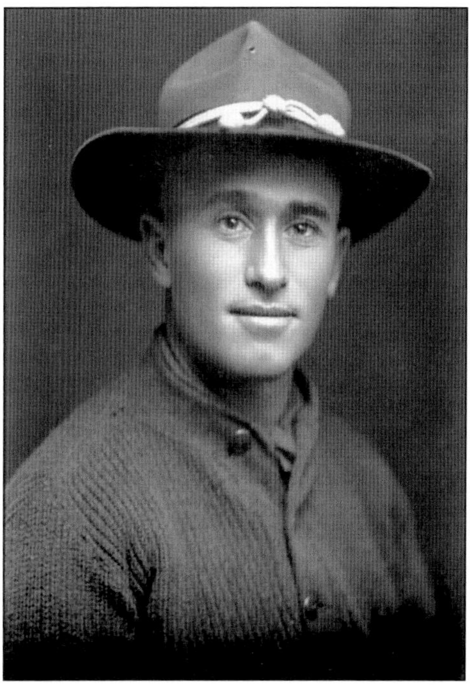

Cpl. Henry Billings, shown here, was one of the many young men from Platteville to serve in World War I. Henry, who served in the Medical Corps, was to write home that "those bombs sure make some noise when they hit the ground. besides they make an awful hole in the ground."

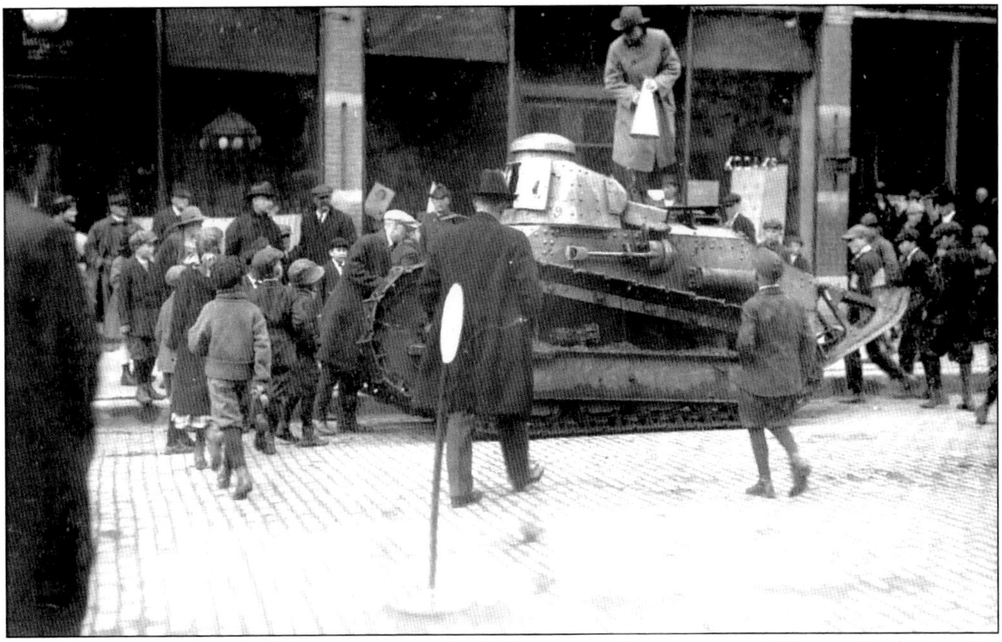

This army whippet tank did maneuvers in both downtown Lancaster and Platteville during the Victory Liberty Loan campaign of 1919. Here it is on Platteville's Main Street on May 1.

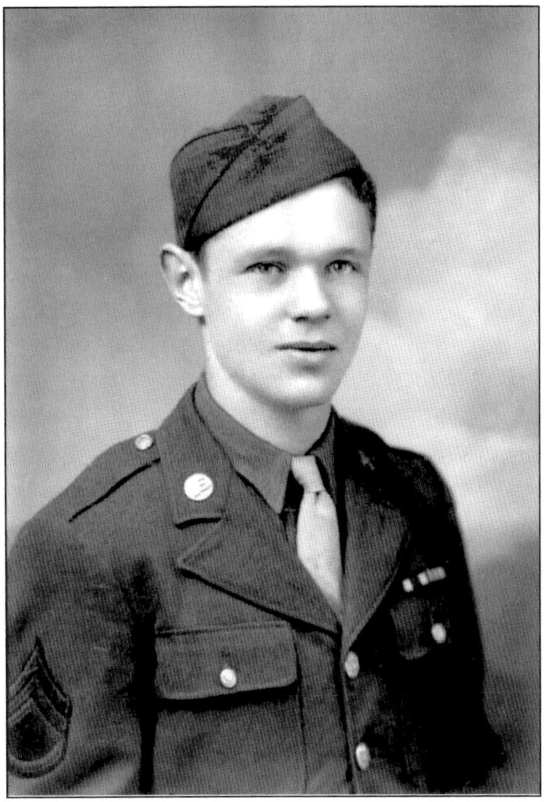

Two decades later, Plattevillians again heeded the call. Here is Staff Sgt. John "Jack" Tiedemann. Jack served as a message center chief in the 20th Corps of the 3rd Army in France and Germany during World War II. This tradition of service continues today with the service of the brave soldiers of Platteville's 229th Engineering Company in Iraq in 2003–04. (Courtesy of John Tiedemann.)

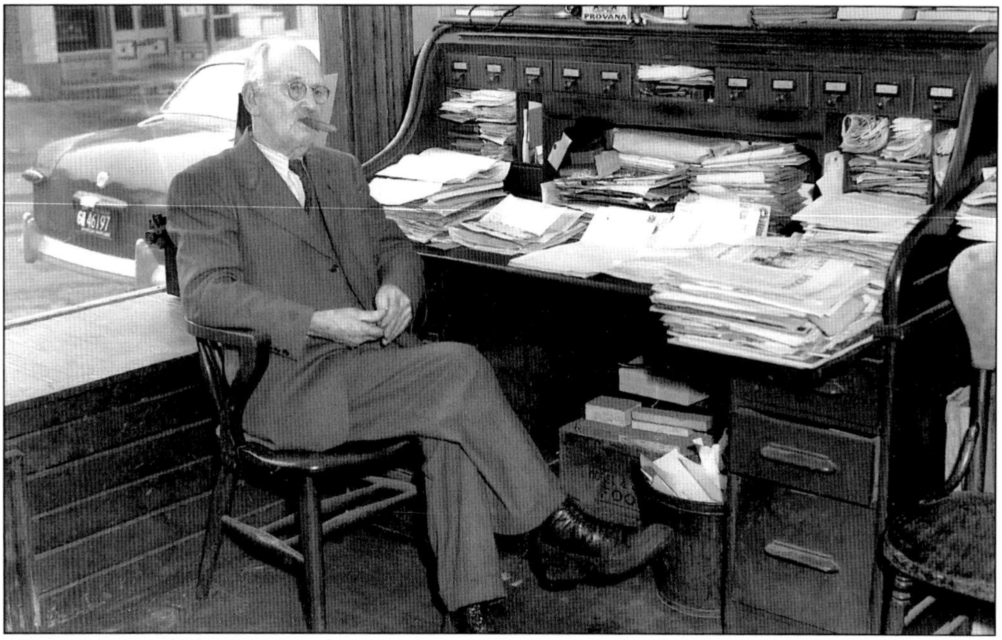

These stories, and many others, were covered by one reporter whose name became synonymous with news, Robert. I. Dugdale, shown here (*c*. 1950) in his office. Born in 1868, Dugdale got his start in the news business when Martin Rindlaub taught "him the printer's trade." Dugdale was the editor and publisher of the *Grant County News*, a Platteville newspaper, for over 50 years. He died in 1956.

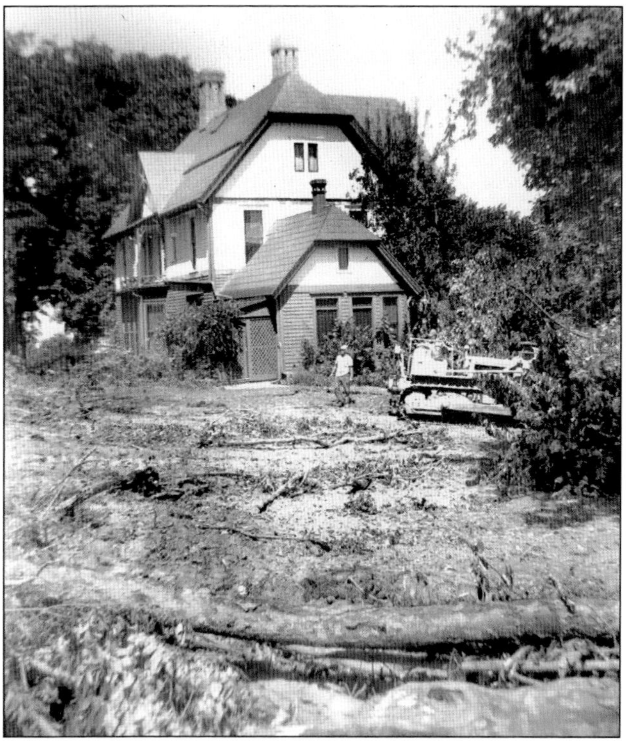

And like every good story, the history of Platteville keeps marching on. Here is an image, taken in August 1961, of the foliage being cleared away from Normal School former President Duncan McGregor's old house. Constructed in 1884 by Harrison Rountree (Major Rountree's son), McGregor lived in the house from 1893 until his death in 1921. The house was razed in the 1960s to make room for McGregor Plaza. Pine Street is to the back of the photographer, placing this house approximately at the main entrance of Dick's Supermarket today.